Heightened Emotions

An Oxfordshire Wedding

Antonia Abbott

Raven Crest Books

Cover Design by www.StunningBookCovers.com

ISBN-13: 978-0-9931909-0-2

ISBN-10: 0-99-319090-1

In memory of my parents Alfred and Joan Gamble. You will recognise Alf as The Crown's landlord, a role he enjoyed. Both my parents always fully supported my ventures and would have loved the fact that I am a novelist. My mother enjoyed reading so much, and it was one of the delights of my childhood to share that enthusiasm with her.

ACKNOWLEDGEMENTS

Firstly, I would like to say a very big thank you to those who bought *Mixed Emotions* and gave me such wonderful feedback. I can't tell you how special all your support has been.

Thank you to those who have helped me - my editor Sarah Williams, who calmly kept me on track on quite a tight writing schedule, Suzan St Maur for her expert knowledge of prison discharge and Duncan Guest for all the information he patiently supplied regarding police procedures.

Last, but by no means least, my husband Karl. Thank you for encouraging me along the way and knowing that I could do this.

ABOUT THE AUTHOR

Antonia Abbott was born in Aylesbury, but lived in Lancashire until she was four years old. Her father was a senior civil servant with entrepreneurial tendencies, buying various businesses, which were then handed over to Antonia and her mother to look after. Antonia clearly inherited these tendencies, as she has turned her hand to many things, including working in a bookie's office (owned by her mother as one of her father's ventures) and running a country pub.

Privately educated in Berkshire, Antonia loathed school and spent as little time there as possible. Subsequently she has spent most of her life in Berkshire and Oxfordshire. Happily married, Antonia still lives in Oxfordshire with her husband Karl. When not writing, Antonia runs a successful IFA practice.

Having always loved reading, Antonia had thought about writing for a long time, but had not had the courage to try. After a chance meeting with a professional writing coach, she decided to write her first book at 58, much to the delight of her husband, who had been telling her for years that she ought to write!

Apart from reading, Antonia enjoys eating out and entertaining, although by her own admission, cooking is not one of her favourite pastimes! She has a passion for cars, and enjoys touring Europe in her BMW convertible. Travelling is also high on the list and she can often be found relaxing on a beach whilst tapping away on her iPad. Formula 1 is another interest and in her late teens and early 20s, Antonia spent a lot of time motor racing marshalling, mainly at Silverstone and Thruxton. When the opportunity presents, she also enjoys dancing.

Antonia is also a collector, particularly of Derby porcelain. She has all sorts of pieces – some dating back to Sansome and Hancock, and on the other side of the scales, a considerable collection of the modern paperweights. She will collect absolutely anything, and has to stop herself from buying! Her collection of silver pill boxes is unusual and fun, but at least they don't take up much space!

She and her husband are very fond of frogs, and have a variety of stone ones adorning the garden, plus one or two in the house. Of course one mustn't forget the Derby frog paperweights.

LIST OF CHARACTERS

Peter Rowlands	Ex-RAF Wing Commander, who used to fly The Queen around
Annabelle Rowlands	Peter's wife, who used to take her clothes off for photos
Susie Rowlands	Their giddy daughter who is engaged to David Timmins
James Rowlands	Gay son of Peter and Annabelle who lives with his partner Greg
David Timmins	Susie's fiancé, who is a whizz with money
George Timmins	David's father. Another whizz with money
Julia Timmins	George's wife. Has own PR Company
Jennifer Timmins	Daughter of George and Julia, sister to David
Sidney Wilkins	Annabelle's father. Lives in Derbyshire
Anne Wilkins	Sidney's wife. Has a secret
Malcolm Neil	Anne's bastard son
Kevin Johnson	Dirty photographer and blackmailer

Greg Somerville	James' partner. Antiques dealer
Simon Somerville	Greg's shady brother who has done time
Stephen Somerville	Bank manager, father of Greg and Simon
Maria Somerville	Stephen's somewhat timid wife
Jonathan Browne	Susie's ex-lover, who fancies his chances
Angela Browne	Jonathan's ex-wife
Emily and Alice Browne	Jonathan and Angela's 8 year old twin daughters
Alex Drummond	Angela's new love interest
Alf Hurst	Opinionated landlord of The Crown
Joan Hurst	Alf's long-suffering wife
Eileen Shaw	Grocer. Owner of Enstone Stores
Mrs Baxter	Annabelle's cleaner
Mark Anderson	Newcomer to Moulsford
Janet Jennings	Prissy headmissy of Woodstock Academy
Grace Noble	Susie's best friend?

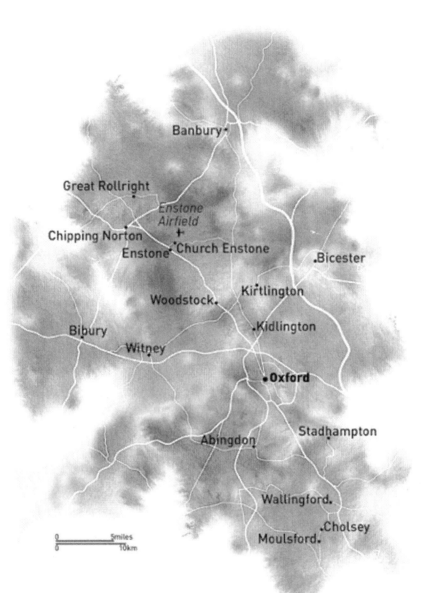

Map of Oxfordshire

CHAPTER 1

The Rowlands family made a very handsome group standing outside Buckingham Palace in the wintry sunshine. There was Peter, looking distinguished in a morning suit with his MBE pinned to his chest, and beside him was his pretty wife Annabelle, stunning in a full-length silver fox coat and matching hat. They were accompanied by their two children, Susie and James, both of whom were feeling very proud indeed of their father. They had posed for a variety of photographs and were just about to leave when a small child rushed up to Susie, saying, "Miss Rowlands, Miss Rowlands, we haven't seen you for ages, and then we see you here! Has your daddy got an honour too?"

Susie looked at the child in amazement. It was Emily Browne, one of Jonathan's children. Jonathan, her ex-lover - what the hell was he doing here? He'd cost her her job at Woodstock Academy and then he'd shoved his way into her house one night when he was drunk, asking her to go and live with him.

Fortunately, David had been there and got rid of Jonathan, as Susie still didn't know how she would have dealt with him had she been on her own. Were he and Angela back together?

"Mummy and Uncle Alex and Alice are over there," continued the excited child. "Why don't you come and say hello to them?"

"Who's Uncle Alex?" enquired Susie, trying her best to smile at Emily, and wishing the ground would just swallow her up. Just as Susie was asking who he was, Uncle Alex, followed by Angela and Alice, walked over to them. Alex was heading straight for her father, hand outstretched, saying, "Rowlands, what a surprise. I was standing there wondering if it might be you, and now Emily has proved that it is as she recognised your daughter."

"Well I'm buggered," replied her father, taking the proffered hand. "If it isn't Alex Drummond. There's no need to ask what you're doing here, but what a surprise that we should both be here at the same time. How many years will it be?"

Susie looked on in astonishment - Daddy actually knew Uncle Alex. How? And what on earth was she going to do about facing Angela? Daddy was introducing them all to Alex Drummond, who in turn was introducing Angela and the twins to the other members of her family. Alice was busy explaining to Mummy that they used to go to Woodstock Academy, which was how they knew Miss Rowlands. Alice went on to tell Mummy that, since her Mummy and Daddy had split up and they had gone to live with

Uncle Alex, they had been going to the Dragon School.

Annabelle smiled at the child, all the while gripped in the chill realisation that it must have been Angela's husband with whom her daughter had had the affair. This was not very comfortable. Horror of horrors, she then heard Peter agreeing to Alex's suggestion that they should all go for a drink and that the Ritz seemed to be as good a place as any. They left the Palace and each family got into a separate cab.

Once safely inside the taxi Annabelle turned to Susie and asked her if it were Angela's husband who was her ex-lover. Susie nodded glumly.

"This is wonderful, Peter," Annabelle said. "We are going for drinks with the woman whose husband Susie was playing around with."

"Sorry, Belle, but how the hell was I supposed to know that?" enquired Peter. "Drummond and I were at Cranfield together all those years ago and I thought it would be fun for us all to have a drink. I wasn't to know that Susie had been shagging his partner's husband, was I?"

James listened to all this with great interest.

"I'm sure no-one will refer to the affair. After all, young children are present," continued Peter. "This is a very special day. Let's enjoy the rest of it."

***

In the other cab, a similar conversation was taking place, albeit somewhat guardedly as the twins were present.

"I can't believe that I'm going to have a drink with Susie Rowlands, after all that has gone on," Angela said.

Alex apologised and said that he couldn't have been thinking straight when he made the suggestion, but he had been stunned to see Peter Rowlands after such a long time. They had trained together at Cranfield and then been sent on their first posting together. They had got on well, but inevitably lost touch over the years, and he had been pleased to see his old friend again. Angela sighed and said that they would have to make the best of things.

It didn't seem long at all before their cab was pulling up outside the Ritz. The twins were very impressed that a man wearing a top hat came and opened the car door for them. They were having such an exciting day!

Uncle Alex had received an MBE for his charity work and Mummy had bought them new outfits for their trip up to London. It was a shame that they hadn't been able to see the Queen for themselves, but Uncle Alex had told them what she had been wearing and what she had said to him, so that was the next best thing.

They were followed into the hotel by the Rowlands, as the cabs had virtually been behind each other. A waiter showed them to a table that was large enough to accommodate them all and, once they were seated, asked them what they would like to drink.

Peter felt that champagne was the most appropriate drink for the occasion and had no hesitation in saying so! Annabelle thought that Angela and Alex looked a little surprised by this, but, gamely, they agreed, and a magnum of Bollinger '97 was ordered.

"What would your little girls like?" Peter asked, turning to Angela.

"They're old enough to answer for themselves," came the somewhat tart reply.

Peter raised his eyebrows in frustration and then turned to the children. Emily said that she would like a Coke and Alice opted for lemonade. Mummy didn't approve of fizzy drinks, so they were seizing the opportunity, as they knew that they wouldn't be corrected in front of other people. That was one of the best things about seeing Daddy, he didn't care what they drank and let them have anything that they wanted.

Thinking about her father, Alice turned to Susie and asked her if she still saw him. Susie had the grace to blush as she shook her head. Hell, she thought to herself, I must get away from these children; surely everyone will be talking about something different by the time I come back. With that in mind, Susie excused herself and headed for the Ladies' Powder Room.

Oh no, she thought, it's going from bad to worse. As she came out of the cubicle, who should she see touching up her lipstick but Angela. Susie smiled at her weakly.

"I've always been fascinated to know more about the woman who caused me such heartache," said Angela conversationally. "Do please tell me why you thought it such a good idea to have a tawdry little affair with my husband and ruin my marriage?"

"I'm sorry," stammered Susie. "I just found Jonathan so attractive and he asked me to meet him after you had viewed Woodstock Academy and things kind of developed from there."

"I'll say they developed," snapped Angela. "I'm just rather surprised that the two of you didn't get together after I threw him out."

At this point the Powder Room door swung open to admit Annabelle.

"You've been rather a long time, Susie darling, and I was beginning to wonder if you were all right," she said.

Susie assured her mother that she was fine, smiled at the two women and scuttled back to the bar and a restorative glass of champagne.

What was said between Angela and Annabelle will never be known, but the conversation that took place in the bar after they both returned was very civil indeed.

***

"The engagement is announced between Susannah Elizabeth, the only daughter of Wing Commander and Mrs P J Rowlands of Riverside House, Moulsford, and David Anthony Timmins, only son of Mr and Mrs D K Timmins of Great Rollright". Kevin was so pleased that he had read that announcement in *The Telegraph* a few months previously, and was still scheming on how best he could use this knowledge to his advantage...

Kevin needed to find out more about Mr and Mrs Timmins of Great Rollright, that was for sure. They might well be interested in what he had. That would be one in the eye for that snotty bastard Rowlands. He hadn't missed his name in the New Year's Honours list. But now that his little girl was about to be wed, things might be different. He might be happy to pay for Kevin's silence. After all, the daughter would hardly want her future in-laws to know that her mother had been photographed nude, would she?

Did the girl even know herself? Where did Susannah Elizabeth live? The Timmins wouldn't be hard to find. He'd looked up Great Rollright and could see that it was only a small village. Directory Enquiries, or 118 118 as they called themselves these days, should probably do the trick. Kevin scratched his groin with enthusiasm. There just had to be money to be made here, and he was going to make sure he got his hands on it.

He didn't know what had made him look through the New Year's Honours list, but when he saw that Wing Commander Rowlands had received an MBE, it had brought that little cow Annabelle to the forefront of his mind. He would make her sweat!

His first job was to find his old drinking pal, Malcolm, Annabelle's half-brother. He had discovered that relationship some while ago. He would never forgive the snotty bitch who had kicked up about taking her clothes off for him, and, to boot, had got him fired from his job at The Buxton Echo when she had gone to the editor and told him about the photo contracts Kevin was signing up on the side. The disgrace had stuck with him, and he hadn't had a decent job since.

Kevin knew that Malcolm was pissed off with Annabelle. He considered her to be a spoiled little rich girl, married to that pillock of an RAF Officer and living in luxury in that posh house on the Thames. What also stuck in his throat was that she had refused to help him out any more. It wasn't Malcolm's fault that he'd been born a bastard and given away, whilst she seemed to have been born into privilege, and married into even more of it.

He'd always liked Malcolm, ever since his schooldays, and when Malcolm had learned what that cow Annabelle had done to him, he had helped devise the blackmailing scheme as the perfect way that the two of them could make some money. He might know where Susannah lived. That would be a very good starting point indeed. Kevin folded his newspaper, scratched his groin one more time, and set off for the local Wetherspoons.

CHAPTER 2

Whilst the Rowlands were at The Ritz, near Arundel in Sussex, a young man was breathing the fresh air very deeply. He was waiting at the main gate of HMP Ford, the open prison, having served half his time for armed robbery. Now he was being released on parole.

He scanned the area anxiously for signs of his parents. Despite what he had done, they knew they had to come to meet him. He had to be released to someone, and although he had spent his initial day and weekend releases with his cousin in nearby Angmering, it was his parents whom he named this time, for this special day.

He felt almost as alone as he had felt on that awful day when the judge had sent him down. Simon wasn't really a bad lad, but he had fallen into the wrong company and been swept along with the idea of getting some easy money. He hadn't expected to be caught though, but he had committed the crime and now he had served the time. All he wanted was to go home, have a bath, get changed and eat food that hadn't been prepared in a prison kitchen.

Yet again, Simon looked up and down Ford Road. There were several cars parked along the kerb, but he didn't even know what car his parents drove these days. Their visits had been infrequent at best, and his brother's very rare indeed. This should be such a happy day, but he was beginning to feel very down in the mouth.

Finally, he saw a female figure, wrapped up against the cold, walking towards him. It was his mother. Where was his father though? Perhaps he was struggling to park the car and his mum was making sure she was there on time. He waved, and then waited patiently as she walked slowly towards them.

The formalities with the prison staff over with, Simon turned his attention to his mother. To say Maria's greeting was cool would be an understatement. Politely, she asked him how he was. Simon assured her that he was OK and then asked after his father and his whereabouts. His mother replied that his father was at work, and wouldn't be coming to meet him.

"Never mind," said Simon, trying to put a brave face on his disappointment. "I'll see him when he gets home. Come on, Mum, let's go home, I'm starving."

Maria took a deep breath. "I'm afraid you won't be coming home, Simon. Your father can't condone the awful crime that you got involved with, and at the moment can't bring himself to see you. He certainly won't have you in the house."

Simon gasped. In his wildest dreams he had never imagined it coming to this. He had expected to be welcomed as The Prodigal Son. OK, he had been involved with a gang who had robbed a jeweller's shop, but no-one had been killed as they'd only had imitation firearms, and he'd served three years in prison with three more years on parole, and hadn't even got any loot to show for it. What the hell was he going to do now?

His mother drove him to Arundel railway station, pushed some money into his hand, said she was sorry again, and drove off, leaving him standing at the entrance to the ticket office, open-mouthed.

Having had a sandwich and a mug of tea in the station snack bar, Simon decided that his best plan of action was to go and look up his brother, who would be bound to put him up. He could get his case sent to the Parole Officers near there. After all, he had nowhere else to go.

His mother had given him a hundred pounds, and he had a little more in the bank, plus a week's Jobseeker's Allowance, but that wouldn't go very far at all. Feeling desperately sorry for himself, Simon caught the next train to Victoria Station in London, made his way by Underground to Paddington Station, where he discovered there was forty minutes before the next train to Didcot. He found somewhere to sit and waited.

***

The Rowlands arrived back in Moulsford feeling very euphoric. Peter, in particular, was pleased with himself. He had collected his gong and met up with his old pal, Alex Drummond. Despite his wayward daughter's misdemeanours, Peter saw no reason why he and Alex shouldn't keep in touch. After all, the fellow only lived in Oxford, half an hour up the road. He knew that Annabelle wouldn't approve, but he didn't need to advertise his plans.

"Right people," he said cheerfully. "Where shall we go for dinner? Susie and James, get your respective other halves over here. We've got some celebrating to do."

James got straight on his phone, but Susie hesitated, pointing out it would take David nearly an hour to drive from Chipping Norton.

"Still ask him, darling," said her mother. "We can't leave David out of our celebrations. He'll be proper family very soon."

Susie did as requested, and was delighted when David said he would be with them as soon as he could.

***

Simon got off the train at Cholsey. It was beginning to get dark, but he

6

didn't have far to walk. Hitching his hold-all up on to his shoulder, he set off. There were no lights on in the house, and repeated banging on the door didn't get a response. Perhaps his brother wasn't back from work yet? He wasn't walking any further, so he slumped down on the back doorstep, out of sight of passers-by.

It was cold for March, and after an hour or so, Simon realised that he couldn't sit there much longer. What the hell was he going to do? He needed to get inside the house and all the bloody windows were closed. He didn't really want to break in, but needs must.

He eyed up the bathroom window which was on the ground floor at the back of the house. That was probably his best bet. His brother would be miffed, but what the hell?

He wished he had a torch. It was now pitch black and Simon couldn't see a thing. He had no tools either. How was he going to get in? Maybe not the bathroom window after all. If the front door was a Yale lock, he might be able to kick it in, but he would have to make sure that no-one saw him. Cautiously, he made his way back round to the front of the building and, having glanced furtively up and down the road, took a run at the door. Bingo! It gave way and he found himself in the passageway.

First things first, Simon thought to himself. He needed to draw the curtains and put on some lights so he could see the state of the front door.

Shit! He had only bust the bloody thing and now it wouldn't close. His brother would go ape. The sodding doorframe had split. The best he could do at the moment would be to put the chain on the door and ram a chair up against it.

That done, Simon decided that a drink and a bath would be in order. He noticed a wine rack in the kitchen and, selecting a bottle of Merlot, unscrewed the top and took a large swig. Bottle in hand, he then made his way through the kitchen to the bathroom and ran himself a deep bath. With a feeling of anticipation, he lowered himself into the foaming water. Taking another gulp from the bottle, Simon decided that things were beginning to look up.

Half an hour or so later, he emerged, wrapped in a bathrobe he had found on the back of the bathroom door. Wandering back into the kitchen, Simon decided that he needed food again. Rummaging around, he found some excellent pâté and French bread, which he wolfed down hungrily. Putting the plate in the sink and the bottle in the bin, Simon walked through to the sitting room to await the arrival of his brother.

CHAPTER 3

The family dinner hosted by Peter following his visit to Buckingham Palace had been enormous fun, resulting in certain people not wanting to get out of bed the following morning. It wasn't far for James and Greg to go home, but David and Susie had to be at work in Chipping Norton, a good hour away.

David, being the kind soul that he was, told Susie to have a lie-in and said that he would get to the office for 9 am. Greg took David's lead and told James not to rush, saying that he would go to the Arcade and keep an eye on everything there. James told him to leave Zizi and said that he would take her and Allsort for a walk along the river.

It was only a minor detour to go to Wallingford by way of Cholsey and Greg decided that he had plenty of time to do just that as it was a cold day and he could do with a warmer sweater. Parking the BMW, he walked up the path and was surprised, and disturbed, to say the least, that, when he tried to put his key in the lock, it became apparent that the door was not properly locked. What the hell was going on? Should he call the police?

As he was deciding what to do, the door opened and a familiar face peeped out.

"What the hell are you doing here and, more to the point, what the hell's going on?" asked Greg.

***

When it had got to midnight, Simon had decided that, for whatever reason, it looked as though his brother wasn't coming home, so thought that he might as well explore the house. Going upstairs, he discovered two bedrooms, one of which was clearly occupied and the other had to be for guests. That was good. He now had somewhere to sleep, but before he did that, Simon felt it would be a good idea to have a bit of a look round to see what he could find out about his big brother's life.

Returning to the main bedroom, it became apparent to Simon that it was occupied by two people, both of whom were male, but then he knew his brother's leaning in that direction. What could he find out about the stranger? Methodically, Simon started to rifle through the drawers. The bank statements were interesting; his brother's lover appeared to be loaded. That could be useful, as he was planning to hang around for a while.

Digging deeper, Simon could see that his brother was not so fortunate.

9

His bank account looked very sad in comparison. He wondered what the pair of them did? Did they work? Did they need to? The little house looked great, but then his brother was artistic and had been on some sort of course to do with art. Simon hadn't been particularly interested in what his brother did, preferring sports to art and crafts. His brother was gay anyway, and Simon had hung around with much tougher guys, who would have been horrified to know he had a bum bandit for a brother.

Moving away from the bedside cabinets, Simon started to pull out the drawers in the dressing table. Mmn, there was some bling here all right. Was it real? Earrings. Bloody hell, had the shirt lifter had his ears pierced? Could some of this belong to the other one? If he played his cards right, there might be some rich pickings.

OK, that was enough of upstairs for the moment. What could he find out downstairs? Simon returned to the sitting room and started to work his way through the paperwork in the bureau. He couldn't find anything particularly interesting and it was getting late. He needed to sleep now. Going back upstairs, Simon turned back the bed in what he had decided was the guest bedroom and, discarding the dressing gown, slid between the Egyptian cotton sheets.

***

Next morning Simon was up with the lark, relishing his first day of freedom. It was great to have yet another bath, but he didn't fancy putting on any of his clothes, so went back to the master bedroom and had a hunt round for something to wear. Satisfied with his choice, Simon returned downstairs and made himself some breakfast.

He was sitting with his feet up, drinking his second cup of tea, when he heard someone trying to get through the front door. Jumping up, he went and opened it and looked his brother in the eye. As Simon had feared, Greg did not look at all pleased to see him.

Simon moved the chair back so that Greg could get into his home. His brother stamped in, shouting, "How fucking dare you break into my house and put on my partner's clothes. You've obviously had a bloody good snoop around, you nasty little villain."

"Steady on, mate," said Simon. "I thought you'd be pleased to see me after all this time."

"Pleased to see you," howled Greg. "You've trashed my front door and you're wearing James' clothes. That suggests to me that you've been here overnight. I suppose you've slept in my guest room too? Where haven't you been in my home? When did you get out and why are you here? Hold on, I need coffee whilst I listen to you."

With that, Greg strode into the kitchen and surveyed the scene. "And you've helped yourself to my wine. What else do I need to know?"

Coffee made, Greg returned to the sitting room, where Simon told his tale of woe about being released, his father wanting nothing to do with him, and having nowhere else to go.

"I wasn't to know that you wouldn't be here, was I?" he said with a pleading look in his eyes. "I had no choice but to break the door down. I couldn't stay outside all night. Look mate, I'm down on my luck and I need somewhere for a while. I've got to have a fixed address with someone reliable or they'll rescind my parole. I've no clothes worth speaking of, and very little money as well. Please help me, Greg. We are brothers after all."

With a sinking heart, Greg realised that he had little choice. "OK," he said. "Here are the rules..."

***

Leaving Simon waiting for the locksmith, and having sorted out the story that they were going to tell James, Greg made his way to the Arcade. It was imperative that he kept James away from West End until the lock was fixed. He would tell him some cock and bull story that he had broken his key in the lock in his excitement at seeing his brother after all this time. He also needed to explain why Simon was staying with them. James had to hear all this from him and not from Simon, who was unreliable at best.

Once he had checked over both shops, Greg rang James.

"Hello, sweetheart, you'll never guess what," was his opening gambit.

"Is there any point in my trying then?" asked James, laughing.

Quickly, Greg outlined the story that he and Simon had concocted about Simon having been travelling and being mugged in Thailand and having most of his things stolen, including his passport. He had managed to get back to the UK with the help of the British Consul, but was now really down on his luck. He had given up the lease on his flat before he went travelling and had nowhere to live. He had come to Greg as he felt that Greg would be more understanding than their parents, and could help him get back on his feet.

James' heart immediately went out to the Somerville brothers and he told Greg that of course he understood, and of course Simon must stay with them, and he would help in any way that he could. Greg breathed a sigh of relief. He was constantly grateful for his partner's generosity – and his naïvety.

"Why don't you come in to the Lamb?" he suggested. "We could work out a plan of campaign to make Simon feel at home." And with a bit of luck, in the interim, the front door will be fixed, he thought to himself.

CHAPTER 4

David had told Susie not to rush and had said that, as he had no client appointments that morning, he would hold the fort, if she could be in for early afternoon; she had nodded eagerly and dozed back to sleep.

Now it was 10 am and the boys had gone, leaving her alone with Mummy and Daddy. "This is a rare luxury," she said, smiling at them. "I had yesterday off work and now I'm getting this morning as well."

"While you're here, it wouldn't be a bad idea to do some wedding planning," said her mother. "Your living in Enstone makes it that bit more difficult."

Peter groaned and said he was going to go and read *The Telegraph* in his study. He had heard enough about weddings to last him a lifetime. There hadn't been all this performance when he and Annabelle had got married. It had been the church in the Derbyshire village where she lived, followed by a reception in a local hotel. He had worn dress uniform and Annabelle had worn a wedding dress – simple as that.

Now there was all this hoo-ha about whether Susie and David should get married in church, and if so, whether it should be Moulsford or Church Enstone, where Susie lived. He thought the latest suggestion had been to have the whole show at Blenheim Palace. He could see himself having to be firm with his two favourite ladies. Although wealthy, there was a limit to how much he was prepared to spend. He had heard his wife and daughter muttering something about wedding dresses costing £2,000 and upwards. For Heaven's sake, it was only going to be worn once. That seemed just a tad excessive to him.

With her husband out of the way, Annabelle turned to her daughter and said that it was time they made firm plans.

"It's almost the end of March, darling. We really do need to find a venue you know. Without the venue, we can't fix the date, and if we don't know what time of year it's going to be, we can't start thinking about dresses. Really all we know at the moment is that you are going to marry David and that Grace and Jenny are going to be bridesmaids. That in itself presents problems with Grace living in Manchester. Couldn't you manage with just Jenny?"

"Not really," replied Susie. "I'm only asking Jenny because she's David's sister and it's the polite thing to do. I don't know her very well; not like I do Grace. I do see what you mean though, Mummy. Look, we've got about three hours, and then I must have some lunch and get to the office. Let's see how far we can get."

Annabelle smiled at the change in her previously wayward daughter. The last year had been hell with Susie having an affair with a married man and losing her job as secretary at Woodstock Academy. Then she had met David Timmins.

James had been at uni with Jenny, David's sister, and had introduced his sister to his friend's brother. David had transformed Susie into the lovely young woman that she was today, and Annabelle was thrilled that they were to be married.

"OK," said Annabelle. "I happen to know that there's a Wedding Fair somewhere Abingdon way on Sunday. I know it's a bit of a hike for you, but if you and David came over for supper on Saturday, the three of us could go to the Fair on the Sunday. We mustn't leave David out of our plans."

Susie said that that would be fab.

The two proceeded to draw up a shortlist of potential venues for discussion with David. All too soon it was time for Susie to leave and make her way to Chipping Norton.

***

Whilst Susie had been happily making wedding plans, her ex-lover Jonathan had been contemplating his forthcoming divorce. He would have to move out of the marital home, because Angela would want her share financially. Everything was looking horribly messy. He still couldn't understand why that silly little cow hadn't wanted him to live with her. She'd been obsessed with him when he wasn't available, and then all of a sudden everything had changed, and when he'd gone round to her house some other bloke had had his feet firmly under the table.

Jonathan wondered whether it might be worth contacting Susie again. Plenty of water had flowed under the bridge now and she might welcome him with open arms. Getting around on a bicycle was tedious - he had lost his driving licence and subsequently his job and company car, due to drinking and driving on the fateful night when Angela had left him and he had gone to find Susie - and his private consultancy work wasn't really bringing in that much money. He went on to wonder how much money this Alex Drummond had. Perhaps he could get money out of Angela as part of the divorce settlement?

He needed some sort of plan, but the first thing he would do would be to get in touch with Susie. Maybe he should start by sending her some flowers?

***

David opened the door of Nag's Head Cottage on Saturday morning to find an Interflora van outside and a young woman holding out a bouquet of flowers. "These are for Susie Rowlands," she said. "The address we were given was Rose Cottage up in Enstone, but her neighbour said that she lives here now. Is that right?"

David smiled inwardly. Good old Mrs MacDonald! She never missed a trick, and never missed an opportunity to meddle either. He replied that Susie did indeed live at Nag's Head Cottage and, thanking the girl, took the bouquet from her and went inside to give them to his fiancée.

"Have I got a rival, darling?" he called.

"Don't be silly," replied Susie, taking the bouquet from him. "Who on earth can these be from, I wonder."

As she read the card, Susie went pale, and turning to David, whispered, "They're from Jonathan. Why on earth has he sent me these?"

David took the card from her shaking hand and read it. "Wondering how you are, Susie, and whether you fancy meeting up? Lots of love, Jonathan."

"Oh just ignore him, he'll go away again. He certainly isn't worth getting upset over," he said with a confidence he didn't feel. "Where shall we put these flowers?"

"In the bin," said Susie, crossly. "I don't want to look at the damn things."

"Tell you what," said David. "It's a pity to put them in the bin. I'll take them next door. Alf can find somewhere to put them in the pub."

Luck was on his side, and Alf was testing his Leffe beer when David walked in to the bar. "Morning, son," he called, jovially. "We don't usually see you this early on a Saturday. Is everything all right?"

David proffered the flowers and explained that they had been sent to Susie and she didn't want them, and they wondered if Alf would like them for the pub. Alf raised his eyebrows, but knew better than to ask any questions. That didn't stop him speculating though!

He felt that there might have been something between Susie and that Jonathan Browne who used to work for Lotus Racing. She had reacted quite strangely when Jonathan had come into the pub with a woman, and let's face it, you didn't get to his age without recognising a bit of trouble when you saw it.

"That's kind of you, son," he said. "I'm sure Joan would love them. I wonder if I can convince her that I've bought them for her."

"I doubt that very much," said his wife, as she walked into the bar. "Good morning, David. How are you?"

David assured her that he was fine and told her to enjoy the flowers that Alf hadn't bought her. "I'd be worried if he had," was her laughing reply.

David went home to find Susie looking very sorry for herself. He did hope that Jonathan Browne wasn't going to come between them.

"What time do you want to go over to Moulsford?" he asked. Hopefully some wedding planning, and a delicious meal cooked by his future mother-in-law, would make Susie forget about that damn man.

CHAPTER 5

Greg managed to leave the Lamb ahead of James so that he could find out about the state of the front door and check that Simon remembered the story about Thailand. Much to his relief, the door had been fixed, and Simon was no longer wearing James' clothes. He had chosen something from the selection of Greg's that his brother had hastily handed over. He had also washed up the dishes that he had used and put the trash outside.

When James got back some half an hour later, the two brothers were sitting with coffee and, on the face of it, having an amicable discussion.

After the introductions, James looked at Simon and said, "You look very pale for someone who has been backpacking around Thailand for the best part of a year."

Bugger, thought Greg. How stupid he had been not to think about the fact that Simon was deathly white after having been locked up for all those years. "Oh, Simon doesn't like the sun," he said quickly.

"Even so," said James. "I wouldn't have thought it would have been possible to avoid it so successfully."

"Plenty of sunblock, particularly on my face," Simon lied quickly, whilst pulling down the sleeves on his jumper as far as possible. Christ, this was getting too close for comfort. He needed to steer the conversation in another direction.

He smiled at James. "Never mind me and my boring story," he said. "Do tell me about yourself, James. I can't wait to get to know the person who has won my big brother's heart. Such a coincidence that you both do antiques. I think I shall really enjoy staying here."

Greg smiled weakly, and listened with half an ear as James talked to his brother about their relationship. How long would the little shit be staying for? He had a nasty feeling it could be quite a while, and could also be quite costly as Simon had no clothes and no job. Perhaps James could help with the former, as he had recently reinvented himself and had a load of clothes that he never wore. He would have a word with him on the quiet and see what he could get James to give away.

"Should we go out to celebrate Simon's safe return?" suggested James.

"That would be lovely. Thank you," was the immediate reply.

Mmn, thought Greg. He and James would be paying for Simon, so he offered to cook something, but was immediately overruled by his lover and his brother. He needed another word with James when the opportunity arose, but he mustn't make him anti-Simon or more inquisitive than he was already.

"OK," he said. "What do we fancy?"

Simon said he would kill for a Ruby, so they set off for the local curry house, where they bumped into a few people that they knew. Again, when introducing Simon, others commented that he wasn't very brown. Greg felt really cross with himself for not coming up with a better story, but it was too late now.

"Must be the lighting in here," he said with a forced smile on his face, whilst attracting a waiter's attention to show them to a table.

"Which parts of Thailand did you visit?" James asked Simon as soon as they were sitting down. Simon muttered something about the Vietnamese border, which set James off again as he had spent a couple of months in Thailand, Vietnam, and Burma whilst he was studying at Brookes.

Greg knew that he just had to turn the conversation and said that although he had never been to Thailand he was beginning to feel that he had spent a lifetime there, and could they please talk about something else?

Simon felt very relieved, whereas James felt somewhat snubbed. Here was he, trying to bond with Greg's brother and show an interest in his backpacking, and all Greg seemed to want to do was change the subject. OK, he'd done his best and he wouldn't mention sodding Thailand again. James turned his attention to the menu.

Conversation became a little stilted, as no-one seemed to know what to talk about and they were all glad when their food arrived. Simon devoured his as it was a real delight for him not to be eating at Her Majesty's pleasure and was finished long before the other two, not that they paid particular attention, as they had their separate thoughts.

James was wondering about Simon and whether there was anything odd about him. He was telling himself very firmly not to be silly, although he couldn't help but think it strange that Greg had never mentioned him.

Come to think of it, he hadn't met Greg's parents either, and he and Greg had been together for just over six months now. Greg had been to Riverside House loads of times, and had also met Susie and David, although it would be difficult for him not to have been to James' home as Greg knew his mother before he knew James.

There was a suitable topic of conversation, surely? "No doubt you'll be keen to see your parents next, Simon," he said. "Do you know there's never been an appropriate opportunity for me to meet them yet, so perhaps we could all go and visit together?"

The two brothers looked at each other absolutely aghast. Greg was first to speak.

"Well, it's not really as simple as it might seem, James," he said. "Mum and Dad were very upset when Si dropped out and went off travelling, and doubtless there's still some bad feeling. It's probably best to wait until he's more sorted out and then get in touch with Mum and Dad."

James nodded his head. He was beginning to feel quite sorry for Simon, who seemed to be the black sheep of the family. That had been Susie's role until last autumn when she got engaged to David. He remembered well how his sister had been heavily in debt, with nowhere to turn, and how cross their father had been with her, and worse still when she had lost her job as a school secretary because she had been having an affair with a parent.

He, on the other hand, had been everything his parents had wanted, except perhaps for being gay, but when he had told Mum she had paved the way with Dad, and he had never had any hassle. Greg was always included in family "dos" and his Dad had even helped him move into Greg's house.

"Forget that then," he said. "Tell you what, Simon, you must come to Moulsford and meet my parents and their dog Allsort instead."

Little did he know.

CHAPTER 6

As David had hoped, going over to Moulsford, and enjoying her mother's delicious cooking, perked Susie up no end. By the time they went to bed that night she was her usual bubbly self. All thoughts of Jonathan seemed to have disappeared.

They were up bright and early the next morning, and the three of them set off to the wedding fair at The De Vere Hotel at Steventon. Peter had looked quite horrified when Annabelle had suggested that he might like to go with them.

"I'm paying for the bloody wedding. Isn't that enough?" he enquired, watching them squeeze into Annabelle's Golf.

Laughing at him, Annabelle waved goodbye and drove off.

None of them had been to a wedding fair before and found it quite an experience. They were amazed by the diversity of the suppliers. There were magicians wanting to entertain guests during the wedding breakfast, pyrotechnic experts wanting to finish the day off with a bang, coupled with the more usual components of a wedding – photographers, cake makers, printers, florists, and a variety of representatives from local venues, all hoping to make a booking or two.

Susie loved it all and was keen to choose all sorts of things. David and Annabelle had to restrain her a little, and suggest that they should just talk to people and take their business cards and then discuss them at home later.

"Surely we could choose just something today, David?" she begged, smiling up at him. "Something little, perhaps?"

David asked her what she would consider to be something little and his wife-to-be told him that wedding rings were small. Annabelle was horrified.

"No, no," she said. "There's so much choice nowadays that you can't rush choosing wedding rings. You're going to be wearing them for the rest of your lives. When your father and I got married there wasn't the same choice for anything, but now weddings are big business, as today is proving. Just get cards and catalogues if they have any and then think very carefully about what you want. From what I can see these people don't seem to have shops, so you can't go in and try on a variety. A rep comes to you and you choose your rings from a catalogue. I'm really not sure about that."

Susie pulled a face, but knew that her mother was right. By the time they left Steventon they were carrying bags full of leaflets and had lots to talk about.

To Peter's dismay they were still talking weddings when they got back to

Moulsford. "Come on, David," he said. "Let's leave the girls to it. We'll take Allsort for a walk down to the Beetle and Wedge."

***

Whilst Peter and David were having a restorative pint or two, and discussing anything but weddings, Annabelle and Susie were sorting through all the catalogues and disposing of those that they didn't want.

"I'll say it again, darling, but we do really need to choose the venue before we can go any further. All right, you can choose your wedding rings and that's about it. Have you thought any more about whether or not you would like to get married in church?"

Susie shook her head. She wasn't particularly religious, so that side of things didn't really come into it. All she knew was that she wanted it to be special and beautiful.

"Well," said Annabelle. "As far as I can see if you get married in any of the hotels that we've got brochures for, they offer you a package. That's simple enough, and you know what it's going to cost, but I'm not sure it's the right way forward. If you wished, I guess we could cater at home if you got married in Moulsford Church. We could have a marquee like we did for James' birthday. To be honest, darling, it also depends on how many guests you would like. Do you think you would like a really big do, or something smaller and more intimate? Another thing we have to think about is where the guests would stay. I can put up Grandma and Grandpa, and James and Greg, of course, but I really don't want a houseful. You also need to consider where you want to spend your actual wedding night."

"Help!" said Susie. "There's a lot more to this wedding lark than I first realised. Today has really opened my eyes."

"It's certainly changed since Daddy and I got married," replied her mother. "We went to the village church and then had a reception in the local hotel. That's what you did then. You can have whatever you want, within reason, darling, but you do need to give it some urgent thought, and discuss it with David, of course. If it's in Moulsford, his parents will need somewhere to stay, as will his sister, and don't forget the Beetle only has three rooms, so people might have to stay in Wallingford."

"But if I picked the church in Enstone, it would be even worse," said Susie. "I think Alf has one letting room! I guess David's parents and sister could go home by cab, but it would mean that the nearest decent place for you and Daddy to stay would be Woodstock. I guess that rules out Enstone Church, so if it is a church wedding it will have to be in Moulsford, and that would then lead on to where we would have the reception – here at home, or in a nearby hotel that has enough rooms for anyone who needs to stay."

"Wallingford, Goring or Streatley would be obvious choices," replied her mother. "The Swan at Streatley has a beautiful setting with all that river frontage, and I'm sure it would have sufficient rooms to accommodate all our guests."

Susie thought about this. "I think that's a good call, Mummy," she said, "and definitely a place to go and have a look at."

***

When Peter and David returned an hour later, they were pleased to discover that the womenfolk had made progress where the wedding was concerned. Susie was all for going to the Swan at Streatley and having a look at it at once.

Peter had a different idea and suggested that the four of them should go and have a meal as that would give them some idea of the quality of the food and the wine list, and if they went for lunch, they might be able to have a look at one or two of the bedrooms if they were interested in progressing things further. That decided, they agreed that the following Saturday was as good a time as any.

Annabelle breathed a sigh of relief. It looked as though they were finally getting somewhere.

***

Back in Kirtlington, Jonathan was disappointed not to have heard from Susie. He had hoped that the flowers would do the trick, but his hopes had been further dashed following a visit from his daughters, who had told him with great excitement that they had seen Miss Rowlands at Buckingham Palace, and that she had been wearing a very pretty ring that she hadn't worn to school. They had chattered on about Uncle Alex's medal and the fact that Miss Rowlands' Daddy had got one too, but Jonathan's attention had been caught by the ring. Could it have been an engagement ring, and could Susie be going to get married? He really did need to see her sooner rather than later.

CHAPTER 7

Simon was having the time of his life in Cholsey. Bit different from the nick! He'd managed to sort out having his papers moved to a parole officer in Wallingford. Slipping over to see him once a week hadn't posed a problem, with Greg covering for him, and the PO was pleased that Simon seemed so settled with his brother. What's more, Greg and James lived like lords and there was always some dosh lying about. Simon made a point of taking notes from the middle of the bundle so it wouldn't be too obvious and he was careful never to take too much at once.

He had also been to Riverside House and met James' parents. They were something else! She dripped bling and he had a posh voice. There was definitely potential there and Simon couldn't wait to be asked to stay overnight to have a good poke about.

He was trying very hard to keep in with Greg and James, because apart from the fact that he had nowhere else to go, he liked the lifestyle. His next plan was to offer to help out at the Lamb Arcade as there had to be lots more potential there. He could pocket something and say that it had been stolen and then sell it on somewhere else, or maybe steal from the other shopkeepers.

At the moment he was trying to be useful with household chores. Shopping was more difficult as the supermarkets were in Wallingford and he didn't drive, but Greg had told him rather tartly that he could catch the bus. That had been a mistake to mention the shopping.

As he drank his cup of tea, Simon wondered if the Rowlands needed any odd jobs doing. He must ask James. That could be a double whammy - he ought to score Brownie points and it might get him into the house on his own. Greg had so kindly pointed out that Cholsey was on a good bus route, and he'd discovered that the Reading bus ran through Moulsford.

Yes, life was definitely good.

***

Peter really hadn't warmed to Simon, thinking that, although he looked rather like Greg, he was nothing like him at all, and, besides, Peter was somewhat suspicious of his Thailand story and having been mugged. So, when Annabelle suggested that they invite him to supper along with Greg and James, he wasn't best pleased.

"Oh, do we have to, Belle?" he enquired. "There's something about that

Simon that isn't quite right."

"It used to be that Greg and now it's that Simon," she replied crossly. "Whatever's the matter with you, Peter? Simon's just a young man who's down on his luck and staying with his brother."

"Why not his parents, and why doesn't he get a job?" retorted her husband.

"Perhaps they feel like you did about Susie when she got herself in a mess and wasn't helping herself," suggested Annabelle. "You were tough on her and perhaps they're being tough on Simon."

"Odd family," was Peter's reply. "James hasn't even met the parents after how many months?"

Annabelle couldn't argue with that, so decided it best to change the subject. Probably the wedding wasn't a good choice, so she decided to pick horse racing and suggested that they go to Windsor the next day. Peter visibly perked up.

***

Peter wouldn't have been feeling so perky had he known what Simon was thinking about, or indeed, had he known that Annabelle's half-brother Malcolm and the ghastly Kevin were busy scheming as to how they could extort money from him.

Malcolm and Kevin were confident that Peter and Annabelle wouldn't want their daughter's prospective in-laws to see Annabelle's glamour photos, and were still chewing the fat as to the best way to approach this. Threatening that smarmy sod again probably wouldn't work, so maybe the daughter herself would be their best bet?

"Where does Susannah live?" Kevin asked Malcolm.

Malcolm shook his head and said that he didn't know, and didn't know how to find out. The engagement notice had announced her address as Moulsford, but Kevin knew from watching the house that the girl didn't live there.

"In that case it'll have to be straight to the in-laws, but maybe with a warning to our little model as to what we're about to do," said Kevin. "Can you think of anything else that we could threaten her with?"

Malcolm said that he couldn't as he really didn't know Annabelle at all. He reminded Kevin that he had been given away at birth, whilst that little cow had had all the privileges, and that he'd only come across her quite by chance after he'd managed to track down his birth mother, who had wanted nothing to do with him either.

"Ah," said Kevin. "That's where we should go. Never mind the in-laws just now. The grandparents won't want nudey pictures of their precious daughter shown around, will they? Now you must have their address. Let's have another pint to help us think straight." With that Kevin scratched his groin and marched up to the bar.

***

Kevin returned from the bar with two pints of IPA, one of which he handed to Malcolm.

"I know where the Wilkins used to live," Malcolm said thoughtfully. "I could get my arse round there and have a look, like you did with my snotty half-sister and her husband. I'm good at watching without being seen. Like you."

Kevin nodded his head in approval. "I've still got plenty of piccies," he said. "Once you've found the old couple, you can leave the rest to me. You won't have to get your hands dirty."

They clinked their glasses and supped silently. Kevin scratched his groin again. Malcolm wiped his mouth on the back of his hand. When they had finished their drinks, they went their separate ways, both deep in thought.

***

Sidney and Anne Wilkins spent a pleasant morning talking about Susie's forthcoming wedding and discussing what they were going to give the happy couple. They thought that life couldn't get any better. After lunch, Sidney went outside to polish his old Jaguar. When Anne came out later to bring him a cup of tea, neither of them noticed the car parked across the road, or the fact that the occupant was speaking into his mobile phone in an animated fashion.

On the other end of the line, Kevin smiled in anticipation. Surely he'd be lucky this time. He congratulated Malcolm on his quick work, then went to hunt through his negatives. He'd show that bitch and her pompous husband, that was for sure.

CHAPTER 8

Susie felt that she had found her wedding venue. She, David, Mummy and Daddy had a fab lunch at The Swan at Streatley, after which they had a look at a couple of bedrooms and had a brief chat with the Wedding Co-Ordinator. She just wasn't sure whether she wanted to actually marry there, or in the church in Moulsford. She rather fancied the bit about the grand entrance on Daddy's arm, when everyone's heads would swivel round to look at her.

"What do you think, David?" she asked her husband-to-be.

"I want whatever makes you happy, Susie," he replied. "I think you should have the opportunity to wear your dress for the longest time possible. Also, if we did get married in the church, we would have a little time for ourselves between the church and the reception. Otherwise our guests are going to want a piece of us all day. I think your Dad would be proud to give you away, too."

Susie could see the sense of that. The church would provide the theatre for her dramatic entrance, followed by her bridesmaids, and the ceremony would be longer, giving people a far better opportunity to admire her. She would ring Mummy and Daddy and suggest it to them.

Peter answered the phone when she rang, and groaned inwardly when he heard the W word, as he now called it. He asked Susie if she would like to speak to her mother.

"Not particularly, thank you, Daddy," she replied. "Let me run this by you first. David and I have been having a chat about the wedding. We do like The Swan, but think perhaps we'd actually like to get married in Moulsford Church and go on to The Swan for the reception. What do you think?"

Peter bristled with pride. He could think of nothing that would give him greater pleasure than escorting his only daughter down the aisle.

"I think that would be lovely, sweetie," he said. "I'll go and get Mummy so that you can tell her."

Annabelle was also delighted. "Now we need to co-ordinate the two," she said. "Would you like me and Daddy to go over to The Swan and suss out availability, and when we have that, you and David could make an appointment to go and see the vicar and see if you can tie the two together. It's the second week in April now, so I don't think we could possibly organise things much before the end of September, beginning of October."

Susie replied that that would be really good. She then went and told

David what had been agreed. They both felt that they were now making progress and soon would be husband and wife.

***

Susie was delighted when her mother called the next day to tell her that the Swan had one or two vacancies in September for Saturday weddings, and that all of October was also available.

"Shall we book an appointment to see the vicar?" she asked David. He agreed immediately and Susie got on the phone and made an appointment for the following Saturday.

The Reverend Collins turned out to be a woman, which of course Susie knew already, having spoken with her. She asked the couple various questions, such as whether they had been christened in the Church of England and whether either of them had been married before. Happy with Susie and David's answers, she took out her diary and asked them when they would like to get married. After some to-ing and fro-ing, Saturday 28 September at 2.30 pm was agreed upon and booked.

The happy pair went straight to Riverside House and shared their news with Peter and Annabelle. Annabelle was delighted that they could now start planning in earnest, although Peter had something to say about the vicar being a woman!

Annabelle told her husband that it was time he limped into the 21st century, as his views were hopelessly outdated. Peter laughed at that and said that maybe she was right, but that he was more than capable of organising a damn good do, and suggested that she phoned The Swan post haste and booked the reception, before someone else got in and picked that date.

That done, Annabelle told Susie that they didn't have that much time to plan a wedding, so they needed to sit down and sort things out.

"Drink, David?" enquired Peter. "I feel Operation W is about to commence and I don't think we need to be involved at this stage."

David nodded his head, so the men folk collected Allsort and set off for a walk to the Beetle and Wedge.

"Don't forget this place only has three rooms, David," said Peter. "You'd better get one booked for the night before the wedding as you can't stay with us. It would be bad luck for you to see Susie on your wedding morning."

David went along to Reception and did just that. Things really were beginning to fall into place. In five months' time he would be marrying the woman of his dreams. He couldn't wait to tell his parents and sister that the date had been set.

Meanwhile, back at home, his bride and future mother-in-law were busy with lists. Annabelle told Susie that she and David must draw up a guest list ASAP and mail it to her, so that she could combine it with hers and Peter's.

"You must also ask George and Julia to do a list, and David must choose his best man and ushers and make sure they know when the date is. You must tell Grace the date; Jenny will know, as you'll be telling the Timmins later today, I'm sure. You need to buy some wedding magazines and get some ideas about wedding dresses and bridesmaids' dresses and how you think you'd like your tables decorated, etc etc.

"You might also like to start choosing your hymns and readings, so that we can think about getting the Orders of Service printed. It would be good to do the invitations at the same time, so have a think about those as well. Once you have some idea about dresses, you and I need to go shopping to have a preliminary look, before involving Grace and Jenny. And of course, you and David can choose your wedding rings now, which I know you're keen to do."

"Stop, Mummy, please," squealed Susie. "I can't take on any more just now. It's all so exciting, but quite hard going too."

"OK," said Annabelle. "Make the guest list your priority and then we can give The Swan an idea of numbers, and they will be able to tell us what they can do for us. We also need to think about how many rooms we should book for the night of your wedding. I think I'll give them another call now to be on the safe side. Obviously I'll book the Honeymoon Suite for you and David, and I think another twenty rooms for starters."

With that, David, Peter and Allsort returned home, the first two enquiring as to what was for lunch?

***

Sidney and Anne were absolutely delighted to receive Annabelle's call regarding Susie and David's wedding and started chattering excitedly. Anne said that she would wait until she knew what colour the bridesmaids were wearing before she chose her outfit, as she wanted to tone in with them. Sidney rolled his eyes to Heaven and wondered if this was going to be his wife's sole topic of conversation for the next five months.

Of course he was thrilled that his granddaughter was going to marry David, but there were other things in life, after all. He felt sorry for Peter, because knowing his daughter as he knew her, and her great organisational skills, he bet the poor fellow was going through hell right now. The wedding would be the only thing on Annabelle's mind and she would be busy making plans. How life had changed since he had married his beloved Anne all those years ago. How many was it? Fifty-three, he thought. He'd have to look out the Marriage Certificate. That would be far more appropriate than asking his wife.

At that point, the phone rang and Sidney went to answer it. A voice he didn't recognise asked to speak with Anne. He offered her the phone, saying he didn't know who it was. Anne took it from him with a puzzled look on her face, which soon changed to a completely different look altogether.

CHAPTER 9

When James and Greg were told the wedding date, Simon asked if he'd be invited. "I don't suppose you'll still be with us in September, will you brother?" asked Greg doubtfully.

"I don't see why not," came the cheerful reply. "I'm enjoying myself here, and you can't say I'm not useful. I'm helping in your antique shop now and I've even done the odd job for James' parents. They were really pleased with those trees that I felled."

Greg couldn't argue with any of that. Simon had really applied himself and was contributing around the house and in the shop. He wasn't paid anything for the hours he put in, but then he didn't pay any rent either. Little did Greg know, but Simon had been filching things from the other shopkeepers at The Lamb and now had a little stash of goodies hidden in his bedroom. He was very careful, and always made sure that, if he was going to steal anything, the Arcade was extremely busy.

He was currently sussing out the Rowlands, and Riverside House, to decide how best he could profit there. He had been paid handsomely for any odd jobs that he'd done, but that wasn't enough. There was more up for grabs there.

He hadn't been to the sister's house, but then that was bloody miles away and like as not a nightmare on public transport. She probably wouldn't have much to interest him anyway. He needed to concentrate on making himself quite indispensable here, so that Greg could see the merit of him staying for the foreseeable future.

There were also James' investments. He'd found some very interesting reading material that first night he came to Cholsey, and he hadn't managed yet to make a large withdrawal from any of those investments. Come to think of it, that might well have to be his swan song. If he could get a few thousand out of one of them, he would then disappear without trace. He'd probably have to! In the meantime, he would just do the best that he could.

Simon suddenly realised that James was speaking to him and saying how good it was to have him around. Simon smirked inwardly. If only the stupid little shirt lifter realised what was going on. His degree in whatever it was certainly hadn't made him streetwise. Outwardly, Simon smiled and said it was just such fun as he hadn't shared a place with old Greg since they were kids, and then Greg had gone off to do his Fine Art course and he had eventually gone to college himself, but dropped out to see a bit of the world. He had found travel addictive, and the rest was history.

James was still droning on and saying how pleased he was that David had asked him to be an usher at the wedding. He'd never been one before and it was a great honour.

Great honour, Simon thought to himself. His brother really had shacked up with a total numpty. Still, that could only be to his advantage. He needed to make James his new best friend.

***

Whilst Simon was busy scheming as to how he could best exploit the Rowlands, Annabelle was having an extremely difficult conversation with her mother.

"Calm down, Mummy, please," she was saying. "Just tell me what's happened. Is Daddy all right?"

Anne tried to take a deep breath and stop crying, but found it impossible. She had just had an awful telephone conversation with some man calling himself Kevin, who had told her that he had taken photographs of her daughter in the nude some thirty-ish years ago. Surely that couldn't be true?

It was now Annabelle's turn to take a deep breath. How had that bastard found her mother? It had to have been by chance. Of course he would have known her maiden name, but there were lots of Wilkins in Derbyshire, so he had either been very persistent or just damn lucky. It didn't matter either way. She had to deal with this.

"I wasn't very old, Mummy," she said, "and I did a bit of modelling for photos for pin money. I was then offered a job as a glamour model, and I assumed that I'd be wearing lovely fur coats and beautiful jewellery. You know the sort of thing. So... I signed a contact with this man called Kevin, which I obviously didn't read properly, and then he told me to take my clothes off. When I refused, he said he would take me to Court for breach of contract, so I just did what I was told. Is he trying to blackmail you? He tried that with me last year, but Peter was wonderful and sent him away with a flea in his ear. I hope he isn't trying to blackmail you, Mummy?"

Anne cringed. She hadn't known anything about her daughter's photographic modelling, and the thought that Annabelle had taken her clothes off in front of a stranger quite disgusted her.

"Why on earth didn't you come and tell me and Daddy?" she asked. "Your father would soon have sorted him out."

"Because I knew you'd be cross with me," came the reply.

"I'm more than cross now," replied her mother. "I have this person called Kevin wanting to show me your glamour photos, as you so sweetly call them, so that I know they exist, prior to him taking them to the village where David's parents live, so that they can see what sort of a family their

34

son is marrying in to. Of course, I can buy the photos for £10,000, but we both know that won't be the end of it, don't we? Honestly, Annabelle, I don't have a clue what to do here. Your father and I can't spare £10,000 for a start. What do you suggest?"

Annabelle turned hot and cold alternately. What the hell was Peter going to say this time?

***

The man in question was at Huntercombe golf course, having had a round with his old pal, Alex Drummond. It had been good to bump into Alex at Buck House and to discover that he was living in Oxford. The men had exchanged mobile numbers and vowed to keep in touch and were enjoying renewing their old friendship. They were now in the 19th hole reminiscing about their RAF days and Alex was discovering that Peter had a share in a light aircraft which he kept at Kidlington. The two men agreed that they should go flying together, although Alex confessed that he didn't have a PPL.

"Never mind, Drummond," said Peter. "I do and I can do the flying."

Peter then went on to say that he was sorry that Elizabeth had died so early, but was delighted that Alex had found happiness again with Angela.

"I'm sure that you know this, but my stupid daughter had an affair with Angela's husband, which cost her her job at Woodstock Academy. I didn't realise who Angela was that day at the Palace when we all went for a drink at The Ritz."

"Don't give it another thought," replied his old friend. "If it hadn't been for your daughter, I don't know that Angela would ever have left her husband as she's such an honourable person. So, inadvertently, your daughter did me a big favour. I couldn't be happier. I also have the children that Elizabeth and I couldn't have, even if I do have to share them some weekends."

"I'm glad about that," said Peter. "Susie caused us great embarrassment, but at least she has brought you and Angela some happiness. She's getting married herself, you know. Operation W, as I like to call it, is well under way. All my wife seems to want to talk about is this bloody wedding. I must say though, that I am looking forward to walking my daughter down the aisle. She's also marrying a thoroughly lovely chap, who hopefully will be able to control her. Susie is rather headstrong. I'm probably guilty of spoiling her, but then that's what you do with girls, as I'm sure you're in the process of finding out."

Alex said that he was, although Angela did positively discourage it.

Peter assured him that you just needed to know when to put your foot down. He had had to do it with Susie, and by God, had she been surprised!

"You'll get used to it, Drummond. Trust me," he said.

At that moment Peter's phone rang. He saw that it was Annabelle, and, deciding it couldn't possibly be urgent, he rejected the call.

***

Annabelle realised immediately what Peter had done, and was very cross indeed. Surely he must realise it was important for her to disturb his precious golf. Should she drive to Huntercombe and look for him? No, that was being silly and just the sort of behaviour that Peter despised. He'd be home soon and there wasn't anything she could do at the moment. She didn't have £10,000, that was for sure.

Her mother was both cross with her and embarrassed, which she couldn't really do a lot about, but somehow she had to stop bloody Kevin showing those photographs to Julia and George. Showing them to her parents would be bad enough, but the Timmins, or her children for that matter, would be even worse. She didn't want them to think badly of her. Why ever had she been so naïve?

Eventually, she heard Peter's key in the lock.

"Go and sit down, darling, and I'll fix us some drinks," she said. "I've got something to tell you that you aren't going to like one little bit."

Peter smiled to himself. What was going on with Operation W, he wondered? Had The Swan thrown them a curve ball? He had no idea how surprised he was about to be.

CHAPTER 10

Whilst various of Susie's relatives were going through emotional turmoil, Jonathan was wondering how the hell he was going to get her back. There had been no response to the flowers, which surprised him. She hadn't even phoned him and told him to go to hell. He'd tried ringing her, but she must have changed her number because the one he had didn't work anymore. He supposed the next thing would be to visit Rose Cottage, but it was a long way on a bicycle and prohibitively expensive in a taxi.

Jonathan really was pissed off. He'd just received divorce papers from Angela and he knew that meant that he'd have to move out of the house by the time she'd had her share. But where would he go? He certainly didn't want to go back to his roots. It had taken some doing for him to lose his Brummie accent and he had the snobby boys at Radley College to thank for that.

Jonathan had been a scholarship boy and his parents hadn't had to pay a penny for his education, which was just as well, because they couldn't have afforded to. He had been a very gifted pupil who had been a good all-rounder. The other boys spoke extremely well and Jonathan had copied them successfully; so much so that no-one could possibly guess where his home town was. He had even added an "e" to his surname as he thought it looked so much better than just "Brown".

Radley had been good for Jonathan in more ways than one. It was at a school dance that he had met Angela Morris and subsequently married her. The marriage had suited him well, as he had felt that as Angela was no raving beauty she was pathetically grateful to be married to such a good looking chap as he was. She had been a dutiful wife and mother and an excellent homemaker to boot, and Jonathan had always thought that she had been unaware of his bits on the side, or if she had known about them, she had chosen to ignore them. Thus he had got the shock of his life when the little mouse had left him for another man, taking their daughters with her. That wasn't really his biggest problem though, where Angela was concerned. Old man Morris had put a fair chunk of money into the Kirtlington property and sure as hell, she was going to want it back. That was serious, because he hadn't a clue where he was going to live and he couldn't get hold of Susie.

Getting a new bird was proving to be more difficult now as he had nothing to offer - no flashy company car, no exotic trips to foreign places and, worst of all, no job and no driving licence. Hardly affair material. If he couldn't hook Susie, he needed to find someone with money who would take him in and look after him. Perhaps the time had come to search for an older woman? He must renew his subscription to that dating site and update his profile.

***

While Jonathan was scheming about women, Susie and David were writing their guest list and making their wedding plans. Susie wanted to send out Save the Date cards, but as David so rightly pointed out, they couldn't do that until her parents had approved the guest list. They had told the bridesmaids, best man and ushers, so all the main people knew about it, and they had also booked them into The Swan for the night of the wedding.

The coming weekend was going to be busy. They were going over to Moulsford to stay with Susie's parents so that they could finalise the guests and get as many other things under way as possible. Once they knew how many guests there would be, they could order the stationery. Susie and David had also been thinking hard about hymns and readings, because the vicar had said she would like to see the Order of Service before it went to the printers.

Susie had a pile of wedding magazines and had been looking at dresses, flowers, table settings and decorations. Her mother had told her that she needed to be ordering the cake, particularly if she wanted traditional fruit. These were very exciting times for the young couple, who were trying to work out the theme of their wedding. Did they want to be traditional or trendy? Susie knew that her father would expect to wear a morning suit. David said he was happy with that and they just had to decide the style and the waistcoats, and whether or not they would have top hats.

Susie told him that her father would expect top hats and asked whether that would be a problem. David pulled a face and said he supposed it was OK.

"Well, we can talk about it at the weekend," said Susie. "I think that perhaps the only things we can do now, totally on our own, is choose the rings and book the honeymoon."

Both those topics sparked off a very animated discussion. Where would the weather be good at the end of September, beginning of October? The Greek Islands seemed rather a nice choice and the pair decided they would get some travel books and have a look. This set Susie off fantasising about getting married abroad. David put his foot down very firmly indeed.

***

"How in Christ's name did that little scumbag find your mother?" Peter yelled at Annabelle. "He's definitely not having ten grand of my money, that's for sure."

"Supposing he shows the photos to my parents and the Timmins?" said Annabelle hesitantly. "Whatever are they going to think of me?"

"I think the best way to deal with that is to tell George and Julia," replied Peter. "After all, we're all adults and I'm sure that George will have been around the block a few times himself. As for your parents, they now know, so I can't see it matters if they see the pictures."

"Daddy doesn't know," replied Annabelle.

"In that case your mother will just have to tell him," was the reply.

"You're not being very sympathetic, darling," said his wife.

"What do you expect me to do?" asked Peter. "Pay the snivelling little bastard £10,000 and then he finds either Susie or James and we have to go through the whole charade all over again? No, Belle, I think the time has come to face up to what you did and rise above it."

Peter's reply both shocked and stunned Annabelle. She didn't know what she had supposed he would do, but it certainly hadn't been that! Whatever would her parents say if they saw the photos? Particularly the one that Kevin had created of her with the donkey. Could she and her parents, between them, find the money without Peter knowing? Could she approach James for a loan? Borrowing off her children, that ought to be unthinkable, but she was in a real predicament here.

"Let's invite George and Julia over for dinner and get that dealt with," said Peter. "There must be things that you need to talk to Julia about regarding the wedding, anyway. We could kill two birds with one stone. You should also ring your mother and tell her that we won't be paying the little bastard £10,000 and to prepare herself to see the photos. That is, of course, if he carries out his threat."

"I couldn't possibly tell her that over the phone," said Annabelle. "She's got to tell Daddy and I really think I should be there when she does."

"Drive up to Derbyshire then," said her unsympathetic husband. "I've dealt with this once, and have no inclination to do so again and again and again, because that's how these people act. You have to understand that, Belle, and to trust my judgment."

If only she knew how frequently he sailed very close to the wind with his share dealings, Annabelle would not be making such a fuss, but for sure he wouldn't be telling her. His wife was very moral and wouldn't approve of some of the things that he did, although she enjoyed the lavish lifestyle that his money provided.

"What night would you like to have dinner with George and Julia?" he enquired, "and would you rather we ate out as that would save you the bother of cooking?"

Annabelle replied that Thursday would suit her fine, and that she would prefer to have that conversation in the privacy of their own home. Peter picked up the phone. When he rang off, he said that George and Julia would be delighted to come to supper and would bring their suggested guest list with them. Annabelle tried to smile, although inwardly she felt sick.

CHAPTER 11

Julia and George were pleased to be invited over to the Rowlands for supper, even though it was a long way to drive there and back. They tossed for the honours and Julia lost.

"Never mind," she said cheerfully. "At least I'll be fully functional in the morning. I know what Peter's cellar's like."

George smiled. He was going to enjoy himself. They got on well with David's future in-laws and he was grateful for that. He was delighted that his son had met Susie and that he had asked her to marry him.

Later that day, in the office, George told his son about going to supper at the Rowlands. David replied that he and Susie were staying there at the weekend and that their main objective was to finalise the guest list.

"Yes, we're taking ours with us tomorrow," said his father. "It looks as though it's going to be a big do. Is that what you and Susie want?"

"I want whatever Susie wants," replied his son gallantly. "We're trying to sort out the Order of Service at the moment, because the vicar wants to see it before we go to print. Once we've finalised that, and the guest list, we can get on with having the stationery printed. The house is full of wedding magazines to try and help us focus on a theme. Susie and Annabelle are very keen on a theme. I'm pretty sure that it's going to be traditional with top hats and tails. Susie thinks that would please her father."

George laughed. "It was so different when your mother and I got married," he said, "but I'm paying attention to all that you say because your mother and I will be going through this one day with Jenny. Anyway, must crack on now, David, I've got an investment report to write for those new clients I saw yesterday, and I'm under pain of death with your mother not to be late tonight."

David laughed too and wandered back to his office.

***

Annabelle dressed with care that evening. She wanted to look good as she was feeling very nervous as to what the Timmins were going to think about her. She had been to the hairdresser that afternoon and had her long dark hair swept up à la Audrey Hepburn.

Looking in her wardrobe, Annabelle chose a cream, long-sleeved, lace dress, which she thought made her look demure, and teamed it with a pair of high heeled gold sandals. It was a particularly warm evening for April and she thought she might be hot under the collar anyway! Jewellery next - her usual gold Omega watch, a gold bangle, and her diamond tennis necklace with marching earrings. Yes, that would do.

After tonight she still had her mother to deal with. Annabelle had spoken with Anne on the telephone the previous day, but hadn't really been able to get any sense out of her, so was planning to drive up to Derbyshire and back the following day. She knew that she was spreading herself thin with David and Susie arriving for the weekend, but it couldn't be helped. She knew that Peter was going into the City which suited her well, as he wouldn't be telling what she ought to say. Not that she had any idea what that was going to be.

Spraying herself with Coco Mademoiselle, Annabelle got to her feet and ran downstairs. She was doing a fish dinner that evening. Crab and brown shrimp salads were to be followed by Scampi Provençale, which was easy to prepare in advance. She found Peter chilling a particularly fine Sancerre, one of her favourites.

"There you are, Belle," he said. "You look very lovely, darling. What would you like to drink?"

Before she had the chance to reply, the doorbell rang, so Peter went and greeted George and Julia instead.

***

George couldn't contain his mirth on the way home.

"Who'd have thought that the very respectable Mrs Rowlands had been a nude model?" He chortled. "Wait till I tell David. I had a job to keep my face straight. Hope it wasn't too obvious?"

"Stop it, George," said Julia. "That poor woman was absolutely mortified when she was telling us. How dreadful that this Kevin person had tried to blackmail her last year and now he's coming for her parents. I don't think David needs to know at the moment. At the very least, you've got to give Peter and Annabelle a chance to tell Susie first. I'm sure if they tell Susie this weekend you'll find out when you see David on Monday."

"Fair enough," replied her husband. "It was a good evening, don't you think? As I've always said, Peter knows his wines and Annabelle is almost as good a cook as you are, my love."

Julia snorted. "Annabelle is a wonderful cook and they entertain to perfection. This wedding should be something else. Apparently, The Swan at Streatley belonged to Danny la Rue in the late 60s, early 70s."

"What's that got to do with the price of fish?" asked George. "Anyway, how and why do you know that?"

"I haven't spent my life in marketing for nothing," was the reply. "You'd be surprised at the things I know. Now, as I've done the driving tonight and by your own admission you've enjoyed Peter's cellar, you can take Honey and Mustard for their late walk."

George groaned.

***

"I'm glad that's over and done with," said Annabelle as she closed the dishwasher door. "All I have to do now is deal with Mummy and Daddy tomorrow."

Peter was feeling particularly benevolent after an excellent dinner with wonderful wines and said that he could leave the City until Monday and go with Annabelle to Derbyshire for moral support, if she so wished. As there was nothing that she would like less, Annabelle assured him that it was quite unnecessary and that she would be fine on her own.

"Well, I think it went well enough with George and Julia, so I'm sure that you don't have anything to worry about," he said reassuringly. "What's more, you should be pleased to have the list of people that they would like to invite to the wedding. It must all be coming together now."

Annabelle gave him an astonished look, so he decided the better part of valour was to shut up and take Allsort for her walk.

When he returned half an hour later, he found his wife in bed but wide awake. He guessed that she was more bothered than she cared to let on about going to see her parents. He did his very best to soothe her with some gentle lovemaking, but she was still awake when he drifted off to sleep.

Peter knew his suspicions were correct when Annabelle went for a run first thing the following morning. That was always a sign that something was troubling her.

CHAPTER 12

James was surprised to find a group of shopkeepers all standing together when he got to the Lamb on Friday morning, and quite shocked when one of them came up to him to ask if he had had anything go missing. He had shaken his head, saying not to his knowledge, and asked why they wanted to know.

To his horror, he discovered that every single one of them had had something stolen recently. The missing items ranged from jewellery, through vintage lace to silverware and porcelain. It appeared that the items were random and there was no particular pattern.

On learning this, James made two phone calls. The first was to his mother who was driving to Derbyshire, braced for a difficult time with her parents and the second was to Greg. Annabelle told him that she was concentrating on her driving and asked if they could discuss it later, and Greg sounded as horrified as James felt.

As soon as he had put the phone down Greg went and looked for Simon. He found him in the garden, throwing a stick for his terrier, Zizi.

"What've you been up to, you little shit?" he demanded.

Simon looked pained, although his mind was racing, and asked his brother what on earth he was on about?

Greg replied that he thought Simon knew what he was talking about and that was that things were being stolen from the Lamb Arcade and that this had only happened since he had been helping out.

"Talk about give a dog a bad name," said Simon with a very injured look on his face. "I've paid the price and done the time for my mistake. Am I likely to be so stupid again? Look, mate, you and James have been very good to me. You've taken me in, which is more than our own parents would do, and James has even given me clothes. In return, I've tried to help out both you and James' parents. I've worked in your shop and I've done some gardening jobs for James' parents. Whatever makes you think I'd cock all that up?"

Mmn, Greg thought to himself. He sounds plausible enough, but I need to get him away from here for long enough to search his room. As he was thinking that, Simon was having somewhat similar thoughts. How could he get Greg out of the house for long enough to move the goodies from his bedroom? That done, his next job was to steal from both Greg and Annabelle as that should definitely divert suspicion away from him.

They both spoke at once, asking each other what their plans were for the day. Simon asked Greg if he thought he should go into the Arcade to see what was going on. Greg replied that James was more than capable of dealing with things there.

"Why don't we do something together?" suggested Simon. "If you've nothing on, that would make a nice change. We could drive out and maybe do some shopping."

That would only work if he got James home to search Simon's room and he didn't want his partner to know what his brother might have got up to, so that wouldn't do.

"No thanks," he replied. "I don't feel like going out today, but don't let that stop you. I'm going to cook up some curries for supper tomorrow. They're much better if left to marinate overnight." Maybe he'd be able to send Simon out for some missing ingredient.

Simon swore under his breath.

***

Annabelle turned off the ignition and took a deep breath. She hoped that she could speak to her mother on her own to start with. She just couldn't imagine explaining to Daddy about being a nude model.

Anne came to the door to meet her daughter. Annabelle was concerned to see how frail she looked. She seemed to have aged ten years. Bloody Kevin had a lot to answer for.

"Hello Mummy," she said, offering the hand-tied bouquet of flowers that she had bought the previous day.

The two women kissed each other warmly and Anne led the way into the little house. "Where's Daddy?" was the first thing Annabelle asked.

"He's walked down to the shops to get a couple of things," replied her mother. "He shouldn't be too long. He knows that you're visiting today."

Annabelle quickly ascertained that her father still knew nothing of Kevin and his photos. She explained to her mother that he had tried to blackmail her the previous summer, but that Peter had dealt with him. She went on to say that she was all for trying to find the £10,000 and paying him off once and for all, but that Peter had said he would come back for more and wouldn't give her any money.

"I'm sure Peter knows best, dear," said her mother, fussing around with coffee and biscuits. "We'll just have to be brave and tell Daddy. He won't like it, but then he doesn't have £10,000 either."

"I did think of asking James if he could lend me some money, but that just struck me as too awful," said Annabelle. "Peter invited George and Julia Timmins for supper last night and made me tell them. I could see George trying hard not to laugh, but I suppose it's better they thought it funny rather than shocking. Once we've told Daddy the only people who won't know will be the children, and I really don't see how Kevin could find either of them. He can't possibly know where they live. If push comes to shove, I can always tell them. I wouldn't want them to find out any other way."

With a nervous smile Annabelle picked up her coffee, and mother and daughter waited, each deep in their own thoughts.

***

Everything considered, Sidney took the news of his daughter's modelling career quite well, but was appalled by the threat of blackmail and wanted to go to the police, saying that Annabelle knew this man, so she could give evidence. Annabelle pointed out that it was some thirty years ago and all she knew was that his name was Kevin and that he used to work for *The Buxton Echo*, and she had been instrumental in getting him sacked from there.

"There we are," said her father jubilantly. "He can be traced via the newspaper. It's still going, you know. We can get him and bring the swine to justice. All we need to do is play him along and get the police involved. Next time he rings, your mother must agree to meet him and then the police can nab him. Don't worry my loves, I shall go to the police and sort it all out, so you can just stop worrying."

Anne looked very relieved, but Annabelle didn't share her confidence and drove back to Moulsford with a heavy heart. She had two concerns - her mother's health, which clearly wasn't as good as it had been only recently, and flaming Kevin. Come to think of it, she must also speak with James. He had been wittering on about some thefts in the Lamb Arcade this morning and she hadn't had time to listen.

As it was rush hour on a Friday she got snarled up in the traffic on the M1, which gave her plenty of time to call James and hear about the goings on at The Lamb. Something else to concern her! James didn't think they'd lost anything, but she'd feel better when she'd looked for herself. She had a busy weekend too, and owed all her time to Susie and David. The kids were already at Riverside House by the time she got home.

Susie was keen to know how her grandparents were. Annabelle assured her that they were both well and looking forward to the wedding. Grandma was eager to know what colour the bridesmaids were going to wear, so that she could co-ordinate with them.

Feeling a full blown wedding discussion coming on, Peter hastily changed the subject and suggested that they should have a takeaway and that he and David would go and fetch it. Anything to get away! The weekend was going to be taken over by Operation W and he was already wondering how essential his presence would be.

They had a lively evening looking at the various guest lists and reminiscing about people they hadn't seen in years. There was also the inevitable question as to whether certain people really had to be invited. In the end they agreed they couldn't possibly look at names any longer and decided to call it a night. Susie thought her mother looked tired and a bit down. She wondered if Annabelle was telling the truth when she said that Grandma and Grandpa were fine, but now wasn't the time to ask. Instead, she said that she and David would walk Allsort so that her parents could go to bed.

***

Once Susie and David had gone out, Peter turned to his wife and asked her if everything was OK and what had happened at her parents. Annabelle told him that her father was adamant he was involving the police, which would in turn involve her as she had known Kevin as a teenager. Peter said that he hoped it wouldn't come to anything and that Kevin would just go away, although privately he felt that was very unlikely.

Annabelle went on to tell him that her mother seemed to have aged ten years recently, and that was worrying her. Peter said he was sure that was the hassle of the photos and Sidney not knowing about them, and now that everything was out in the open, he was confident that her mother would feel better and therefore look better. Annabelle hoped he was right, although she was still doubtful. Once again she vowed that she must make an effort to see her parents more often.

"And finally," she said to Peter, "there's the little matter of the Arcade. James phoned me today to tell me that there's been a load of thefts, but that to the best of his knowledge we haven't lost anything. It never rains but it pours. I'm going to be so busy with the wedding coming up, I was wondering whether perhaps Greg's brother might be able to help me out. He's helped out Greg and James now that they've got the double unit next door to me, so he does know a bit about the business, and there's always plenty of people around to ask if he's unsure. What do you think, darling?"

"Belle, it's always been your business and nothing to do with me, now please come to bed before Susie and David get back, otherwise it'll look as though you're unappreciative of their efforts in walking Allsort. Also, I would enjoy spending some time with you alone."

With that, Peter took Annabelle's hand and led her towards the stairs.

CHAPTER 13

The weekend passed in a flurry of wedding preparations, and after some minor squabbles the guest list was finalised. With help from Annabelle, Susie and David sorted out their hymns and their readings. Phone calls were made to a couple of people to check that they were happy to read, and then Susie left a message for the Reverend Collins asking when it would be possible for her and David to go and discuss the Order of Service.

Despite superficially functioning on all levels, Annabelle's mind was in turmoil. She was worrying about her mother and her shop in the Lamb Arcade. Nevertheless she cooked delicious meals and guided her daughter and future son-in-law in the right direction with their wedding plans. She always had been a natural organiser and was enjoying planning a wedding. Peter spent a lot of the time closeted in his study with the weekend *Telegraph* for company, coming up for air at mealtimes.

When they had waved the couple off, fairly late on Sunday afternoon, Annabelle turned her mind to her antiques. The Arcade was closed, so she rang James to see what was going on, and for the latest news. He told her that he had been there all day with Simon, looking after the two shops between them, and horror of horrors, they had had the pair of Derby dwarfs stolen, and neither of them knew how it could have happened. Annabelle swore. Those Dwarfs were late eighteenth century, pristine mint and had cost her £2,000. They were worth £2,500 of anybody's money.

***

The previous day, to Greg's delight, Simon had announced that he was going to catch a bus to Oxford and take in some culture. The evening before, when everyone had gone to bed, he had packed his rucksack with all his goodies, having taken off the labels and memorised the information written on them. That was the good thing about these thefts, he had all the information he needed about each piece, so no other dealer would be able to pull the wool over his eyes.

Walking to the bus stop, Simon felt pleased with himself. He was sure that Greg would go through his room in his absence and as he wouldn't find anything, that should put him in the clear. Simon was quite right, half an hour after he had left the house, his brother was methodically searching everywhere.

However, the fact that he didn't find anything didn't convince Greg of his brother's innocence. He knew that Simon could have gone to Oxford to dispose of the stolen items. Question was, should he jump in the car and go to Oxford himself and see if he could catch the little git in action? But then again, it was a Saturday and it wasn't really fair to leave James with the two shops when he knew that Annabelle would be busy in Moulsford, wedding planning.

Greg made himself a cup of coffee and sat pondering. He didn't want to ring James and tell him of his suspicions, so why could he suddenly need to go somewhere? The only emergency he could think of was a dental one. Could he swing that? It might work, because his dentist was in Oxford. He called James.

"Oh poor you," said James, on discovering that Greg had lost a filling. "I can manage here if you can get an appointment today."

***

Greg parked in the Westgate car park and set off down the High Street. There was a variety of antique shops there and it could be where Simon had headed. He drew a blank everywhere he looked, and then he thought he saw his brother about a hundred and fifty yards ahead. He quickened his pace and tried to push through the Saturday crowds. By the time he had done that, the figure had disappeared, but Greg was sure that he hadn't been mistaken. Where, oh where, had the little shit gone?

Simon had had a productive couple of hours and had sold everything. He had spun a yarn about his mother having recently died and that he needed to sell some of her things to pay for her funeral. That worked well and dealers were perhaps a little more generous than they would normally have been. He had over £5,000 in his pocket and Greg had lost him when he had gone to deposit the major part of it in Barclays Bank.

Coming out of the bank, Simon smiled to himself. Wasn't that his big brother up ahead on the opposite side of the road? Now, should he cross over and catch up with him or not? Whilst he was thinking about what to do, Simon screwed up his paying in slip and tossed it into a wastepaper bin. He couldn't risk leaving any evidence lying about.

"You could have told me you were coming into Oxford and given me a lift," Simon said when he finally caught up with Greg.

"I wasn't planning on it, but then a big filling came out of my tooth and I managed to get an appointment with the dentist," was the smooth reply. "I then thought I'd take a quick stroll down the High Street and have a look at what was going on in the Oxford antiques world."

I'll bet you did, thought Simon to himself. No doubt you were looking for me. Well, I'm smarter than you big brother. You'll have to get up early to catch me.

"And did you see anything worth buying?"

Greg shook his head and told Simon that if he'd had enough culture he'd give him a lift back to Cholsey.

***

Greg made a point of saying that he had toothache that evening, as he wanted his story to be believed by both lover and brother. He had made curries the previous day so dinner was both quick and simple to prepare. He was still worried by the thefts and told James that he felt they needed a minimum of two people between the two shops at any one time. Simon immediately suggested that he and James should go the following day, giving Greg a chance to nurse his poorly tooth. Fate seemed to be playing into his hands.

Simon had two objectives that Sunday. One was to nick at least one thing from either Greg's or Annabelle's shop and the other was to make James his new best friend. He started as soon as they got into the Mini by telling James how much he liked his car. James preened and told Simon that it had been a birthday present and all about his party the previous year. He explained that was where he had met David, who was his Financial Adviser. He had met David through David's sister Jenny, who James had gone to college with, and then in turn, Susie had met David and now they were to be married.

"What a lovely story," said Simon with a big smile, although in actual fact he wasn't in the slightest bit interested. "Weren't you lucky when you turned twenty-one? Didn't you inherit some money?"

James told Simon about both his inheritance and his lottery win, which had helped him and Greg to take on the larger shop in Wallingford.

"Don't you and Greg just have a fab life," he said as James parked the car, more determined than ever to take what he could. Yesterday had been pleasing, banking five grand, but he was going to have to be careful here now, as people were noticing that things were going missing.

When James went to get them coffee, Simon sized up the two shops. Some jewellery from Greg would be easy, as not all of it was in locked cabinets, but he did rather fancy the odd pair of pot-bellied figures in silly hats in Annabelle's shop. They were marked up at £2,750, so why mess about with piddling bits of silver when he could have one good hit? How was he going to get them out? That was the next question. He felt his pockets would bulge if he shoved one in each. Could he hide them and come back for them later? Yes, that was it.

Just as they were nearly out of the door he'd tell James that he'd forgotten something and go back for the dwarfs. There was still the problem of concealing them though. If he could buy something cheap that was fairly large, he could hide the dwarfs in the bag with that. Yes, that was what he would have to do.

Simon's opportunity came later. He said to James that he fancied a walk around the Arcade now that it had gone quiet, as he'd never really had the chance to have a proper look. Now, what to buy? Finally he saw some cushion covers. He didn't particularly like them, but they were nice and big and would protect the dwarfs from damage. Handing over £60, Simon made his purchase.

He made a great show of letting James see the cushion covers and then when James was busy helping a young chap choose a present for his girlfriend, having made sure that no-one was watching him, Simon stuffed the dwarfs into the cushion covers and put his carrier bag under Annabelle's wrapping table. He then sauntered over to James to see how he was getting on. The customer eventually chose an armful of silver bangles and went on his way looking very pleased with his purchase. Simon felt it was about time that it was noticed that the Derby dwarfs had gone AWOL. He walked ahead of James back to the shop next door where he gave a gasp of horror.

"Have you sold those ugly little chaps with the peculiar hats?" he asked James. "I could have sworn they were there a minute ago."

CHAPTER 14

Susie and David went to see the Reverend Collins the following week for approval of their Order of Service. They called in at Riverside House afterwards and agreed upon wedding stationery. Susie was desperate to send out Save the Date cards, so they were ordered as well. Peter had no hesitation in saying that they would only be thrown away, and couldn't see the point of them at all, but then that was Peter!

After Susie and David had left to go back to Enstone, Annabelle explained to him how exciting it all was for the young couple.

"You bought me a ring and turned up at the Church, and that was how it was done then," she said, "but this is now and weddings are big business. It's going to cost a lot of money, so it has to be right."

"Don't I know it," replied her husband, "but Susie's my only daughter and I want to do her proud."

How things had changed from the previous summer, when they had both despaired of their daughter and her antics.

In the car, Susie and David were also talking about their wedding.

"We seem to be almost living with your parents," David said to his fiancée.

"It's unavoidable at the moment. As they're paying for the wedding, it's only fair that they should be involved in the decisions. You don't mind, do you, David?"

"Of course not," he replied, accelerating up the hill out of Woodstock. "It's just all the travelling backwards and forwards. It's not so bad when we go for the weekend, but there and back on a week night is a bit much. Poor old George will think we've abandoned him."

George was Susie's large ginger cat.

"George is in cat heaven being looked after by Alf and his gang," replied Susie. "I know Alf slips him minced steak and chicken and salmon. He's an old softie where that cat's concerned."

"Let's call in and have a quick drink before bed," said David. "It would also give us a chance to say thank you for services rendered to George."

The pub was busy when Susie and David went in and Alf was looking flustered. He'd had a member of staff go off sick and in his words he was dashing about like a blue-arsed fly, which was no good to him at his age.

Susie was very fond of the old chap, who had been kind to her when she had had all her problems.

"If you'd like to sit down and talk to David, I'm sure that I can remember how to run your bar," Susie said to him, and within seconds they had changed places and she was the one dashing about with pints of beer and large gins and tonics.

***

Kevin and Malcolm were drinking to their good fortune. They were confident that Anne Wilkins would come good with the ten grand. Kevin agreed that he would give her another bell the following morning to see if she had the money. They were now discussing where the handover should take place. They didn't want it to be anywhere sinister or difficult as they didn't want to frighten the old biddy.

"I think you should just arrange to go to the house," said Malcolm. "She'll be comfortable there, and it'll also give you the chance to count it."

Kevin scratched his groin thoughtfully.

"Yeah, I suppose so," he said. He raised his glass. "Here's to our success. This time next week, we'll be rich, mate. What you going to spend yours on?"

***

The following morning Kevin rang the Wilkins and was pleased when Anne answered the phone. He was more pleased still when she agreed to him going round on Thursday afternoon. That would give her plenty of time to get the money.

When she had replaced the receiver with shaking hands, Anne wondered what she should do. Should she contact the police as Sidney wanted, or should she just tell this villain to go to hell? Sidney hadn't heard the phone ring as he had been putting out the rubbish, so she had time to think. Two days in fact, as it was only Tuesday. Perhaps she would start by ringing Annabelle and seeing what she thought. Sidney was playing bowls that afternoon, so she would have the opportunity to do that while he was out.

Just after two o'clock, Anne rang her daughter. With a trembling voice, she explained that Kevin was coming to collect his money on Thursday and should she go to the police as Annabelle's father wanted her to do, or should she just tell him to go to hell? Annabelle said that she would have a word with Peter and ring her back.

Peter said he was glad that his wife and her mother weren't trying to find the money, but he was a bit worried about a vulnerable couple telling the brute to go to hell. He could become nasty and try and beat them up and then rifle through the cottage to see what he could steal. He felt that he should go up there, once again armed with a tape machine. He really would like to stop the slimy little bastard once and for all.

54

Annabelle gave him a kiss and went and phoned her mother, who was very relieved that her son-in-law would be visiting on Thursday.

***

On the day in question, Peter was at Daffodil Cottage bright and early, telling Anne and Sidney exactly what he would like them to do. Anne was to go to the door and invite the obnoxious chap into the hallway, whereupon Sidney could go through. It wouldn't take the little rat long to demand the money, but Anne must ask to see at least one photograph just to make sure that he did in fact have them. Peter would put his Dictaphone in a place where it couldn't fail to pick up the conversation and he would join them when he felt the moment was right. That would shake him all right! He had taken the precaution of leaving his BMW in the next street, in case Kevin should recognise it.

Promptly at two o'clock, there was a knock on the door. Anne went and opened it and let Kevin into the hallway.

"I can see where your pretty daughter got her looks from, darlin'," he said in his obnoxious nasal whine. "I'll bet you were a right looker in your time."

"How dare you speak to my wife in that manner?" demanded Sidney, entering on cue. "Show us your photographs and then you can go."

"Not without the ten grand, I don't," snivelled Kevin, having a scratch. "Show me the lolly."

"Photographs," snapped Sidney.

This wasn't really going as Kevin had planned. He'd expected the old girl to be on her own and to be easy meat. It looked as though the old man might have a bit about him. He hoped he wouldn't have to turn nasty. He didn't want to duff up the old codger. Fishing around in the scruffy case that he was carrying, Kevin extracted a large brown envelope.

"They're in here, mate," he said, shoving the envelope into Sidney's hand.

As Sidney was opening the envelope and looking with horror at a photograph of his naked daughter, Peter strolled through.

"Not you again, you snivelling little wretch," he said contemptuously. "I thought I made myself clear last time. No-one is going to pay you any money for your dirty photos, because no-one's interested in them. Would you like to watch while I throw them on the fire? You'll run out of copies of the bloody things eventually. I've recorded your demand for money again in case I need to involve the police, but for now you can just piss off."

Kevin made the mistake of hanging around for that bit too long. Peter opened the front door, pushing Kevin through it, perhaps with slightly more force than was required, so that the wretch fell face-down on the driveway.

Blood running from his nose, Kevin staggered back to his car. That snotty bastard Rowlands again! What would Malcolm have to say? No doubt he would find out very shortly.

Malcolm in fact had quite a lot to say and it wasn't complimentary.

CHAPTER 15

Simon walked over to Annabelle and said how sorry he was that the dwarfs had been stolen, and from under his nose too.

"Yes," she said. "They're a strange choice. It has to be a specific collector. No-one would be able to pass those within the trade. There aren't that many pairs of them and mine were absolutely pristine. I've rung round a lot of the dealers and alerted them and I've also told the police. Not that I expect much help from them. My lovely Mansion House dwarfs probably have pride of place on someone's sideboard by now."

Oh no, they don't, thought Simon. They're wrapped in my underpants at the bottom of a drawer, hopefully away from prying eyes. The bugger of it was that it didn't look as though he'd be able to move the bloody things on. Not yet anyway. He needed to make himself indispensable to Annabelle so that he could get a good shuftie inside Riverside House. There had to be pickings there.

"You must be so stressed out with the wedding and all the things that you have to arrange," he said. "Is there anything at all I can do to help you? You and your husband have made me feel so welcome."

Annabelle smiled. "The Baxters are going away the week after next. I wouldn't expect you to do housework, but perhaps you could do some of Mr B's jobs, such as clean the cars?"

Simon said that indeed he could, and that housework was no trouble to him either. He found it relaxing, so if she would like him to have a flip through the house, he'd be more than happy to do so. It would make a change from cleaning for Greg and James. It would be even better were Peter to be out, he thought to himself, because then he could have a good scout round. The question now, though, was what to do with those bloody dwarfs? Could he allegedly find them somewhere and be a hero by returning them? No, too obvious. He might just have to dump them somewhere. Then inspiration hit him! He would dig a hole in Greg's garden and bury them carefully. The fuss would have to die down eventually and then he'd be able to dig them up and do something with them.

***

Malcolm had been furious with Kevin.

"That's twice you've cocked things up," he had said. "I could do better myself."

That was how he found himself driving the long distance to Great Rollright the following morning. He'd show that silly arse Kevin. He'd get some dosh out of the Timmins's. Luckily for him, Great Rollright wasn't a large village and he soon found his way to The Barn.

Julia was irritated when she heard the knock at the front door. She was busy working on a deadline for a project she was delivering in London the following week. Reluctantly, she put her glasses down on her desk and went to see who the caller was.

Malcolm had spruced himself up for the occasion as he wished to create a favourable impression.

Sadly, he failed miserably to do so.

"Good morning," he said to Julia as she opened the door. "We haven't met before, but I'm Annabelle Rowlands' half-brother. I understand that your son is going to marry her daughter."

"He is, but I fail to see what concern that is of yours," replied Julia.

"Ah, well, there are certain things that I think you should be aware of," said Malcolm, with what he hoped was an ingratiating smile. "Could I perhaps come in, rather than talk here on the doorstep?"

Julia felt obliged to show the stranger through to the sitting room, where she offered him a seat, but nothing else.

"Now, how may I help you?" she enquired. "I'd appreciate it if you could get to the point quickly, because I am rather busy today."

Malcolm smiled again.

"I think you'll find it is I who can help you," he replied.

Julia's eyebrows shot up. How could Annabelle's half-brother possibly help her?

"You see, Mrs Timmins," he said, "I was born a bastard and my mother had me adopted. However, I managed to find my birth mother, who is also Annabelle's mother, but neither of them want anything to do with me."

I wonder why? Julia thought to herself. Malcolm was getting on her nerves.

"Now, me and my friend have got disgustingly obscene photos of Annabelle, supposedly modelling, and I'm quite sure that you wouldn't want your son to see them, would you? What's more, do you want your son to be marrying into that kind of family? You strike me as a nice, sensible sort of woman, and I'm sure we could come to an amicable arrangement where your son doesn't get to see any of the nasty pictures. Otherwise, I think I might go and introduce myself to him. You wouldn't want me to do that now, would you?"

"To be quite honest, I don't care what you do and where you go as long as you leave here immediately," said Julia, rising to her feet. "I've no idea how you found this house, but I strongly advise you not to return here again. You might not be so fortunate next time. My husband might be at home and he likes potential blackmailers even less than I do. I can quite understand why Annabelle and her mother want nothing to do with you."

After Malcolm had left, Julia made two phone calls. The first to Annabelle, and the second to George.

***

Annabelle was in the Arcade when Julia phoned. She left her shop in the care of Simon, who immediately pocketed a silver snuff box while she went up to the Coffee Shop where she could talk more freely. Feeling horrified by what Malcolm had done, she couldn't apologise enough. Julia assured her there was no need to apologise; she was merely alerting her to the fact that Malcolm, instead of Kevin, was now trying his hand at blackmail, and wondered whether Susie and David ought to know about the photos. Julia went on to say that she didn't know how Malcolm would find either of them, but then he'd managed to find her. Annabelle told her not to worry, as Susie and David were staying in Moulsford again for the weekend, and she would tell them then.

"What are you sorting this weekend?" asked Julia, relieved to get away from Malcolm.

"Susie and I are having a preliminary look at dresses on Saturday and then we're going to another Wedding Fair on Sunday in Oxford. They enjoyed the last one and I'm hoping we might find a photographer and a cake maker. Peter will spend as much time as possible in his study with *The Telegraph*, but at least he'll have David for company on Saturday whilst Susie and I are out. They can talk things financial. That's after they have completed the little task that I'm setting them.

"Look, Julia, I'm really sorry about Malcolm. We've been pestered by Kevin. It sounds as though the two of them are in some sort of partnership and determined to fleece my family. Happily though, they aren't doing too well."

With that the two women said goodbye to each other. Julia phoned George and Annabelle phoned Peter to let him know that Malcolm was now involved in the scam too, but had drawn a blank with Julia.

***

Susie and David arrived at Riverside House that evening bubbling with ideas. Susie had seen a few dresses that she liked and was laden with bridal magazines. They had also seen some fabulous wedding rings and table layouts with the most beautiful decorations.

"Calm down, darlings," said Annabelle. "One thing at a time. I've made four appointments at bridal shops tomorrow, Susie, and then we're going to the Wedding Fair on Sunday. I've even got a job for you too, Peter. You can go over to The Swan, which you will enjoy. I've made you an appointment with the Wedding Co-ordinator to look at menus and drinks packages. I've made the appointment for tomorrow at 11.30, so while Susie and I are looking at dresses, you and David will have something to do. You can report back over supper."

Over the supper table that night Annabelle told Susie and David about her half-brother, her modelling career, and the various blackmail attempts. They were stunned, and said it would be interesting to see if either Kevin or Malcolm managed to find them.

In bed that night, Susie asked David if he was upset or offended by what he had heard. "Not at all," came the sleepy reply. "I'm just sorry for your poor mother having to confess all to my parents, and now to us as well. She's still got James to tell too. I think your dad has been brilliant; not allowing anyone to give in to the bullies and for going up to help your grandparents. Come to think of it, Mum did well too. Mind you, she's not got where she is today with her marketing career by being a wimp."

Snuggling up to him, Susie confessed that she was somewhat shocked by her mother's antics and amazed that she had a half-uncle she'd never heard of, but then she understood that things were different in those days and you just didn't have a child without being married.

"You wouldn't have been sharing your room with me in your parents' house before we were married either in those days," said her husband-to-be. "I'd have been somewhere down the corridor, and as for James and Greg, heaven knows what would have happened there!"

"I'd have been tiptoeing about to find you," she replied, turning up her face for a kiss.

CHAPTER 16

The weekend whizzed by. Susie had an idea of what style of dress she would like, but wasn't at all sure about the colour for her two bridesmaids. They had arranged for three photographers to come and see them the following Sunday, and bring some photos and albums of weddings they could look at, and Susie and David had made an appointment for a cake maker to visit them at home in Enstone on the Tuesday evening.

As next weekend he and Susie would be having their first Saturday at home for a while, David suggested that they should go on a wedding ring hunt, and they could also look for bridesmaids' and groomsmen's gifts at the same time. They drove back to Enstone feeling very happy indeed and decided to have a celebratory drink in The Crown.

It was unusually quiet for a Sunday evening and Alf came over to chat to them.

"How are the plans for the wedding of the year going?" he asked jovially. "You'll never guess who was in here this lunchtime asking for you, Susie love. That Jonathan chap from Lotus, or who used to be from Lotus anyway. They sacked him after he was done for drink driving. Don't know how he got here, either. He appeared to be on his jack jones."

Susie's face blanched to match her tee shirt. "What did you tell him, Alf?" she gasped.

"Nowt," was the reply. "A good landlord, which of course I am, doesn't discuss his customers. I can be daft as a brush when I need to be." He tapped the side of his nose. "Mum's the word, Susie love."

Susie smiled at that, breathed again and took a restorative gulp of her wine. David squeezed her hand reassuringly.

***

Jonathan had received his decree absolute the previous day, with all the bits and pieces that entailed. As he knew it would, the house in Kirtlington had to be sold and split 65/35 in Angela's favour. He had no maintenance to pay, as his consultancy business was not doing very well, but finding somewhere to live was the big stumbling block.

He wasn't doing too well on the dating site and he was beginning to wonder if he should try his hand at being a male escort; they were well paid for accompanying some old bag to the theatre or somewhere similar, and he understood that you could charge a fortune for sex.

Meantime, he was going to have one more go for Susie. The taxi to Enstone would be bloody expensive, but he was damn sure that he wasn't going there on his bike. Saturday would be a good day as she wouldn't be at work.

Arriving at Rose Cottage, Jonathan was disappointed not to see Susie's red Mini parked outside. Nevertheless, he walked up the path and knocked on the door. It was eventually opened by a woman he didn't recognise. Jonathan explained that he was looking for Susie Rowlands, but was met with a blank stare. The woman told him that she and her friend lived there. Thanking her, Jonathan walked back down the path and up the one next door. She had always been a nosy parker, and was bound to know where Susie was living now. His luck was out there too. No-one answered his knock.

Swearing under his breath, a disgruntled Jonathan turned away. Why had he let that taxi go? He had been so certain that he would find Susie and charm his way in, and he certainly hadn't wanted to pay waiting time.

There was only one thing for it; he would have to walk to the pub. That cantankerous old landlord was sure to know where she was. As he set off, it started to rain, and he hadn't got an umbrella. Great! So to add insult to injury, he was going to look a bedraggled mess when he did find Susie. What a day this was turning out to be.

When he got to The Crown, Jonathan dived straight into the Gents to check that his appearance was as good as it could be. Reasonably happy with what looked back at him from the mirror, he proceeded to the bar. Oh yes, the old boy was there, no doubt forcing his opinion down some unsuspecting throat.

Jonathan greeted Alf convivially and even bought him half a pint of Leffe. They exchanged pleasantries, for what seemed an eternity to Jonathan, and then he cut to the chase, asking Alf about Susie. When Alf replied that he hardly saw her these days and knew nothing about her other than that she had worked for him for a few months the previous summer, Jonathan really could have poured the beer over Alf's head.

"Isn't that her Mini parked down the road?" he enquired.

"No idea," replied Alf. "Cars and who drives what doesn't interest me in the slightest." With that, he turned away to greet another customer.

Could Susie be living down the road? Jonathan wondered. He was positive that was her car. Should he put a note under the windscreen wiper asking her to get in touch? But then the flowers hadn't worked. There was the cottage that adjoined the pub and then a couple more lower down. Perhaps her boyfriend lived in one and she was living with him? If that was the case, he could hardly burst in on them. He needed to get Susie on her own and charm the pants off her.

He'd have another drink and go in the garden to order a taxi. He didn't need the whole world to hear him do that. It really did look as though he was going to have to step up his activity on that dating site, and maybe an ad in the local paper to the effect that he was a male escort. He certainly wasn't paying an agency a hefty cut of any money he made.

***

Simon had been wondering how the hell he was going to remember where he had buried the dwarfs, and he wanted to bury them sooner rather than later, when he had a brainwave.

Greg looked at him in amazement when he arrived home with a magnolia tree, which he insisted would look lovely in the back garden and said he knew just the place for it. Asking Greg where he kept his spade, Simon made a great show of digging a hole and planting the tree. He'd bury the dwarfs when the other two were out. The magnolia would be a good marker for him to find them when the time was right. He felt a bit like he was playing a part in an old film, where the robbers buried their ill-gotten gains to dig up at a later date.

"What on earth made you buy us a magnolia tree?" Greg asked his brother. "It's a very strange present."

"It'll be something for you to remember me by after I've gone," was the only reply he could think of.

"I wasn't aware that you were leaving any time soon," said Greg drily. "Have you got something to tell us?"

Simon said that he hadn't got anything to tell him, other than that he thought a magnolia tree would look good in the garden, which in his opinion was a bit neglected. If Greg and James would like, he'd be happy to spend some time out there and knock it into shape. The boys exchanged glances and said that would be great.

He got his opportunity to bury the dwarfs on the Sunday. Both James and Greg had gone to the Arcade as Annabelle was messing about with Susie and her wedding plans. He had even bought some bedding out plants in case the next door neighbour noticed him digging. What should he do with the snuff box he'd nicked from Annabelle, he wondered. It appeared that neither she nor her silly son had missed it. He decided that should be easy enough to sell on, so he'd hang on to it.

Armed with the spade, a trowel and the bedding-out plants, Simon went into the garden. He had wrapped the dwarfs in cling film to protect them, and then put them back in a pair of his underpants. There! They should be safe enough.

As he was planting the bedding-out plants, Greg and James' neighbour came out and called to him over the fence.

"Good morning," Simon called back cheerily. "I'm making it a project to get this garden looking lovely."

"You're making a good start there," replied the old chap. "Nothing like a show of petunias, but are you sure you've put that magnolia in the right place? I don't think it'll get enough sun there. I'd move it to the other side if I were you."

CHAPTER 17

"In all the wedding preparations, we've almost overlooked James' birthday," said Annabelle to her husband. "Obviously we won't be giving him a party this year, but how about a dinner? We could invite Susie and David, and Simon and Greg, and Simon's parents too. It's about time we met them."

"If that's what you'd like to do, Belle," Peter replied. "I must say I'd like to meet the mysterious Somervilles. There's something odd about that Simon and we might see where he gets it from."

Annabelle wrinkled her nose and decided to ignore Peter's comment. She had to admit that she was curious too. She thought Simon was a nice boy, who seemed to go out of his way to be helpful, but she would be interested to meet his parents. They did indeed seem mysterious.

Annabelle made the phone calls to her children and invited them and told James to include Simon. She then asked to speak with Greg and asked for his parents' phone number. He immediately offered to invite them on her behalf, but Annabelle was having none of that. With a sinking heart, Greg relayed the number.

Stephen and Maria Somerville were very surprised to receive a phone call from Annabelle Rowlands, inviting them to dinner for James' birthday and saying they were welcome to stay the night if they would like to. Stephen answered the phone and said he would have to consult with Maria, who wasn't in just at the moment. Annabelle went on to say how much she and Peter were looking forward to meeting them, and hoped that they would be able to make it.

When Maria came in, Stephen told her about the phone call. They were both cagey about going, but felt it would be rude to decline the invitation, so Maria rang back, thanking Annabelle and saying they would be delighted to be there.

Greg was not delighted when he learned that his parents had accepted the invitation. What might come out over the dinner table once the wine started flowing? How would his dad react to Simon? He could warn Simon to be on his best behaviour, but there wasn't much he could do about his dad. He really could do without the prison business coming out in front of the Rowlands. That could scupper everything.

Simon was, on the other hand, delighted. He was going to get an opportunity to make his father squirm. You never knew, this might be his way back to London. A few more bits and pieces from here and it could be a good time to move on.

"How kind of your parents to include not only me, but my parents as well, and to think we'll all be staying over," said Simon to James. "I'm really looking forward to it."

"It'll be a good evening," replied James. "Mum's an awesome cook and I know she'll pull out all the stops. My twenty-first party last year was something else. We had a marquee in the garden and a live band."

"Your presents were something else too, from what you told me," said Simon with more than a tinge of envy. "I wonder if you realise just now privileged you are?"

James was a bit taken aback by that remark. "You don't seem to have had too bad a time dropping out of college to travel," he replied. "Come to think of it, when will you be going back and picking up your course again?"

Simon shrugged his shoulders. "I'm having too much fun here to rush back," came the reply. He must be careful with what he said. He needed James on his side.

Greg quickly steered the conversation away from Simon's gap year. He didn't need James to be suspicious. "It will be a lovely evening," he said. "Like James said, his mum is a phenomenal cook. I'm really looking forward to it."

"What do you think of my efforts in the garden?" enquired Simon. "The old chap next door was quite complimentary."

"Is that magnolia getting enough sun?" his brother asked. "I would have thought it would have been better on the other side."

Not you as well, thought Simon. "I thought it looked good there," was his reply. "Let's see how it does before we start thinking of moving the poor thing. It'll only upset it if it's dug up again."

***

Stephen and Maria were concerned about the forthcoming dinner at the Rowlands. They had accepted the offer to stay the night as it would be a long drive back home. They weren't sure how they would react to Simon. They understood from Greg that he was staying with him and James, who they hadn't met either, but they didn't know what his story was. Maria said that she would ring Greg and find out, as they didn't want to drop any clangers.

"I'm going to find it hard to be civil to him after what he's done," said Stephen. "Time seems to have made it worse, not better. I think I was so shocked that my son was in prison to start with, that I managed to visit. However, with time, all I can think about is what a terrible thing he did."

"You're going to have to do your best to put it all behind you," replied his wife. "We might well end up with him living back with us."

"Over my dead body," growled her husband.

Maria groaned and went and phoned Greg. He told her that, as she knew, Simon was staying with him and James. The story was that he had dropped out of uni for a year to go travelling, and had been mugged and had everything stolen in Thailand. Simon was now helping out in his antique shop and in James' mother's shop too. He had also done some odd jobs for the Rowlands family and everyone seemed to like him. He was going out of his way to be obliging, and Greg didn't see why his parents couldn't now have him back, as he'd been out of jail for a couple of months.

This situation couldn't go on forever. He'd paid his debt to society and his father should man up and cope with that.

"It's not as though he even profited from the crime," Greg went on. "Work on Dad and see what you can do. It's not right that he should live with me and James indefinitely."

Maria knew that her son was right, but she also knew how difficult Stephen could be if he dug his heels in. She was between a rock and a hard place. She loved all her family more or less equally and didn't like there to be any unpleasantness amongst them. That said, at Stephen's request, she had had very little to do with her younger son following his conviction, and only visited the prison with Stephen at his suggestion.

Stephen was set in his ways. He was the manager of the local branch of Barclays and had been in banking all his life. He only saw black and white, and no shades of grey. Maria had been a clerk in his first bank, and he had been her senior. Once they had been going out together for a few months and things had got to the stage where Stephen was thinking of asking her to marry him, he also asked her to leave the bank, as it wasn't the done thing for them to be going out together and working together.

Ever obliging, Maria had done as she had been asked, and had continued to do so ever since. Now that she was coming up to fifty, it was a bit late for her to change her ways. She loved and respected her husband. He had always been a reasonable provider and a good father to the boys, who were only a year apart in age.

She was very much looking forward to seeing Simon. That March day outside the prison had been really difficult. There had been Simon looking forward to coming home and she had had to send him on his way. Thank goodness Greg had done the decent thing. Little did Maria realise that Greg had had no option as Simon had broken into his house. Given the choice, he wouldn't have taken in Simon either.

Simon was looking forward to the evening very much. He was longing to see his father squirm and he felt quite sure that he'd be able to make him. Let's face it, he was going to be wondering all the time what Simon might say next. As for his mother, he was sorry that she seemed to be so dominated by his father. OK, she'd given him a hundred quid when he came out of the nick, but she'd never bothered to write to him and had rarely come and seen him when he was inside, and never on her own, always with his dad. What was more, he could count on the fingers of one hand the number of visits he'd had from them.

His main plan was to have a good look round Riverside House to see what was there and what he dared pick. He had been keen to nose about from the word go, but just hadn't had the opportunity. Being invited to stay the night was the icing on the cake. He'd be able to go all over the place without anyone being any the wiser. If he could get back in with his parents, the time might be approaching for him to leave Oxfordshire. He had over £5k in the bank, buried Derby dwarfs and a couple of opportunities - James Rowlands' investment portfolio and Riverside House. If he couldn't make a killing, there was something wrong with him.

CHAPTER 18

Jonathan had thought very carefully before placing his ad in *The Oxford Times*. He wished to appeal to discerning ladies, regardless of their age. He felt that being thirty-nine was useful, as he could appeal to both older and younger women. He didn't want to appear in the least bit sleazy, and wondered if he could go for an air of mystery.

After much pondering and scribbling, and even more crossing out, he finally came up with "Non-Agency discerning and discreet male escort available. Based between Bicester and Woodstock, but will travel any reasonable distance. Services include escorting ladies to theatres, black tie affairs and business functions. I am thirty-nine years of age, tall and attractive. Please contact me on 07956 772397 for more details." He had bought a pay as you go mobile, as he didn't want to use his normal number or his landline either.

What should he call himself? He certainly wasn't using his real name. What would have universal appeal? Something foreign? Jacques? Pierre? Jean? No, they all sounded affected. Justin? He really was struggling here. He hadn't had to reinvent himself before. As a PR man, he should find this easy. Charles! That was it. Depending on the situation, he could be either Charles or Charlie.

Once he had placed the advert, Jonathan sat back and waited for the paper to be published. He was a little disappointed to find that it had been squeezed in between the premium sex chat line numbers. He hoped that it wouldn't get overlooked, or attract the wrong clientele – i.e. those who couldn't afford him.

He needn't have worried. By the Sunday evening, he had had four tentative enquiries, ranging from a young girl who wanted to be accompanied to a ball to a lady in her sixties who wished to be escorted to the Opera at Covent Garden. He had quoted the young girl £300 to be taken to the ball, as he thought it unlikely that she would have much money and she sounded like fun, and the opera lady £500. Both were going to let him know. The other two had hung up quickly when he said his minimum charge was £200, and that was for 2-3 hours.

Then, joy of joys, he got his first booking, to take a lady out for the evening. She explained to him on the phone that this would be a trial run, as she had a very important function coming up and she needed to see if he would be a suitable person to take her.

With that in mind, she suggested dinner at The Feathers in Woodstock

(Christ, he hoped there was no-one in there he knew in case she turned out to be an old boiler!) on the coming Friday. She went on to give him her address so that he could pick her up. At this point Jonathan had to interrupt the woman, who was in full flow, to explain that the procedure was for her to send a taxi for him and then he and the taxi would collect her.

For the evening, his charge would be £100 per hour, which would start when the taxi collected him and finish when the taxi took him home. He would want an up-front payment of £200 transferred by BACS to his account. (He had opened a new one in the name of Exclusive Escorts, which had made the bank manager raise his eyebrows.)

On top of that, his clients were responsible for paying for the taxi and for the dinner and drinks. If the client preferred, she could give him cash in order that it looked as though he were picking up the tab for dinner and his final price could be adjusted accordingly.

Jonathan almost collapsed with relief when the caller agreed to all his terms and said the money would be transferred the next morning and that a taxi would collect him at 6.30 pm on Friday. Her keenness made him wonder what kind of a woman she was going to be.

***

As usual, Janet spent a large part of the weekend reading the newspapers, leaving *The Oxford Times* until she had finished with the broadsheets. Sitting with her feet up and enjoying a glass of Bristol Cream sherry, she had been thinking about the up and coming function to which she had been invited once again and feeling somewhat inadequate because she didn't have a husband or suitable gentleman friend to be her companion for the evening. How she hated going on her own, year in, year out.

Taking another sip of her sherry, Janet turned the page in *The Oxford Times*, whereupon an advertisement caught her eye. A gentleman escort, who purported to be discreet. Could she... did she dare to contact him?

Of course, she couldn't risk him taking her anywhere so important without trying him out first, but that wasn't an impossibility as there was still three weeks to go. She finished the glass of sherry that she was drinking and then, pouring herself another one for Dutch courage, Janet picked up the phone and dialled the number in the advertisement.

"Good evening, Charles speaking," said an educated voice.

"Good evening, Charles," she replied, hoping she sounded more composed than she actually felt. "I'm ringing to enquire about you and your services. Would you be kind enough to tell me a little about yourself?"

"What is it in particular that you would like to know?" Charles enquired smoothly.

Janet swallowed a large mouthful of sherry before replying. "What sort of age are you, and what is your background please?"

Mmn, Jonathan thought to himself, class is clearly important here. He told her that he was a Radleyite and had left Oxford with a Masters in history. Since that time he had done a variety of consultancy work, and had recently set up as an escort as he felt there was a gap in the market for a discreet and confidential service such as the one he was now offering. He was thirty-nine, tall, fair (sounded more interesting than light brown) and good-looking, and knew how to treat a lady. He could be openly affectionate and hold her hand and take her arm when appropriate, or equally he could be more reserved and formal. That was entirely the client's choice.

Janet blushed at the thought. It would be exciting to have a good-looking man take her by the arm, particularly at her important function. She could never quite bring herself to call it by name. However, perhaps for the practice run she and Charles should be more circumspect. She told Charles she would see how things went before she committed herself to anything physical. He smiled to himself.

Taking yet another mouthful of sherry, Janet asked Charles how much he charged. It was probably just as well she was on her second glass when he told her his prices! With a sharp intake of breath she agreed to everything he said. After all, if it turned out that he cut the mustard, it would be worth the money to see the expressions on the faces of the others.

She told Charles that she wished to be taken to dinner at The Feathers in Woodstock on the Friday evening and that she would send a taxi to collect him at 6.30 pm. Wishing him a good evening, Janet finished the call; part of her wondering what on earth she had committed herself to.

***

Jonathan dressed with care on Friday evening. He felt that Janet was an older woman, to whom background was important and that she would appreciate him dressing formally. With that in mind, he selected a pair of light coloured trousers, which he teamed with a blue and white striped shirt and a navy blazer. Tie? Yes or no? He figured that yes would be a safer bet.

After pushing a pair of cuff links through the buttonholes on his shirt cuffs, Jonathan ran his hands through his hair and then surveyed himself in the mirror. Yes, he thought he would pass muster, no matter how discerning and fussy Janet was.

Just before 6.30, a white Peugeot taxicab arrived and took Jonathan to Janet's address in Bladon.

***

Janet felt a frisson of excitement as she got ready for her evening out. She'd never done anything like this before. She'd been to the bank on the way home and withdrawn £250. That should more than cover their dinner and pay for the cab. She intended to give the money to Charles, so that it didn't look to the rest of the world that she was buying his company.

She had managed to leave work early so that she could get ready at her leisure and had treated herself to the hairdresser at lunchtime. Janet was pleased with the result. Her naturally curly hair had been coaxed into loose waves that framed her face very nicely, even if she did think so herself. She very carefully tucked it up under a bath hat so that she could have a good soak without doing it any damage. Getting out of the tub, she indulged totally and massaged Madame Rochas body lotion all over and then added a little spray of the matching Eau de Toilette.

Walking into her bedroom, Janet looked at her dress and jacket hanging ready on the outside of the wardrobe. Yes, that would do nicely - linen was classy, and pale pink suited her. She applied a little make-up, not wanting to overdo it so that she appeared as mutton dressed as lamb, and then stepped into the frock and zipped it up.

She carefully shook her head so that her hair fell back into place and added a mist of Elnet to keep it that way. Picking up her handbag, and checking that she had put the cash inside, Janet went downstairs to await Charles' arrival. She trusted he would be punctual.

Sure enough, dead on the dot of 7 pm, her doorbell rang. As calmly as she could, Janet got up and went and opened the door. Her intended greeting of "Good evening, Charles," quickly changed to "Good God! I don't believe it!"

CHAPTER 19

The weekend before James' birthday was an extremely busy one for Annabelle. She took Susie wedding dress shopping and they looked again at bridesmaids' dresses. Annabelle had been all for having Grace and Jenny to stay so that the three of them could go shopping, but Peter had put his foot down saying that she would have a house full on the Monday for James' birthday and that she was trying to do too much.

In her heart, Annabelle knew that her husband was right. She was just anxious to get the dresses on order because the average lead time was three months and the wedding was on 28 September. She agreed with Peter with the proviso that the girls could come and stay the following weekend. With this in mind, she and Susie hit the shops with a great sense of purpose.

Being tall and with a good figure, Susie fancied a simple, fitted dress and they managed to track one down that she liked in a small wedding boutique in Oxford. Annabelle explained to her daughter that it would be really useful if they could get the bridesmaids' dresses from the same shop, because then it would be possible to look at them all together, and get a general idea of whether they complemented each other.

Susie wasn't sure quite what she wanted and kept wavering on the colour. Her two bridesmaids were so different – Grace was petite with shortish blonde curly hair and Jenny much taller with long brown hair. She suddenly panicked and said to Annabelle that the three of them would look ridiculous as they were so different.

Annabelle drew in a deep breath. "Well, darling, Grace and Jenny are very different heights. I think that is perhaps the most awkward thing, but there's nothing you can do about it, so you have to work with it. You can't adjust their heights by giving them different shoes, because that won't work at all. They need to match. Don't let Jenny put her hair up, because that will make her look taller still. She must do something pretty with it down. Or, you just have one bridesmaid."

"I've asked them both," replied her daughter, "and told them the date of the wedding, so I know that they're both free. I can't now tell one of them that I've changed my mind."

"As usual, Susie, you rushed into things in the excitement of the moment without thinking them through properly," said her mother, "so we're going to have to do the best we can. Who are you going to have walking behind you to hand your bouquet to?"

Susie pulled a face and said she hadn't thought about that bit. Annabelle raised her eyebrows and said that her daughter really did need to start to think. This was her big day and it needed to be orchestrated correctly.

"Grace is my friend and Jenny is going to be my sister-in-law," said Susie. "Who should I choose? I feel it should be Grace, but then I don't want to upset Jenny, who I've really only asked out of politeness because she's David's sister."

"Grace it is then," replied her mother. "That officially makes her the Chief Bridesmaid. Now let's concentrate on colour and style, or do you need a coffee break?"

They slipped down the road to Costa where they continued their conversation.

"What colour do you think, Mummy? You're so good at this type of thing," asked Susie.

"Well," said Annabelle, "it's the end of September, so you perhaps don't want too summery a colour in case the weather isn't that good, so I would go for a strong colour, but one that won't overpower either of them. A deep blue, pink or turquoise perhaps? Maybe with little jackets or long sleeves just in case it is chilly."

Susie nodded. She felt they were getting somewhere and didn't know what she'd do without her mother. Suitably revived, she suggested that they return to the bridal shop, as there was also the matter as to whether or not she should wear a veil and she hadn't yet looked at shoes, and maybe a bag for the evening.

After more deliberation, the colour for the bridesmaids was finalised. Susie chose a deep turquoise, which she felt would flatter both girls. Her mother coaxed her to try a long veil, and yet another decision was made. They returned to Moulsford satisfied, but exhausted. Annabelle was very touched to find David in the kitchen, putting together a lasagne and salad for supper. Needless to say, Peter was buried in his study with *The Telegraph* and a large gin and tonic.

***

Susie didn't go into work on the Monday of James' birthday party. She stayed on at Riverside House, ostensibly to help her mother prepare for the dinner. As she knew Susie was no cook, Annabelle relegated the more basic tasks to her daughter. She was asked to check the guests' bedrooms and bathrooms and make sure they had plenty of towels and toiletries. When she had done that she was instructed to lay the table in the dining room and then go and ask her father about wine, so that the red could be uncorked.

"Gee whiz, there's a lot to doing this entertaining lark properly, isn't there?" she said to her father when she ran him to ground in his study, smoking a cigar and reading the financial part of *The Telegraph*.

74

Peter laughed. "It's one of the things that your mother does really well," he said to her. "You could do a lot worse than try and learn from her."

"Oh Daddy, I'm useless in the kitchen and David knows that," she replied. "He's a pretty good cook, you know."

"I'm sure he is, Susie," replied her father, "he made us a lasagne on Saturday night which was very tasty, but never forget the saying about the way to a man's heart. Now, what have you come in here to pester me about?"

"Wine," replied Susie. "Mummy wants to get some red breathing, but doesn't know what you want to serve, so please can you fetch some bottles up for her?"

Grunting, Peter folded *The Telegraph*, rested his Havana in the ashtray, and went to do his daughter's bidding.

Susie wandered back to the kitchen, where her mother asked her to start peeling vegetables. Really, she thought to herself, I would have had a far easier day in the office.

***

As the evening approached, the various guests had different feelings of anticipation. James was really looking forward to it all. It was his birthday and he was spending it with his family. His mum would cook a superb dinner and everything would be great. He was looking forward to meeting Greg's parents too.

Greg was somewhat apprehensive of how Simon and his parents would get on, and was praying that nothing contentious would be said either by his father or his brother.

Simon was bursting with excitement. He was pretty sure he'd be able to wind his father up and he was going to get a chance to have a good look round James' parents' house to see what was what and what might be up for grabs.

Stephen and Maria were anxious on all sorts of fronts. They didn't know the Rowlands, but it was clear they had money and were in a different league; they hadn't seen Simon for ages and didn't want it to come out that he had been in prison; for that matter, they hadn't seen Greg for a while either, and they'd never met James. Was the gift of a bottle of champagne that they had chosen suitable? Were they dressed correctly? This could be the evening from hell.

Stephen had had to leave the bank early and wouldn't be in again until the following afternoon, and that hadn't particularly pleased him. Maria's fussing was also getting on his nerves. They knew the way to Cholsey, and Moulsford was only just up the road from there, so he couldn't see why she kept worrying about them being late.

"Yes dear, you look fine," he said for the umpteenth time without even looking at her. "Just put the overnight bag in the boot and then we can think about getting on our way."

David was quite tired and a bit fed up with constantly driving between home, Moulsford and the office, but felt that an interesting evening was in store, and he'd be getting his fiancée back too. His bed had felt empty without Susie the previous night.

Susie was her usual bouncy self. She was doing her best to help her mother, but was quite stunned by how much work there was if you did "proper entertaining".

Peter had relaxed for most of the day, contemplating his investment portfolio and thinking about what his next move might be. He knew the evening would go well as Annabelle was in charge and she did everything to perfection. He was particularly looking forward to meeting the Somervilles, as it would be interesting to know something about the parents of the man his son was living with. They might also give him some insight into that lad Simon. There was something peculiar there, but he couldn't quite put his finger on what it was.

And as for Annabelle, she was delighted to be entertaining James on his birthday and was looking forward to an enjoyable evening, surrounded by her family. Of course. she had no qualms about everything running smoothly; she just took it for granted. Little did she know.

CHAPTER 20

Janet couldn't believe her eyes when she opened the front door. That Browne man who had been sleeping with her secretary, which had resulted in her losing two promising pupils, was standing on her doorstep, a smile plastered all over his face, and leaning forwards as though he was planning on kissing her. How dare he? How could he? She visibly recoiled.

"Good evening, Janet," he was saying. "Your carriage awaits. Shall we?"

Clearly, he hadn't a clue who she was. Well, she was going to have to make the best of it. He didn't seem to have seen her shocked expression, or heard what she had gasped, and was just standing there with that silly smile on his face. It was a shame she had used the taxi company that she used for the school, otherwise she would have told him to go to hell there and then, but she wasn't giving the taxi driver the satisfaction of seeing her cause a scene.

Making sure she had her handbag, Janet closed and locked the door and followed Charles down the path to the taxi. He opened the door for her and she got in. They travelled to The Feathers in relative silence, making very little small talk.

Once inside the restaurant, Janet tried hard to relax. She would make the most of these awkward circumstances, without making it obvious that anything was amiss. She was in the driving seat here.

Nursing a glass of Bristol Cream, Janet turned to Charles and asked him to tell her more about himself. Jonathan balked and insisted that she should tell him about herself first. Should she tell him who she was, Janet wondered. No, not yet. Charles was going to have his comeuppance and she was going to enjoy herself.

She turned to him and smiled, fully aware that she was being appraised.

"I'm a teacher, here in Woodstock," she said, studying Charles' face carefully. He showed no emotion, so Janet was quite certain that he still didn't know who she was. "I've lived in the area now for about ten years. I enjoy my home and my garden, and country pursuits in general. There's usually something interesting going on at Blenheim, and if there isn't, there's the beautiful park, which is always delightful for a walk."

Jonathan nodded.

"Do you enjoy walking, Charles?" enquired Janet.

He turned his face towards her and gave her the benefit of a dazzling smile.

"Like you, I enjoy outdoor pursuits," he said. "A round of golf, a day's shooting, a walk in the countryside. They all hold a certain appeal." He felt that was an appropriate answer, as he was very conscious that he was on trial, and wanted to be the kind of person that he felt Janet would like and want to be taken out by again.

Leaning towards her, Jonathan enquired quietly whether she would prefer to slip him some cash so that he could settle the bill? Janet cringed at the phrase and assured him that she was fine paying it herself. Little did Charles know it, but he wasn't getting any more of her money. She would confront him later, but for now she was playing the game.

A waiter came and took their order. Janet noticed that Charles wasn't holding back, and really went to town when presented with the wine list. She had to admit that he seemed reasonably knowledgeable, but then sending his twins to Woodstock Academy hadn't been cheap, so there had to be some money somewhere.

However, it was fascinating that he was now a male escort and that the girls had left the school. She felt confident that his wife must have left him following the Susie debacle and he now needed to make some extra money. She couldn't for the life of her remember what he did for a living, and it was quite certain that Charles wasn't going to tell her.

After about a quarter of an hour, the waiter came back and escorted them to their table. Janet was pleased to see that the dining room wasn't as busy as she would have expected for a Friday evening. She might be able to say what she needed to over coffee.

***

The meal and the wine were excellent and Jonathan was enjoying himself, flirting gently with this older lady. She was quite plain, in his opinion, but had obviously gone to a lot of trouble for the occasion. He wondered what he was being auditioned for, and seriously hoped that he got the job. After all, getting several hundred pounds for taking an old biddy out to dinner really was a nice little earner. It certainly had the potential to bring in more than his PR business was doing right now.

He was quite flabbergasted when Janet asked the waiter if there was somewhere quiet where they could go for coffee and wondered if she was going to ask him for something extra. Dinner was fine, but he really didn't want to have to go to bed with her. Bracing himself, Jonathan stood up and followed Janet into The Study.

"What liqueur would you care for, dear?" he enquired, hoping he didn't sound nervous, and in the same breath asking the waiter for a Hennessy XO for himself. Janet replied that she would like a crème de menthe frappé. Jonathan rolled his eyes.

Once the coffee and liqueurs had arrived, Janet leaned towards Charles and said, "There's something I've been longing to say to you all evening."

Oh Christ, thought Jonathan, she does fancy me and she wants extras. What the hell am I going to do here? Sex had always been on his terms and been risky and fun. The thought of this mature woman in her pale pink linen removing her clothes filled him with dread.

He forced a smile to his face and said, "Really?"

"Oh yes, really," replied Janet. "I recognised you immediately, but it was blatantly obvious that you hadn't the slightest idea who I was. For your information, I am the headmistress of Woodstock Academy, the school that used to be attended by your daughters, Alice and Emily. Yes, Charles, I know exactly who you are. You are the deviant who was fornicating with my secretary, Susie Rowlands, which in the end resulted in her losing her job. Your extra-marital affair caused an uproar in one of my classrooms, causing deep distress to your daughters. I am assuming that your wife and daughters have left you. I only know that the children never returned to Woodstock Academy after that day. I am presuming that you are now working as a male escort because you are desperate for money. I was naïve enough to phone you and ask you to take me to dinner as a trial for an important occasion I have to attend. I'm sure that you will realise that you won't be taking me anywhere else after tonight."

Jonathan opened his mouth to speak, but Janet held up her hand imperiously to command him to be silent.

"Rather than lose face with the cab driver, who I know through the work that he does for me at the Academy, I allowed you to bring me here tonight, as when you arrived on my doorstep you completely threw me out and I wasn't sure what to do. However, I am now extremely positive as to what I shall do. I shall pay for the meal and the cab, which will only be taking me back to Bladon, and I shall be leaving you to find your own way back to Kirtlington. Goodnight, Charles. You made a silly error in not recognising me, but then I wouldn't be glamorous or young enough to be worth noticing, would I?"

With that Janet looked at her watch. As she expected, she had timed everything to perfection. She would pay the bill at Reception and then her cab would be waiting outside. It was almost worth the horrendous amount that she had to pay to see the look on the face of that dreadful Charles. How he had tried to charm her and all to no avail!

***

Jonathan sat staring into his brandy balloon and wondering what the hell he was going to do next. He put his hand into his inside pocket and discovered that he hadn't got his wallet. Neither had he brought his phone, because it only made his jacket pocket bulge and he hadn't imagined needing it. The signal in Woodstock was crap anyway, so that had been another good reason for leaving the damn thing behind. OK, think about this. The taxi driver wouldn't know he hadn't got any money until they got back to Kirtlington and he could write him out a cheque if he didn't have enough cash in the house to pay him. He just needed to get the girl on Reception to call him a cab. That shouldn't be too difficult.

Sauntering out to Reception, Jonathan eyed up the receptionist, gave her his most disarming smile and asked her if she would call him a cab, as he couldn't get a signal on his mobile. That proved to be a foolish thing to say, as she smiled back and told him if he just stepped outside and walked a few yards, he would definitely get a signal. She went on to say that it wasn't hotel policy to call cabs for non-residents.

He smiled and thanked her and left the premises. What next? Could he go back in and say that it still wasn't working and ask again if she would help him? It had just turned 10 pm and Woodstock was busy. Young people were spilling out of The King's Arms on to the pavement and the air was full of noise and laughter. Jonathan felt utterly defeated.

No, he wasn't going back into the hotel and talking to that snotty receptionist again. He was amazed that she hadn't fallen for his charm. Normally that type of girl couldn't get enough of him. Christ, he hoped he wasn't losing his sex appeal.

Standing there, he longed for Susie and thought back to that first afternoon when he had bought her a bottle of champagne in The King's Arms and how she had fallen for him hook, line and sinker. Now she didn't want to know him and was going to marry some chinless wonder. He'd lost his wife and children and was going to have to move out of the house soon as Angela wanted it sold, or at least her share of its value.

He had no driving licence and no job to speak off. He had just utterly fucked up his first date as an escort and was now stuck in Woodstock. He looked back towards The Feathers and saw that the snotty receptionist was standing at the glass door, peering out at him with a puzzled expression on her face. Feeling unable to stand there any longer, Jonathan started to walk in the direction of Kirtlington.

CHAPTER 21

Because they were anxious not to be late, the Somervilles, much to their horror, were the first to arrive at Riverside House to celebrate James' birthday.

"Doesn't it look a lovely house?" said Maria to her husband as they drove up the gravelled drive.

Riverside House did indeed look beautiful on that May evening. The early evening sun was shining on all its Georgian splendour and it looked mellow and welcoming.

"It certainly does," replied Stephen. "Obviously a wealthy family that Greg has got involved with. I'm glad one of them seems to be turning out all right. Now, I wonder where I should park the car?"

He needn't have worried about that, because Peter had heard them arriving and had come outside to greet them. He indicated where they should park.

"Over there, if you don't mind, please, Stephen," he said, pointing in front of the garage. When the Somervilles had got out of the car, apologising profusely for being the first to arrive, Peter introduced himself and assured them it was no problem at all and that someone had to be first. He showed them into the house, where he introduced them to Annabelle, who said that she would take them to their room.

When Annabelle had left them, Maria turned to Stephen and remarked in awed tones that the guest room they were staying in had an en-suite bathroom. She looked around admiringly - the pale pink carpet, the beautiful white broderie anglaise bed linen, and the tasteful antique furniture. The room was exquisite. She hoped she never had to entertain the Rowlands. Maria was out of her league and knew it.

"Greg's definitely punching above his weight here," remarked Stephen. "Good luck to him, that's all I can say. I hope Simon behaves himself tonight. I wouldn't like him to spoil things for his brother. Anyway, enough of gazing at the bedroom, let's get downstairs, otherwise our hosts will wonder what on earth we're doing."

With that, he opened the bedroom door so that Maria could precede him down the stairs. They had been told to make their way to the conservatory, where drinks and pre-dinner nibbles would be waiting. As they walked into the room, they could see that Peter and Annabelle had been joined by a young couple and were introduced to Susie and David.

Maria struggled not to feel self-conscious. These really were the beautiful people and she felt quite insignificant. How on earth would Simon cope with all this after his time in prison? Talk about from the sublime to the ridiculous, except it was the other way round. She smiled shyly at Peter and accepted a glass of champagne. Taking a sip, she marvelled at the flavour. This was different from the one that she bought at Tesco.

She could see that Stephen was beginning to enjoy himself. He was deep in conversation with David, talking about quantative easing, for goodness sake. Susie walked across to her, with a plate of canapés in her hand.

"Do try one of these, Maria," she urged. "The smoked salmon ones are Mummy's speciality. I see your husband and David are engrossed in the world of finance."

Maria smiled at Susie. "Looks like Stephen's found a kindred spirit," she said. "Are you involved in the world of finance too?"

Susie told her about her job and went on to say that she and David were going to be married on 28 September.

"Daddy's very into stocks and shares too," continued Susie. "He does something part-time in the City which I don't think Mummy really understands. She concentrates on antiques and is actually rather knowledgeable. That's how she met Greg, because they both have shops in the Lamb Arcade in Wallingford, and that's how Greg met James, when James was helping Mummy out in the shop in his last year at college. Oh, speak of the devil," she continued, "the birthday boy and your two sons are just arriving, Maria. That's a first. I'm usually the one who's last, or at least I used to be, until I met David."

With that, Susie turned to greet her brother. "Hello James," she said, giving him a big hug. "Happy birthday." She continued to greet Greg and Simon, and then introduced James to Maria.

They both took stock of each other. Maria saw a rather glamorous young man, tastefully but trendily dressed; James saw an attractive woman who looked a bit unsure of herself.

"We can be a bit much when we get together," he said kindly, "but we're OK when you get used to us. My father is something of a control freak, but don't let on that I told you. Anyway, you must want to talk to Simon, not to me, as you haven't seen him for ages. I'll go and introduce myself to your husband."

Stephen was, by now, more anxious than his wife, as he could see Simon talking to Peter. His prison sentence mustn't come out, it really mustn't. It would be too degrading. Before James could collar him, Stephen crossed the room to where Peter and Simon were standing.

"It's good to see you looking so well, Simon," he ventured.

"Yes," replied his son. "I was just filling Peter in on the gaps in my life story. We've only met a couple of times before. He knows Greg quite well, but not me, you see."

Stephen inwardly panicked. Surely the stupid little sod wouldn't say he'd been inside, but it might be a good idea if he could come between the two of them, so there was no opportunity for Simon to embarrass him and Maria. Simon could see how uncomfortable his father was and began to enjoy himself.

"I found the conditions very tough indeed," he said to Peter. "It took some adapting to, I can tell you."

"I can imagine," replied his host. "I don't think it would do for me."

Before Stephen could come join the conversation, Peter excused himself and went to ask Annabelle when she would like people seated. As always, he smiled inwardly when he saw her in the kitchen, calmly arranging the starters. He was a very lucky man. Not only did he have a beautiful wife who he was proud to have on his arm, but he also had one who was a wonderful cook and homemaker. With that, his thoughts turned to Susie and David. He hoped that their marriage would be as good as his.

Meanwhile, Stephen was asking Simon through gritted teeth what he and Peter had been talking about.

"Wouldn't you just love to know, Dad?" he asked. "I was telling Peter about my recent experiences. He seemed very interested indeed, but then you came and interrupted us. You could at least pretend that you're pleased to see me you know. I've paid my debt to society."

"Will you keep your voice down, Simon," hissed Stephen. He was beginning to feel very hot indeed under the collar. He tried to smile and look as though he was pleased to see his son, when in fact he had a nasty suspicion that this was going to be the evening from hell. Why had they agreed to come? He answered his own question. It would have been rude not to and he also needed to keep an eye on his younger son.

At that moment, Peter came back into the conservatory and asked his guests to take their seats in the dining room.

***

The Rowlands had no idea how strained all the Somervilles were feeling as they took their places at the table. Apart from Simon, of course. Being an odd number, it had been difficult to sort out who was going to sit where. In the end Annabelle had decided to sit people opposite their partners, and put Simon, as the odd one, at the bottom of the table, with his parents on either side of him. Next to Maria was Greg, with James next to Stephen. Next to James was Susie, with Peter on her other side, Annabelle opposite him and David between her and Greg. The other awkward thing had been the shortage of women.

Stephen felt relieved that Peter and Annabelle were as far away from Simon as possible, but James was certainly in earshot of any indiscretions.

As he expected, Simon was as controversial as he dared be, making lots of references to where he had been recently, the awful food he had had to eat... When he mentioned food, Susie piped up that she has always been told that the food was delicious.

"Have you been inside then?" Simon asked her. Stephen almost choked on his stroganoff.

"Inside? Inside where for heaven's sake?" he asked. "What are you talking about?"

"Asia," replied Simon smoothly. "I spent a good deal of time inside Vietnam and Thailand. You must remember that it was Thailand where I got mugged and lost everything, Dad?"

Before Stephen could open his mouth, Greg turned the conversation to James and his birthday. Stephen stopped holding his breath and did his best to smile.

From there on, the party proceeded calmly, without any more controversy. Once Simon had stopped tormenting his father, Maria began to enjoy herself. She thought James was very charming, and delighted that he and Greg seemed to be in a good, stable relationship. She was enjoying the food and drink too, and literally drinking in the convivial atmosphere. These were indeed the beautiful people and it was lovely to be part of them, albeit for a very short while.

It was a very good evening indeed. James was pleased with his birthday gifts and delighted to meet Greg's parents at long last. He particularly warmed to Maria, whom he thought very sweet and somewhat in awe of her husband. He couldn't see why though, as he didn't find Stephen particularly imposing.

Peter too was fascinated to meet the Somervilles. He picked up on the underlying tension between Simon and the rest of the family, and felt that the boy was trying to embarrass his father, which was interesting. He would have to dig deeper when the opportunity presented itself, because there was something about Simon that he didn't quite like, and he still couldn't put his finger on exactly what.

As for Simon, he knew what he wanted to do. As it became apparent that the party was breaking up, he offered to take the dogs for their last walk. Zizi had come to the party too, and was snuggled up under the kitchen table with Allsort. Both dogs had been very hopeful that some tasty morsel might come their way, but had been out of luck, as no-one had left any of Annabelle's delicious cooking.

Simon smiled as he let himself out of the back door. The dogs were going to get a very long walk tonight. He wanted to make sure that everyone would be asleep when he got back to the house. Looking at the amount of booze they had all drunk, they were bound to be.

CHAPTER 22

Breakfast next day passed off without incident, and by lunchtime all the guests had gone home, leaving Peter and Annabelle on their own. Peter just had to discuss Simon with his wife.

"There seemed to be some tension between that Simon chap and his parents, in particular his father, don't you think, Belle?" he enquired.

"Oh darling, I really do think you imagine things," she replied. "I thought the evening went off very well indeed and everyone seemed to enjoy the food. There wasn't a thing left! As for Simon, I think he's a very kind boy. He took the dogs out so that the rest of us could go to bed. I never heard him come back, so they must have had a lovely long walk. How thoughtful was that?"

Peter couldn't disagree over the dogs, but still felt very uneasy as he went through to his study. What was the problem between Simon and his father? He had found Stephen pleasant enough, if a touch boring, but as the man had worked for Barclays Bank since he was eighteen, Peter could understand why. It had almost seemed that Stephen didn't like his son talking to him, and was concerned as to what he might say. What could it be? He really did want to get to the bottom of it. That aside, he was pleased to have met the Somervilles as James was sharing his life with their older son. He had been wondering for some months what kind of people they were and he had now come to the conclusion that they were an ordinary, pleasant couple.

***

On their way back to London, Maria asked her husband if he felt he could now forgive Simon and let him come home. As he was sitting in a traffic jam on the M40 and was anxious to get back to the bank, Stephen wasn't exactly at his most receptive.

"Let him stay where he is for a bit longer," was all he said.

Maria sighed to herself, even though the remark was more promising than it had been last time she asked. That had been "Over my dead body." She had been pleased to see Simon, and wondered if she would now be able to visit him. She would leave that discussion for another day.

The post was on the mat when they got home. Picking it up, Maria handed Stephen his then went into the kitchen and switched on the kettle. Stephen was very relieved that she couldn't see the expression on his face when he opened his mail. Refusing her offer of coffee, he ran upstairs and changed into a suit and then made his way to the bank as quickly as he was able.

Once there, he told the staff in no uncertain manner, he didn't wish to be disturbed under any circumstances. They looked at each other in surprise. Mr Somerville was normally so helpful. What could be the matter, they wondered. Perhaps he had some important report that he needed to write?

They couldn't have been further from the truth. Stephen was busy investigating a substantial deposit into a particular bank account. He knew the gentleman in question very well indeed, and the deposit didn't make sense. Stephen was trying to find out if an error had been made. He was hoping fervently that one had. If not, things could become very uncomfortable indeed.

***

"That magnolia tree really isn't doing very well at all," remarked James to the two brothers. "I think you and next-door are right, Greg. We ought to move it to the other side of the garden. Shall I do it now?"

"I'm about to head off to Wallingford and as your mum's not coming in today I could really do with some help," was the reply. "But then I guess you'd be happy to do that, wouldn't you, Simon?"

"I kinda feel responsible for the magnolia as I bought it," was the swift reply. "If you really want it moved, I could do that while you two go antiquing. I'm sure James doesn't want to get all dirty messing about with it. Anyway, I rather fancy myself as an ace gardener."

"Then why did you plant the bloody thing in the wrong place?" was the sarcastic retort.

Once Greg and James had gone, taking Zizi with them, Simon sat down and thought about the previous twenty-four hours. It had been fun winding Dad up in front of the Rowlands, and he felt that he had endeared himself to Peter and Annabelle by taking the dogs for that walk. He'd achieved a lot when he got back too. As he had expected, everyone had been asleep and he'd been able to wander at will. It was interesting what people left lying around.

Putting all that from his mind, Simon went into the shed to fetch the spade. Oh fucking hell, the nosy neighbour whose name he couldn't remember, was in the garden, and was calling to him. Forcing a smile to his lips, Simon walked across and agreed that yes, it was a lovely day.

"Going to move the magnolia, are you?" enquired Mr Nosy. "I did say that it wouldn't do any good there. Never mind, I'll give you a hand. We don't want the poor thing getting damaged now, do we?"

How in Christ's name did he get out of that one? At the speed of lightening the bloody man was out of his garden, through his house and already walking into Greg's garden. Shit, shit and more shit! Simon couldn't possibly let Mr Nosy dig, in case he hit his package. What was he to do? Stall him, somehow.

"Can I offer you some coffee before we start?" he suggested.

"No, no, thank you," replied Mr Nosy. "I've just had some with the missus. Don't let me stop you, though. I could start digging."

Over my dead body, thought Simon. Then he had a brainwave. "Tell you what. Why don't you find a place that you think would suit it and dig a hole, while I dig up the magnolia and then I'll bring it over to you."

Mr Nosy headed to the opposite side of the garden looking for an appropriate space, whilst Simon dug as fast as he dared, being very careful not to catch the precious Derby dwarfs with the end of his spade. However, Mr Nosy was more than a match for him and had his hole dug and was coming back towards Simon, saying, "It's all right. I'll give you a hand to lift it. We don't want to break the roots now, do we?"

Simon really didn't know what to do. He did his best to stand over the package of the dwarfs so that the neighbour couldn't see them, when to his horror, his foot slipped and he heard a horrible cracking noise. Silently, he prayed it wasn't a broken dwarf, but he was in no position to look. He just had to get the damn magnolia tree out of the earth and re-situated on the other side of the garden without Mr Nosy seeing anything suspicious.

"What was that noise?" Mr Nosy enquired.

"Oh, it must have been a twig I stepped on," said Simon quickly.

That seemed to satisfy Mr Nosy, so the two of them carried the magnolia across the little garden and re-planted it.

Simon then scuttled back and quickly filled in the hole where the magnolia had been, whilst Mr Nosy patted the earth level on the other side of the garden and then watered the shrub.

***

The Lamb Arcade was quiet that Tuesday morning, and James was casting an eye over Annabelle's shop when he noticed a gap in one of the displays. They always took photos of all the displays so that they could see if anything had gone missing. Getting out the latest photos, James soon discovered that the missing item was a silver snuff box.

He walked across to Greg and asked him if he had sold it. He hadn't. James next rang his mum and asked the same question. He got the same answer, but could tell from the tone of her voice how upset she was that something else had disappeared. The box had to have been stolen, but when? First the Derby dwarfs and now the snuff box; it appeared that

Greg's was one of the few shops where nothing had gone missing. It was a mystery.

A thought was going through Greg's mind that it could be his brother who was the thief. If so, how was he going to catch him? He'd been through his room and followed him to Oxford and he hadn't discovered anything, but he still couldn't help being suspicious. Why did life have to be so complicated?

CHAPTER 23

Jonathan had had a miserable time walking home from Woodstock. It had rained on and off for the entire journey, so his tan loafers were soaked through and would probably never be the same again. Janet had completely humiliated him and that was not something he was used to. He made a pathetic figure creeping along the roads between the two villages. Cars swept past him, frequently spraying him with water, and it was so bloody dark. How had his life got to be such a mess?

He had lost his wife and children, courtesy of Susie bloody Rowlands, who appeared to be having the time of her life. He would put money on the fact that she was living with that pillock she'd been having dinner with that night he went to see her, and as for his own dear little ex-wife, she was lording it up somewhere in Oxford.

What about me? What about me? The words kept going round and round in his head as on he trudged. The next awful thing to happen would be the loss of his house. Where the hell was he going to go? Could he have another play for Susie? If tonight was anything to go by, he wasn't going to make a fortune as a male escort. The dating site wasn't turning up any rich old biddies either. He was going to have to try harder. He could also do with a proper job. This freelance work certainly didn't bring in anything like enough.

Left, right, left, right, on and on he walked. Would he ever get to the end of this sodding road? Then all he had when he did get to the end of it was an empty house and an even emptier bed. When was the last time he had had sex? Even that seemed to be a thing of the past. He was the man who used to be able to charm any girl he wanted, but that was when he was part of Team Lotus and jetting off all over the world. Never in his wildest dreams had he thought that life could come to this. Susie, who'd sworn she loved him, had turned on him. Surely it was within his power to get her back?

Finally, he reached Kirtlington and rounded the corner into the Mews. Once inside his front door, he kicked off his sodden shoes and threw his wet clothes in a heap on the floor. Rubbing himself dry as best he could with the kitchen towel, Jonathan poured himself a large Scotch and then headed upstairs for a hot bath before bed. Life really was shit.

***

Angela, Jonathan's ex-wife, had had a simply splendid evening. Alex was a natural with the twins and the three of them had bonded exceptionally well. Of course, they still liked to visit their father, and being scrupulously fair, Angela would never try to discourage that, even though she knew that Jonathan spoiled them in ways she didn't approve of, such as letting them have sweets with too many E numbers. Alex, on the other hand, took an interest in what they were doing at school, and encouraged them to play educational games, such as Scrabble.

Jonathan's idea of a good evening was plenty of booze followed by sex, whereas Alex was quite different. Generally more cultured than Jonathan, he had a wide variety of interests. He also enjoyed the children's company. They, in turn, were very fond of him. They loved living in Oxford and going to the Dragon. They were very proud that Uncle Alex had been to Buckingham Palace and received his MBE from the Queen herself, and took great delight, if presented with the opportunity, of telling everyone about their day in London.

The age gap didn't worry Angela. Alex made her feel safe, just like Daddy used to. Angela hadn't realised how much she had missed that feeling whilst married to Jonathan, and was now basking in a wonderful sense of security. She would soon have more money too, because now that the divorce was absolute, the pressure was on Jonathan to sell the house in Kirtlington. Daddy had already said that he didn't want any money from the proceeds of the sale; however, he wanted to make sure that Angela received her fair share of two thirds of the property. She would only inherit the money after he died, so he felt that she might as well enjoy it now. Not that she actually needed anything. Alex made sure of that.

Alex, too, was happy. He couldn't believe that he had found another wonderful woman. His marriage to Elizabeth had been almost perfect - the only thing they had lacked had been children. Now, here he was in his mid-fifties helping to bring up Alice and Emily, and enjoying every moment of what he considered to be real family life. However, having very strong moral beliefs, Alex did feel slightly uncomfortable "living in sin" as the old saying went. He had wondered for a while what to do about it, and now that Angela was a free woman, knew that he had to do something. No, not had to, wanted to.

This was why Angela's evening had been so splendid. She had been sitting in the drawing room, having put the twins to bed, enjoying her hot chocolate when Alex had come and sat down beside her.

"I've something to ask you, and hope fervently that the answer will be yes," he said to her. Angela turned to him and smiled, whilst raising her eyebrows enquiringly. What could it be, she wondered. Was Alex perhaps planning a holiday somewhere that he wasn't sure would meet with her approval? That seemed unlikely, but she really couldn't think of anything else. Besides, she was feeling lazy and satisfied after a delicious dinner and really didn't feel the need to tax her brain.

All her senses came alive, however, when Alex did ask his question.

Would she marry him? The question came as a complete surprise. That said, it was the most wonderful surprise. She could hardly believe her ears. She was completely overwhelmed. Alex took her silence as a refusal and was beginning to stutter an apology that maybe it was too soon after Jonathan and that he quite understood and he hoped he hadn't offended her, when he suddenly realised that Angela was, in fact, smiling.

"Of course I will, you silly thing," she said. "Your question took me by surprise, that's all. No, it's not too soon after Jonathan. It will be wonderful for us to be a proper family. Thank you so much for asking me. I love you very much, Alex."

Putting down her hot chocolate, Angela leaned over and kissed Alex gently. "I can't wait to be Mrs Drummond," was all she said.

"I'm delighted," her husband-to-be replied. "Don't move. I'll be right back."

With that, he went upstairs and came back with a little box which held a beautiful solitaire diamond ring. Sitting down again, he gently removed Angela's wedding ring and replaced it with the diamond.

"I haven't liked looking at Jonathan's ring," he said. "I think that's much better. What do you think, my love?"

Angela told him that it was just perfect and that the evening was perfect too.

***

The twins were very excited the next morning when Angela told them that she was going to marry Uncle Alex. They wanted to know if they could be bridesmaids and where the wedding was going to be. Angela explained to them that she and Uncle Alex hadn't thought about any of the arrangements yet, as they had only decided to get married the previous evening.

"Have you told Daddy?" asked Emily. "I'm sure he'll want to know,"

Angela had already decided that she would go to Kirtlington and tell Jonathan face to face, as she didn't feel it an appropriate conversation to have on the telephone.

"Not yet," she replied. "I shall go and see him after breakfast, and before you ask, no, you can't come with me. Uncle Alex is going to take you into Oxford. You can see Daddy next weekend, as arranged."

With that, Angela concentrated on preparing the breakfast, all the while wondering what she was going to say to her ex.

***

On arriving in Kirtlington, Angela was surprised to find all the curtains drawn. There was no reply when she knocked on the door, so as she had keys to the property, she let herself in. She couldn't believe it when she immediately tripped over a complete set of Jonathan's clothes, lying screwed up in a wet bundle on the floor. Stopping herself from picking them up, she went to the bottom of the stairs and shouted up, asking Jonathan to please come down as she needed to talk to him.

Eventually a very dishevelled Jonathan appeared, asking her what the hell she wanted. "Good morning to you too," Angela replied, somewhat tartly. "You look as though you have a prize hangover. Perhaps I should make some coffee?"

Jonathan merely grunted, so she walked past him into the kitchen, and came back a few minutes later with two steaming mugs.

"Before we start, you need to get this house tidied up so that it sells quickly," she said. "Don't think you can stall things by being obstructive, because I'll have my solicitors on you faster than fast. Anyway, that's not what I came to see you about. I've come round as a matter of courtesy to let you know that Alex and I have decided to get married, and I thought you should hear it from me."

Jonathan was aghast. Not only had the cow left him, she was getting married again, to a man who obviously had money, and she was going to get a large slice of his pie too. Life was so unfair. He'd felt sorry for himself last night after the Janet debacle, but he really was at rock bottom now. Somehow he had to get back with Susie Rowlands or find himself a rich woman. He was supposed to be the glamorous, sexy one, and here was his little mouse who'd left him and found herself a bloody good meal ticket.

Mechanically, Jonathan nodded his head. He was sitting in the same position, staring gloomily into his coffee mug, half an hour after Angela had left.

CHAPTER 24

Susie was looking forward to the weekend. She and David were going to stay in Moulsford, as were Grace and Jenny, and the girls were all going shopping, without David of course, for wedding and bridesmaids' dresses.

The cake man had been and they had chosen a fantastic wedding cake. He preferred to call them sculptures. It was made entirely of chocolate, with four cakes covered in chocolate swirls. It was definitely different and very unusual. The cake designer had said that they could have edible flowers, again made of chocolate, that would pick up the colours in Susie's bouquet. She thought this to be a wonderful idea and once she had chosen the dresses would get on the trail of flowers. There was so much to do!

Currently they were struggling with both the photographer and the stationery designer. Two photographers had not turned up for appointments, which was amazing. The new plan was that David and Susie would see them at home first, and if they liked them, then they would arrange a meeting in Moulsford for Annabelle and Peter to give them the once over. The same was happening regarding the stationery.

Susie had met someone at a wedding fair and she had visited them at home and said she would go away and come back with a design, which she had failed to do, and now wasn't responding to e-mails or phone calls. Why not just say she didn't want the job, for Heaven's sake?

Susie was struggling to find another stationery designer as she didn't want just run of the mill stuff, or anything that was too formal either. As June was approaching, she and Annabelle were beginning to get anxious. David, typically, was laid back, saying that everything would come together on the day.

Whilst Susie was going shopping with Annabelle, David and Peter were going to go and choose morning suits. Peter was of the opinion that it could also be a good idea to pop into the Swan and have another meal. If they were going to have a buffet in the evening, it might be as well to try out the bar snack menu.

The week whizzed by and it wasn't long before Friday evening came and, once again, Susie and David were in the car heading for Moulsford. Jenny was with them too and Grace was on her way, driving down from Manchester.

***

Crawling along the M6, Grace wasn't sure what to make of the goings on. She hadn't heard from Susie in ages, then out of the blue she got a phone call with Susie wanting to talk about some married man she'd been having an affair with. Now here she was driving down to Moulsford to be Chief Bridesmaid and Susie was marrying someone else. Grace looked forward to meeting him.

Deep down, Grace was really quite hurt by the way Susie had blown hot and cold with her. They had been so close as children and had still been on the best of terms as they grew up. Grace had moved to Manchester to work, but they had still kept in good contact. The girls visited each other for weekends, when Grace had a sudden realisation that it was always she who rang Susie, so decided to leave it a while to find out what would happen.

What had happened was that Susie had never called, clearly because she was embroiled with this married man. However, she had been quick enough to call when the chips were down.

Grace ran her hands through her blonde curls. It was very hot in the car and the traffic was hardly moving. The M6 on a Friday night was not a good place to be. That would be followed by the M42, then the M40 and then she would have to get round Oxford before finally getting to Moulsford.

It would be good to see Susie's parents too. She hadn't seen them for a long time either. Grace hoped that they could choose the dresses over this coming weekend as she didn't want to have to be making this journey too often. She understood that there was another adult bridesmaid, who was David's sister. She hoped that they could find a dress that suited the two of them, but wondered what the odds of that were.

Three and a half long hours later, Grace finally drove through the gates of Riverside House. That didn't seem to have changed much over the years, and here was her old friend coming to greet her.

"Gracie, Gracie, it's so lovely to see you," enthused Susie, throwing her arms around her. Grace could not fail to be caught up in her friend's enthusiasm and hugged her back.

"You must come and meet David and Jenny," Susie burbled on. "I expect you're starving too. I know I am. Mummy's held back supper so that we could all eat together."

Grace followed Susie into the house, where she was soon greeted by Peter and Annabelle and introduced to David and Jenny. She was slightly perturbed to see that Jenny was tall and dark like her brother. They'd look a right pair following Susie down the aisle – she was short with shoulder length blonde curls, and Jenny was tall with long dark hair. Where was Susie's head in all this she wondered. Maybe she should have a word and get her to change her plans?

Grace really wasn't bothered whether or not she was a bridesmaid. She lived in Manchester and had a high profile job with Granada TV, so didn't need the hassle of fiddling about coming down to Oxfordshire several times for dress fittings. She would have to get Susie on her own and explain that to her. After all, they had grown apart over the years, mainly through Susie's lack of communication.

Susie was oblivious to Grace's thoughts as she chattered on incessantly about her plans and where she and David were up to in sorting everything out. Eventually, she commented that her friend seemed quiet. Grace explained that it had been a long day and she was tired. The journey from Manchester had been horrid and she had been up since the crack of dawn. She went on to say that her job was also very demanding. Susie pulled a face at this. Despite having come a long way from the spoilt brat of the previous year, currently she was only interested in her wedding and her plans.

When the time came for everyone to say goodnight, Grace asked Susie if they could have a quiet word before bed. Very calmly, she explained to her friend why she thought it might be better were she not to be a bridesmaid, majoring on the fact that both Susie and Jenny were tall and dark and would look good together, whereas she would only spoil the look of things, due to her colouring and her height.

"If there were a lot of us, Suse, that wouldn't matter, but with only two I think we'll look silly and I'd hate to ruin your special day. There's also the hassle of coming down from Manchester for all the fittings etc."

Sadly, Susie's worst side surfaced once again, as she told her friend that she felt she was extremely selfish, thinking about herself, when after all, it was her big day. Grace tried to point out that actually she was thinking about Susie, but Susie was having none of it.

"Why did you bother to come if you didn't want to be my bridesmaid?" she yelled at the bewildered Grace. "Perhaps you don't even want to come to my wedding? Is it such a long way from Manchester? Are you jealous that I'm getting married before you? Yes, that must be it."

Grace told her to stop right there, before she regretted something that she said in anger, as she didn't want to spoil their friendship.

Like the spoiled girl that she used to be, Susie told her that she had already ruined their friendship and if that was how she felt she needn't bother coming to the wedding at all. She really didn't care either way!

Grace shook her head sadly and said that they would talk again in the morning.

Angrily, Susie went up to bed, where she complained long and hard to David about what Grace had said. It did not go down well at all when he said that he could see her friend's point – that Susie and Jenny were a similar height and colouring and she wasn't.

Ever the diplomat, David went on to suggest that she should patch things up with Grace, thank her for offering to stand down, and ask if she would go shopping with them tomorrow to see how the three of them looked together when dressed in their finery before anyone made a hasty decision. Then, and only then, could they make a decision as to how to move forward.

Susie knew the wisdom of David's words, but wondered if she might have let things go too far with Grace. She had been very cross and rude, as all she was concerned about was her wedding – her special day. She would have to see what the morning brought. With that thought in mind, she snuggled up to David and very soon drifted off to sleep.

CHAPTER 25

Jonathan was stunned by Angela's news. He supposed it didn't affect him really, one way or the other, but nonetheless he was surprised. Of course, he'd had a bit on the side now and then, but that wasn't the same as being unfaithful and actually having a love affair as Angela had done. There he'd been, slaving away, keeping everything ticking over, while all the time, behind his back, his quiet little wife had been cementing a new relationship, ending up in marriage.

That was bad enough, but last night had been quite awful too. How had he been supposed to know that the woman he had been escorting to dinner had been the twins' headmistress at Woodstock, and that she would recognise him and kick off?

Thinking about Woodstock made him think, again, of Susie Rowlands. She had been so entertaining and given him so much pleasure. What could he do to get her back? She'd moved house and he reckoned she was living next door to the pub in Church Enstone with that drip she'd been having dinner with the night Angela had left him and he'd gone charging round.

Would a letter work? He hadn't heard anything after the flowers, so probably not. He really had to get her to meet him, as he was sure that face to face he'd be able to charm her, but the question was how. Maybe he should look to rent a property in the Enstone area, as he would have to move once the house in Kirtlington had been sold. Then he could do his best to bump into Susie.

Yes, that was a plan. He'd have to look for property somewhere. Enstone would do nicely. Putting his coffee mug in the dishwasher, Jonathan picked up the tangled bundle of his clothes, sorted them between what could go in the washing machine and what would have to go to the dry cleaner, then went upstairs, showered, shaved and dressed.

Feeling a bit more human, Jonathan walked to the village store where he bought a local newspaper, bacon, eggs, mushrooms, and bread. After a substantial brunch, he turned his attention to the rental properties. Anything half decent was expensive. It looked as though he might have to rent just a room in a house with other people. He shuddered at the thought. Susie really was his answer, in more ways than one. Apart from her obvious personal attributes, she owned her cottage, so that made her doubly attractive.

Suddenly an ad caught his eye. "Flat to let above Enstone Stores. Low rent in return for assistance in shop." Quickly, Jonathan dialled the number and made an appointment to go and see the owner, Mrs Shaw, on Monday. It would be the cost of a taxi, but so what. He would make the most of his time in the village and visit The Crown as well. He might learn something, or he might even see Susie. It would be one in the eye for Angela if she had to sell an empty property because he had already moved out.

***

Susie couldn't believe her eyes when she looked out of her bedroom window the next morning. Grace's car wasn't parked in the drive where it had been the previous evening. Surely it couldn't have been stolen? She flew downstairs to find Annabelle in the kitchen, preparing breakfast.

"Grace's car is missing," Susie gasped.

"So is Grace," replied her mother. "She asked me to give you this note. She explained to me why she wasn't staying, and I couldn't persuade her to change her mind."

Susie tore open the envelope. "Dear Suse," she read, "I'm sorry, but I don't think it's right that I should be your bridesmaid. I'll only spoil the photos because I'm short and you and Jenny are both tall, so I think it best that I go home and don't go shopping with you today. Love Grace xxx"

Susie was both angry and upset. "How could Grace do such a selfish thing?" she asked her mother.

"Grace sees it as being selfless," was the calm reply. "She's aware that you and Jenny are similar in height and colouring and that she is completely different. Grace believes that she has done the right thing and you have to respect that, Susie darling."

"Respect that?" Susie screeched. "I'm now stuck with David's bloody sister, who I hardly know. All because I did the decent thing and gave the damn woman an important role in my wedding."

Annabelle could see the start of a full-scale tantrum, something she certainly didn't want either Jenny or David to be party to. "Calm down, darling," she said. "It'll be much easier with just you and Jenny and you will look stunning together. Now perk up, take drinks upstairs for the both of you and get ready for a lovely day shopping. After all, you don't have to have a turquoise bridesmaid now, if you would prefer another colour."

Susie took the mugs of coffee that her mother was holding out to her, popped them on a tray and went back to the bedroom. David was just waking up.

"You'll never guess what's happened," she said to him. "Grace has only gone and buggered off, thanks to your sister."

"What's Jenny got to do with anything?"

"What Jenny has to do with it is that I felt obliged to ask her to be a bridesmaid because she's your sister, and because she and I are both tall and dark, Grace said she'd spoil the photos, so she's gone home."

David made the mistake of laughing, which really whipped up Susie's fury.

"There you are," she yelled at him. "I do what's right and nice to please other people and I end up being crapped on. It's just not fair! It's my wedding, after all."

David groaned inwardly. The Susie he had originally met, who had been hostile and angry, was beginning to creep out of the woodwork again. Where had the lovely girl she had become gone, he wondered. He really didn't like this side of her at all.

"It'll all be fine on the day," he said soothingly. "Just you wait and see."

"And what the hell do you know about it?" enquired his wife-to-be. "It'll be fine for you, with your best mate as your best man, having a laugh and no doubt a few pints as you get ready, but what about me? I shall be stuck with someone I hardly know, helping me into my dress and getting ready with me. That person should be Grace, and if it wasn't for your flaming sister, it would be. And now I'm stuck with her. It's just not fair." With that parting shot Susie flounced off into the bathroom and ran herself a bath. David lay in bed, drinking his coffee and thinking.

***

Annabelle had had better shopping sprees. Susie was surly and not very pleasant to Jenny, who was looking rather uncomfortable. She felt like taking hold of her daughter and giving her a good shake. Here was she, laying out for expensive dresses and accessories, and Susie was barely interested. Nothing was quite right, be it the shape, the colour, the material - you name it and there was something wrong with it. Finally, Annabelle decided to be firm.

"We're getting nowhere," she said. "Let's have a lunch break and decide what it is we're looking for." With that, she dragged the girls off to the nearest Café Rouge, immediately ordering a bottle of Sauvignon Blanc. "Now then, Susie," she said, "you've been reading bridal magazines until they're coming out of your ears, so would you like to tell me, please, exactly what sort of dress you're looking for? I thought we'd found it the other week, but clearly not, as you didn't like it this morning."

Susie glared at her mother. "It's not as simple as that," she started to say.

"OK," said Annabelle, "well, I'd like you to humour me in the next shop. We're going to Beautiful Brides, which is extremely exclusive. Let the shop owner make suggestions and you agree to try on whatever she comes up with. She's used to dressing brides and their attendants, so let's see what she can do for you and Jenny."

Susie opened her mouth to argue, but, seeing the expression on her mother's face, thought better of it.

Lunch over, the trio set off for Beautiful Brides, where they were soon being attended to by the owner, Mrs Copeland. It wasn't long before Susie was looking at herself in the mirror, wearing a stunning vintage lace dress with a low back. Sulky as she was, she had to admit that the dress really suited her and that Mrs Copeland certainly knew what she was doing. Next came a pair of shoes and a long veil.

"You look absolutely entrancing, darling," said a very relieved Annabelle. "And now for Jenny."

It didn't take Mrs Copeland long to come up trumps again and soon Jenny was in a deep violet dress which went beautifully with her colouring. "What do you think?" Annabelle asked, turning to the two girls.

Very tactfully, Jenny said how wonderful she thought Susie looked and what a beautiful bride she was going to be. Susie thawed slightly at this, as she did think she looked rather good in the lace confection, which fitted her to perfection, skimming her figure beautifully. She turned to Jenny and explained that she had been thinking of turquoise for her bridesmaids, but now that there was only Jenny she could see that the violet blue was a perfect colour.

Mrs Copeland preened, saying that she hadn't run Beautiful Brides for twenty-two years without learning how to dress brides and their attendants perfectly. "Obviously your bridesmaid will need shoes dying to match the dress," she said, "and we do need a slight adjustment to the bodice. That is, of course, if you're going to go ahead with these dresses."

Annabelle asked her if she would put them to one side for an hour, told the girls to get dressed and said that they would have a discussion over coffee. With that, the three women headed back to the Café Rouge. Within the hour, they were back at Beautiful Brides, where, to Annabelle's great relief, an order was placed for the two dresses and various accessories. Something she could now cross off her list. Everything was coming together. Finding her own outfit would be so much simpler!

CHAPTER 26

Greg was first up. It was a beautiful June morning with the sun streaming in through the windows. He let Zizi out into the garden whilst he pottered about in the kitchen, making coffee and warming up pains au chocolat. Looking through the kitchen window he smiled as he watched Zizi scampering about, doing a garden survey as he liked to call it. The garden was looking good and Greg felt somewhat annoyed with the dog when she started digging frantically. He went outside in an attempt to dissuade her, but Zizi was having none of it and was scrambling away as though her life depended of it.

"That'll teach me to choose a terrier," Greg thought to himself as he walked towards his little dog. "What are you up to Zizi?" he asked her. Suddenly the digging stopped.

"Thank goodness for that," Greg thought, when he saw, to his amazement, what appeared to be some sort of package being dragged across the lawn by the dog. Greg went to investigate and found two Derby dwarfs wrapped in a pair of underpants, then stuffed in a cushion cover before being crudely wrapped in a newspaper. The top of the hat of the one carrying the stick was broken, although that was the thing that concerned Greg the least. He realised that they had to be Annabelle's and that they must have been stolen by Simon. What the hell should he do? He didn't want James to know just yet, as he didn't want him to realise what an utter bastard his little brother was turning out to be. Where should he hide the damn things he wondered? The other two could be up at any minute. That was the first thing to do and worry about how he was going to tackle the actual theft later. Shoving the dwarfs back in the cushion cover, Greg quickly hid them at the back of the shed, before going back to the more mundane task of preparing breakfast.

He thought it probably best to get Simon on his own and give him an almighty bollocking and then ask him to leave. Whether he came clean and told Annabelle and James about what had happened, he really wasn't sure. What a way to start the day, but at least he had found them rather than James.

At that moment his lover came out of the bathroom. "What were you and Zizi doing in the garden a moment ago?" James asked.

"Oh I think she was looking for a bone and couldn't remember where she'd put it. That was all," came the reply.

James seemed satisfied by that and went off upstairs to get dressed.

Greg was still wondering what he was going to do, when his phone bipped and there was a text from his father saying "Need to speak with you urgently in private. Ring me when you can. Dad."

***

Annabelle was hunting for her long diamond earrings. Where on earth could they be? She was normally so careful with things and they weren't in their little box in the safe. Had she left them on her dressing table or pushed them in a drawer? She wasn't one to leave jewellery lying around. When did she last wear them? Was it the night of James' birthday? If so, she had vague recollections of taking out her earrings and putting them in a little dish on the sideboard. That must be where they were.

Going downstairs to the dining room Annabelle was mystified to find that the earrings weren't there. She didn't want to tell Peter that she might have lost them, because, understandably, he would be annoyed. They were a pair that had come to her from his mother and were particularly beautiful and valuable. Peter never misplaced anything either, so would go on and on at her should she mention the fact that she couldn't find them. He was meticulous.

Little did she know that at that precise moment her husband was himself searching for something and getting in quite a lather about it. For his fiftieth birthday Annabelle had given him a beautiful cigar cutter and matching cigar lighter. They were from Aspreys and were 18 carat gold. They seemed to have disappeared off the face of the earth. He always left them in the crystal ashtray on his desk and he had just noticed that they were missing. Neither Annabelle nor Mrs Baxter, the cleaning lady, would have moved them, because that was where they lived and they both knew that. Surely they couldn't have been stolen? The only strangers to the house that he could think of had been Greg's and Simon's parents and he hardly thought that they would be thieves. If the things didn't turn up, he might just have to ask Annabelle if she'd moved them.

***

Stephen had been very concerned by what he had discovered at the bank. It had all started the morning after James Rowlands' birthday dinner when he had opened that bank statement addressed to Mr S Somerville that wasn't his. After closeting himself in his office and making enquiries, his fears had been confirmed. The bank account belonged to Simon. More worryingly still, his son had recently deposited £5,000 in cash at the High Street, Oxford branch. Stephen didn't like to think where the money could have come from. He had a nasty feeling that it had to be stolen, as where on earth could Simon have got it from legitimately? He didn't want to tell Maria of his suspicions just yet. He felt it might be better to have a word with his other son, hence the reason for the text. He appreciated that a private conversation could be difficult in Greg's little house, so it was much better for Greg to ring him at a convenient time.

Stephen didn't have too long to wait before Greg was on the line. Once again he had told his staff that he didn't want to be disturbed until he told them otherwise.

"Hello Dad, what's up?" came his son's voice.

Stephen told Greg about the money in Simon's account, saying that it had been deposited in Oxford and asked him if he knew anything about it. Greg's heart sank.

The little shit must have paid it in that day he had followed him to Oxford and then lost him on the High Street. He must have sold the things that he'd nicked from the Arcade and that Greg had been unable to find. First the Derby dwarfs and now this.

What a start to the week! Should he tell his father of his fears regarding Simon or should he just kick him out? Simon had enough money stashed to be able to rent somewhere, but if he made a big thing of this, he could stop him from getting a job, when basically all Greg wanted was to get Simon out of the house so that he didn't queer his pitch with James. He decided to tell his father nothing, but agreed with him that it was definitely most peculiar.

James and Simon had gone to the Lamb, so Greg was left with plenty of time to think.

He needed to get Simon to leave the house, without James knowing that his brother was a thief who had stolen Annabelle's dwarfs. He had to get Simon on his own to confront him. That might be easier said than done. Perhaps he could work it so that the two of them did the Lamb together the next day.

However, fate was not that kind. That evening after supper James decided he would mow the lawn. Both brothers were aghast when he came in and plonked the dwarfs on the coffee table demanding to know what the hell was going on. Greg spoke first, explaining that Zizi had dug them up from the garden where the magnolia tree had been planted originally and he had pushed them to the back of the shed as he hadn't known what to do.

James was upset by this comment. "Didn't know what to do?" he echoed. "It's bloody obvious to me that your brother stole them from my mother and buried them in the garden. That's why he bought the magnolia tree, so he could remember where he'd put them. I'm really disgusted with the pair of you. Greg, I thought you loved me and you've been horrid and deceitful. You've chosen your brother over me. As for you, Simon, words fail me. When I think of all the clothes I have given you for example and welcomed you to my family home as well and all the time you were stealing from my mother. You're probably responsible for all the other thefts from the Arcade too. I don't know how much you knew about this, Greg, but I do know that I can't stay here tonight with you two. I'm going to pack a few things and then I'll be off. I need time to think. I appreciate this is your house, Greg, and that Simon is your brother. I feel as though I'm the outsider here now."

With that James ran upstairs, threw a few things into a bag and roared off in his Mini Cooper. Not knowing where to go, he rang Susie and asked for a bed for the night.

CHAPTER 27

David was somewhat irritated when Susie came off the phone and told him that James needed a bed for the night. First he had had her weekend of tantrums over Grace and the wedding and now James was coming. He had nothing against James personally, but the spare bedroom was above his and Susie's and the only way to access it was by walking through their room. He told Susie that it just wasn't practical to have James to stay and that he was popping next door to see if Alf's spare room was available.

Fortunately, it was. David explained to Alf that he didn't know how many nights it would be for, but it seemed as though Susie's brother had had a fall-out with his boyfriend, which of course Alf didn't know.

"Don't worry, son, Mum's the word," he said cheerfully, tapping the side of his nose. "Just send James round when you're ready and I'll look after him."

David thanked Alf and went back and told Susie what he'd done. She pulled a face, but said she could see where David was coming from. She hadn't thought about James having to trample through their bedroom to get to his, but then that was fairly typical of Susie. She didn't always think. On a good day, David found this charming, but not so on a bad one.

"Let's eat at The Crown," she said. "I don't know that I want to listen to James droning on all night. I've got enough problems of my own with Grace and the wedding. We could make the meal our treat."

"I don't know what problems you've got, darling," her husband-to-be replied. "You've chosen your wedding dress and all the bits that go with it and Jenny's dress is organised too. The church and the reception are booked and organised. We've also chosen our cake and stationery, which reminds me; shouldn't that be here by now?"

Susie shrugged her shoulders and said she would chase it up the following day as she supposed it was time the invitations were written and posted.

It wasn't long before James arrived and the three of them went next door to The Crown. Alf's hospitality was up to its usual standard and they ate and drank very well indeed. David could see that Susie had no intention of asking her brother why he had felt it necessary to uproot himself from home, so over coffee he turned to James and asked him what had happened.

James replied that something awful had happened and that he just didn't know what to do. David raised his eyebrows in an effort to encourage

James to continue, but the younger man really wasn't forthcoming.

"If you don't want to talk about it, then don't," said Susie unsympathetically. "God knows I know what it's like to have problems. Look at the mess I was in last year. At least you have money. That solves most things. I was desperate."

"Yes and I helped you out," retorted James, stung by his sister's lack of sympathy, "and I came to court with you when you were caught speeding, so please don't come the victim here. At the moment, I am the one who has a serious problem."

"But you don't want to talk about it," repeated Susie. "So if you don't mind my asking, why exactly are you here? Mummy and Daddy only live three miles away. Why didn't you go there?"

"Because at the moment, I don't want to confide in them, as it's rather complicated," came the reply.

***

After James' abrupt departure, the two brothers sat looking at each other. Greg spoke first.

"You've excelled yourself this time, haven't you, brother dear?" he said. "First you break into my house, which I cover up as I can't bring myself to tell my partner I have a gaol bird for a brother. Next, you ingratiate yourself with my partner's parents, pretending to be such a helpful soul, when all the time you're working out how you can steal things from the Arcade and sell them on. Your coup de grace is the sodding dwarfs buried in my garden, which you stole from James' mother. Oh yes, I have also had Dad on the phone regarding the little matter of the £5,000 you deposited in Barclays in Oxford. I was following you that day, you know, and that must have been where you went to when I lost you. I haven't told Dad about the thefts, because I want you to leave here and be able to rent a place and get a job. He's convinced though that the £5k is from ill-gotten gains."

As Greg paused for breath, Simon opened his mouth to speak, but didn't get the chance.

"You may now well have buggered up my relationship with James," Greg went on. "He found his mother's dwarfs hidden in the back of the shed and thinks that I may have had something to do with their disappearance. He's now stormed out of here because of you. Do you hear what I'm saying? You could have cost me my future with James. Now piss off out of here and don't come back again. Take the clothes that James gave you, but just piss off. I'll have your door keys too - now."

Silently, Simon handed over the door keys, then went upstairs to pack. He certainly had more now than would fit in the rucksack that he came with, so he went and asked Greg if he could lend him a bag.

106

"Lend you a bag?" exclaimed his brother. "I'll give you a bag, because I never want to see your sorry arse again."

"Where do you expect me to go tonight? It's getting late. Could I go in the morning please? You haven't even heard my side of the story," Simon wheedled.

"I don't want to hear it. You've turned into a common little thief and I want no more to do with you," Greg replied. "As I said earlier, just take my bag and piss off."

Simon knew when he was beaten. He went back upstairs, packed his rucksack and the bag that Greg had given him. Silently, he came downstairs, and left the house without so much as a backward glance.

Greg sat staring into space after his brother had left. What should he do now? Should he ring James? No doubt he had gone home to Moulsford. That could make life difficult in the Lamb with Annabelle, depending upon what James had said. This could be the end of a very promising relationship as Peter and Annabelle would be unlikely to welcome him to their home ever again if James had told them the story about finding the dwarfs in the back of the shed. Bloody Simon!

Life had been running along quite wonderfully until he had turned up. On balance, Greg decided it best not to make a phone call and to see what happened the following day. He got Zizi's lead and decided to take her for a long walk to see if it would help him think.

***

Alone in his bedroom at The Crown, James was feeling both unhappy and confused. Susie's indifference to his problem had upset him too. She had been very dismissive when he said he didn't want to talk about things. He supposed he had hoped that she would try and find out what was wrong, but she hadn't. He felt alone, unloved and unwanted.

Susie and David had gone home, saying they couldn't really have him to stay because of the layout of the rooms in the cottage and here he was, sitting alone in a room in a pub. He had no idea what would happen regarding Greg. Again, he felt let down. He had welcomed Greg's brother into his house, but then, it wasn't his house, was it? It was Greg's.

Maybe he should consider buying with Greg? That would put him on an equal footing. Then there was the incident of the sodding Derby dwarfs. Was Greg dishonest? Was he in league with Simon? Unable to cope any longer with the thoughts that were whirling round and round in his brain, James decided to go down to the bar and see if another drink would help.

Alf was very surprised indeed to see his guest again so soon. "Is everything all right, son, or do you need something?" he asked as James walked into the bar.

"Fine, thank you," James replied. "Not particularly keen on my own company, that's all. Could I have a pint of Stella, please?"

Alf sent Nick to fetch James' pint, then settled down to talk to him. "How long do you think you'll be staying, son?" he enquired.

James shrugged his shoulders and said that he'd had a bit of a falling out with his partner, so wasn't really quite sure what he was doing, just at the moment. Alf nodded his head, and told him that the room was available as long as he needed it. Curious as he was, Alf could see that James was troubled, so decided not to pry. Tactfully, he moved on to speak with another customer, leaving James hunched over his lager.

CHAPTER 28

Jonathan swung his legs out of bed and went to the window as soon as he woke up on Monday morning. Looking out, he could see it was a glorious day for his trip to Enstone. He pushed back the curtains and drank in the air. This could be the start of the rest of his life, as the saying went. All he had to do was make a favourable impression on Mrs Shaw and hopefully the flat and the job would be his. He wasn't particularly keen on the idea of the job, but needs must and he knew that. He could then start on his campaign to win back Susie.

He arrived at Enstone Stores in plenty of time for his 10.30 am interview. All the way there in the cab he had been playing games with himself, imagining what Mrs Shaw would be like. He wasn't kept waiting long before the lady in question appeared. Jonathan did a double take. Not at all what he had imagined!

This lady was groomed and elegant, and didn't look at all like any of the women he had been dreaming up, or even how he expected a shopkeeper to look. Smiling, she held out her hand to him and then led the way through to the back.

Passing through what was clearly a stockroom, Mrs Shaw continued until she came to her office, where she invited Jonathan to sit down. Next, she offered coffee, which he accepted gratefully. Whilst Jonathan was looking around him and trying to size up Mrs Shaw, she started speaking, saying she was quite surprised by who he was. Jonathan regarded her quizzically.

"The name Browne didn't mean a lot to me," she said. "After all, it's hardly uncommon, but I do recognise your face from television. Some sports programme, I think? Do please tell me about yourself. Why do you want to live in my flat and help out in my shop?"

Christ, thought Jonathan. She didn't beat about the bush. He gave Mrs Shaw what he hoped was a disarming smile and started off by telling her that he was recently divorced, his wife having left him for another man after carrying on behind his back, unknown to him, of course, for a number of years. That was a good start. Mrs Shaw had a sympathetic expression on her face. Sighing, Jonathan continued, yes she had seen him on television, as until very recently he had worked for Team Lotus, but with the break-up of his marriage he had found the job too demanding, so had resigned. The other thing was that he only had limited access to his children, so just couldn't be out of the country attending a Grand Prix if it was his weekend for seeing them.

Warming to the part, Jonathan told Mrs Shaw that he had twin daughters who were eight years old, and that he missed them dreadfully. He was currently doing freelance PR work, and would have to move out of the marital home when it was sold, so the combination of a flat and some steady work was extremely attractive. So are you too, my dear, he thought to himself, all the while wondering if there was a Mr Shaw.

When Jonathan had finished speaking, Mrs Shaw nodded, saying she would show him round the flat.

"Nothing like being taken upstairs by a glamorous lady," he joked. Mrs Shaw's look froze him out.

Whoops, Jonathan thought to himself. Not too much sense of humour here. How old was she, he wondered. Looking at her, Mrs Shaw was smartly dressed and well groomed. Women were difficult to age these days. Jonathan guessed that she could be in her mid-sixties. He would have to find out if there was a Mr, but in the meantime he must concentrate on getting the flat and the job.

Mrs Shaw gave him a tour of the flat. Jonathan was pleased to see that there were two bedrooms, so there would be room for Alice and Emily to come and stay. There was also a fairly large lounge diner, a small kitchen and a bathroom.

Mrs Shaw motioned him to a chair in the lounge and continued her conversation cum interview. She explained that the store was staffed by locals, who were all part-time. None of them needed accommodation, so she had decided to let out the flat for a low rent in return for some hours in the shop. The person living in the shop would also be the second port of call should the burglar alarm be activated. Naturally, she would be contacted first. Jonathan asked Mrs Shaw if she lived close by. She said that she did, but wasn't forthcoming with any details.

As she was talking, Eileen Shaw was trying to get the measure of Jonathan. She had realised quickly that he was desperate for the flat and would therefore accept the fact that he had to put in some hours in the shop in return. She had also been advertising for over a month with very little take-up as the majority of people seeking accommodation were youngsters, who had no inclination to do shop work.

This Browne chappie really was quite fascinating. He could clearly tell a tale and what was more was down on his luck, which should make him obliging. He fancied himself as a lady's man, but she was more than capable of dealing with any advances he might make towards her. On balance, he could be a useful addition to her little team, and she really did prefer to have the flat occupied for insurance purposes.

"I'm interested in your application, Mr Browne," Eileen said, "and am wondering what sort of references you could supply me with?"

Jonathan was horrified by this question and felt it showed. "References," he echoed. "I can't supply you with any that would be of interest to you. I'm a home owner, so don't have anyone who can vouch for me as a tenant and I've never worked in a shop before."

"How about a character reference then? That shouldn't be too difficult, and providing it's suitable I'm sure we could come to a mutually satisfactory arrangement. I'll show you back to the shop and leave you to have a look around. I'm sure Michelle would be only too pleased to answer any questions you might have. I'll expect to have that reference within the week."

With that Eileen, escorted him smartly downstairs, shook hands again and left Jonathan with Michelle.

***

James had a restless night, tossing and turning and thinking about Greg and Simon. What should he do? He had hoped that Greg would have phoned him, but he hadn't, so should he phone Greg? Perhaps things would seem clearer after breakfast. He had to admit that Alf did indeed serve a scrummy breakfast. There was plenty of everything, beautifully cooked. Should he go to The Lamb? James really didn't know what to do.

Sadly, he felt there was little point in going next door to ask his sister. Besides, he would have to tell her what had happened and he wasn't sure that he wanted to do that just yet. Why didn't Greg phone? Sitting gazing into his empty coffee cup wasn't going to help, so James got to his feet, and went in search of his car keys. Where to? That was the next question. Not Cholsey. Not yet, anyway.

James drove to Woodstock and had a wander around the antique shops, but his heart wasn't in having a serious look. He went into Hampers where he had a cup of coffee and a scone and wasted the best part of an hour. He then decided to go back to The Crown and have some lunch.

James and Jonathan arrived at the pub together. Whilst James was parking his car, Jonathan went inside and ordered a pint. He was on a fact finding mission and determined to find out what he could about Susie. He was steering the subject around to her when James walked in, taking Alf away to serve him. Jonathan cursed under his breath. Alf was now deep in conversation with the newcomer.

Draining his glass, Jonathan called for another one and was infuriated when Alf sent a girl to serve him. Normally this would have suited Jonathan, who would have started flirting with her, but right now he wanted the landlord's attention, which he most certainly wasn't getting. Taking the bull by the horns, he strolled across to James and Alf and asked if he minded if he joined them. James felt rather irritated by this intrusion, but what could he say? Manners dictated that he smiled and welcomed the chap.

"Hello," he said. "I'm James Rowlands. How do you do?"

Jonathan did a double take, whilst shaking the hand that was offered to him. Could this be a relative of Susie's? How common a name was Rowlands? He responded mechanically to James, whilst wondering what his next move should be. Bugger it! Now that he had moved across to talk to James, Alf had left them to it, and it was Alf he wanted to talk to, to see what he could find out about Susie. Maybe if he chatted to James he could discover something.

Jonathan opened the conversation cautiously, saying that he hadn't seen James in the pub before and asked if it were his first visit. James explained that he had been once or twice before with his sister. Jonathan's ears pricked up - there was a sister, but was the sister Susie? Surely it had to be? That would make sense, as why else would this boy be in the pub?

He decided to ask if James was waiting for her. James said that he wasn't but that he had seen her last night and that he was staying over in Church Enstone for a couple of days and would be seeing her again that evening. Jonathan was stuck. He could hardly ask James Rowlands what his sister was called and where she lived. Alf seemed to have disappeared off the face of the earth, so he might as well make tracks for Kirtlington. He had a character reference to sort out, after all.

As he walked out of the pub, preferring to call a cab when no-one would be listening, Jonathan wished wholeheartedly that he had paid more attention when Susie had been waffling on. He knew that she had a brother, because he remembered him having a twenty-first birthday party, but for the life of him, he didn't know what the man was called.

James finished his drink, ordered another and sat thinking about Greg and what the hell he was going to do next.

***

Greg was also wondering what to do. He had kicked Simon out and was now in his shop in the Lamb Arcade wondering whether James would turn up, with or without Annabelle. He didn't have long to wait before Annabelle arrived on her own. Greg wondered if James had gone to Moulsford the previous evening. He couldn't ask of course, but would have to wait and see if Annabelle mentioned the fact. She didn't and seemed to be her usual charming self. Surely she would mention if James had gone home?

The day over, Greg and Zizi returned to an empty house. It was no good, Greg decided. He couldn't let this drag on. Taking out his phone, he called James.

CHAPTER 29

James had thought long and hard for most of the day and wondered whether he had enough money to buy a small flat somewhere, or whether he should go in with Greg. Since walking out of the house in Cholsey, he realised that it belonged to Greg and not to him and Greg. Maybe that was part of the problem? He would go next door and have a word with David and get his opinion.

When he arrived, Susie was in the middle of a hissy fit regarding wedding stationery. It would appear that it hadn't arrived as promised and now she couldn't get hold of the supplier. To avoid her ranting, David suggested that they go and have a pint next door and discuss things quietly. Settling themselves in a corner of the bar, James explained to David that he and Greg had basically fallen out over Simon and that he had felt he was as much a guest in the house in Cholsey as Simon. Having spent the day thinking, as he had nothing else to do, James was wondering whether it was time that he either bought a small property for himself or that he and Greg bought something larger together.

"I know what you said about me not getting a mortgage, David, but that was before my lottery win. I must have about £200,000 invested, so I should be able to buy something small without a mortgage, or else go in with Greg."

David agreed that that should be possible, but advised James against putting more into a property than Greg was going to put in, to keep things on a level footing. "I know you think I'm a doom and gloom man," David went on, "but you are my client, not you and Greg, so it's you I'm interested in, and it's your interests that I want to protect."

James said that he understood and would have another think and talk to Greg. Meantime, he suggested that David go and fetch Susie and that dinner tonight would be his treat.

Susie was still ranting, only more quietly, when she came in with David. "Everyone seems determined to ruin my wedding," she wailed. "First Grace pisses off and now my bloody stationery woman's gone and disappeared. I need it and I need it now."

"For Heaven's sake," said a very unsympathetic James, "there must be literally thousands of companies who print invitations, or can't you just go and buy them from Smith's?"

Susie glared at her brother. "Actually, it's a whole suite of stationery and no, you can't buy the sort of thing that I want from Smith's."

"Oh, get off your high horse and stop being such a drama queen, Suse," retorted James.

"Huh! Drama queen's good coming from you," Susie all but yelled. "A little tiff with your lover and you come crying over here, but won't tell us what the problem really is. You make me sick at times."

James excused himself, left the table and went upstairs to his room. He didn't need to be spoken to like that. His life was a mess and now his sister was being an utter cow. Well, David could have the pleasure of her all to himself. He'd had enough.

"Now look what you've done," David said to Susie. "You've driven poor James away."

"Poor James, my arse," was the rude reply. "What about me and my wedding stationery? Don't you care about our wedding and the problems I'm dealing with?"

David winced. This was reminiscent of Susie's behaviour when they first met. The excitement of the wedding was making her horribly self-centred. He didn't like this side of her at all. She had just been dreadfully rude to her brother, who was in something of a sorry state himself. Was this her typical pattern if things didn't go her way? David sincerely hoped not.

***

Back upstairs in his room, James was in another quandary. He was hungry, but he certainly wasn't sharing a table with that cow of a sister. Could he ring down and ask someone to bring something up, he wondered? He knew it was cheeky, but short of going out in the car to another pub he couldn't see that he had much option. Taking his phone out of his pocket, James noticed that it was on silent and that he'd missed a call from Greg. No message though. Bracing himself, as he didn't know what to say, James dialled Greg's number.

His boyfriend answered quickly. Taking a deep breath, James said he was sorry to have missed Greg's call. Greg asked him where he was and James told him.

"Shall I come over so that we can talk?" Greg enquired.

James replied that he was hungry but had just walked out of the restaurant because he'd had a bit of an argument with Susie. Greg laughed at that and asked him why he didn't come home then? James replied that he felt very much that it was Greg's home and not his; that he was a visitor and in some ways more of a visitor than Simon. At this point, Greg reassured him, telling him that he had thrown Simon out and he most certainly wouldn't be coming back again. James breathed a sigh of relief.

"So, how about it kid?" asked Greg at his most seductive.

James was relieved that Greg obviously wanted him back, but wasn't going to roll over that easily. After all, there was still the question of his mother's dwarfs and the fact that Greg appeared to have been involved in their disappearance. That really hurt. Could he be less than honest? Life had been fantastic until Simon had appeared and the best of it was that he had liked Simon, because in a lot of ways he was similar to Greg. Certainly to look at.

He did need to talk to Greg at length and James didn't think The Crown was the right place. Should he go back to Cholsey tonight? He could leave a note for Alf and ask him to send the bill, but that was a bit cheeky. He didn't want to go back into the bar because of Susie and he felt it would be sneaking off if he just left a note. Better to go home tomorrow. Greg couldn't come to Church Enstone as he had suggested, because of Zizi. Alf didn't allow dogs. Besides, if he stayed tonight, he might get the chance tomorrow to talk some more to David about a mortgage.

How to explain this to Greg? James started by telling him about Alf's no dogs policy, which stopped Greg from coming and staying with him. He then went on to say that it would be helpful if he could have a meeting with David before coming home, and finally, he didn't really want to slip away from the pub without saying goodbye to Alf.

Greg's antennae shot up at the mention of a meeting with David. What could James be up to? Nothing that would affect him, surely? Still, James was at least agreeing to come home the following day, so he'd best settle for that. Telling James how much he missed him and how much he was looking forward to seeing him the next day, Greg finished the call.

James was relieved that everything was sorted out, but he was still hungry! He looked at his watch. It was a little after 8 o'clock. Alf took his last food orders at 9 pm, but would Susie and David have finished eating and gone home by then? His room overlooked the lane at the front of the pub, so he could sit and watch for them to leave, but if they left late, he wouldn't get anything to eat at all. There was nothing for it, he would have to ring down and ask if something could be brought up. Alf answered the phone, told him that he was a bleedin' nuisance, but that he would send someone up with a pint, steak with all the trimmings, and cheese and biscuits. James sighed with relief for the second time that evening.

**

The following morning, after he had had another splendid breakfast, James thanked Alf profusely for his hospitality, but told him that he would be checking out that morning. Alf winked at him and said he was pleased that things seemed to have sorted themselves out, but to come back and see them all again soon.

Next, James rang David and asked him if he could come and see him in his office. An appointment was made for 11.30 am.

As he parked his car in Chipping Norton, James realised that he would also have to see Susie as she worked on the Reception desk. Not surprisingly, she had a sulky expression on her face and her greeting wasn't particularly friendly either.

"Oh, look what's turned up," she said sarcastically.

David was really cross with her. James might be her brother, but at this moment, he was a client of George Timmins and Son and deserved to be treated with the utmost respect. He dashed out of his office to greet James warmly and asked Susie to bring them coffee. She wrinkled her nose, not realising that David had seen her do it. He was simmering with rage by now, but far too professional to show it. He would have to speak with Susie later.

"I was surprised to see that you had made a large withdrawal from your portfolio without talking to me first," was his opening gambit to James.

CHAPTER 30

Sitting quietly after supper, Alex and Angela were busy with wedding plans. The twins were so excited at the prospect of being bridesmaids that it was unbelievable. Alex had decided to wear the Ancient Colours Drummond tartan and Angela was still thinking about her outfit.

Unlike Susie and David, this wedding would be relatively low key. They had considered marrying in a Scottish castle, but decided that was too far to expect Angela's parents, who lived in Cornwall, to travel. There wouldn't be many guests - mainly family. Alex had a sister and husband who lived in Edinburgh, so there again they didn't want to go too far south. Blenheim Palace? One of the Oxford colleges? Angela was refusing to stress over it. She had a calm, placid nature and was not easily ruffled. All she knew was that it would be very different from her wedding to Jonathan.

"How about St Hilda's?" said Alex suddenly. "Fiona studied there and I do believe that they have a chapel in the college. We could get married in the chapel and then have the reception in the college itself. We live in Oxford, for goodness sake, and it's probably about an equal distance between Cornwall and Edinburgh. Would you like me to look into it, Angela dear?"

Angela said that she would, thinking that it could be a lovely setting which would also be peaceful and dignified. She wanted a tasteful, quiet wedding. It would be her second time, after all. As indeed it would be for Alex, but his circumstances were completely different. It would be splendid if they could marry in the chapel itself, because then Emily and Alice could actually follow her down the aisle and her father could give her away - again!

Life with Jonathan had been all go. There had never been a dull moment with him jet-setting all over the globe latterly with Team Lotus. They had done very little together as a family, as it had always been the weekends when he had been away. Things were so different now. With Alex, they did things as a proper family and Angela felt very content. The twins had settled happily at The Dragon School, Alex was appreciative of her home-making, and what was particularly lovely was the fact that he didn't work and was there with her most of the time.

The wedding would be the icing on the cake. Angela hadn't been proud of her affair with Alex, but really Jonathan had brought all that upon himself, always chasing after some bit of skirt or other. She would feel much happier being Mrs Drummond and having what she considered to be a proper relationship.

Alex had also said that he would like the girls to take his name, as he was looking upon them more and more as his daughters. Angela hadn't broached that with them yet, but she did hope they would want to change.

"Time for bed now, girls," Angela said, looking at her watch. "You've got school tomorrow and I don't want you being over-tired. Clean your teeth and into bed and then Uncle Alex and I will be up to say goodnight."

Obediently, Alice and Emily kissed both Angela and Alex and then headed off upstairs.

"I do hope they decide to become Drummonds," Alex said to their departing backs.

***

Who the hell could he get to give him a character reference? The question went round and round in Jonathan's head. No-one from Team Lotus, that was for sure. He had left there under a big cloud after losing his driving licence. He hadn't got any particular friends in positions of authority, so that left such people as his doctor, who he never saw, his solicitor who had dealt with his divorce, where clearly he had been the guilty party, or the bank manager who had looked surprised when he had opened his new bank account for his escort business.

That wasn't doing very well either. After that dreadful hike back to Kirtlington from Woodstock, that cow Janet had refused to pay his bill. When he had tried to pursue it, she had suggested he took her to court. It was tempting to call her bluff, her being the headteacher at such a posh school, but he would probably only lose and he didn't have money to throw away. He was eternally grateful that Angela hadn't asked for maintenance for Emily and Alice. Much as it went against the grain, he had to admit that she had been scrupulously fair all the way through the divorce and it was only right that she should have the lion's share of the house.

Reminiscing about Angela didn't sort out his reference. He needed that desperately. Who was he going to ask? On balance, Jonathan decided that he would ring the bank manager first thing the next morning. That decided, he logged on to the internet to search for eligible women. He couldn't make anyone contact him via the escort agency, but sure as hell he could be proactive here.

After ten minutes or so, he came upon a rather classy looking blonde in her early fifties. She looked worth a punt, so he sent her a mail. To his surprise, he discovered that she had to be online, because within seconds a reply had popped up in his in-box.

From the mail, Jonathan could see that she was called Claire, lived in Chipping Norton and owned a beauty salon. That would account for how good she looked. Chipping Norton would also be very convenient when he was living in Enstone. Not if, but when. He started to type a reply, explaining that he was a freelance PR guy with expertise in the motor sport industry, somewhat busy at the moment, but that he would love to take her for lunch (public transport would be easier during the day) in a week or so's time. What did she think? He was surprised by the rather curt reply that she would consider it if still available.

Time to move on, there were plenty of others out there. What was the German expression? Something like "other mothers have beautiful daughters too". Jonathan started scrolling carefully, until he came to another interesting looking bit of stuff. This one said she was forty-eight and actually admitted to being wealthy. Get in there, he thought to himself. Must word this one carefully though.

He'd just start off by saying hello and see where that took him. Unfortunately, it appeared that she wasn't online as no reply came back. Pity, he thought. Maybe the shotgun approach would be best. Blast out a message to about twenty women, leave it and see what happened. Decision made, he started trawling once again.

**

"I haven't seen you use your lighter recently," Annabelle said to her husband, watching him light a cigar with a match. "Come to think of it, I haven't seen your cigar cutter either. Don't you use it anymore?"

"I don't use either of them, because I can't seem to find them," was the reply.

"That's not like you, Peter. You never lose anything." Annabelle took a sip of her drink, wondering whether this would be a good time to tell him that she too had lost something precious - his mother's diamond drop earrings.

"I know I don't. I really can't understand it. The two of them live in the crystal ashtray on my desk. As you're asking about them, it's obvious that you haven't moved them, Belle, and I can't imagine Mrs Baxter would. She knows that the things on my desk are sacrosanct."

Mrs Baxter was the cleaning lady who had worked for the Rowlands ever since they had moved to Moulsford.

"I presume that you've looked all through your study for them?" Annabelle asked.

"Of course I have," said Peter. "They're not there, which begs the question where the hell are they?"

"Surely no-one can have stolen them?" said Annabelle.

"Where the hell are they then?" asked her husband, somewhat crossly.

"It's funny that your smoking accessories should be missing," Annabelle continued, "because I don't seem to be able to find your mother's drop diamond earrings. I kept thinking I must have put them somewhere peculiar - you know what I'm like, but now I'm beginning to wonder. If someone has got into the house and stolen your cigar bits and pieces and my earrings, what else could have gone missing?"

"I very much doubt anyone's got in to the house," said Peter. "It's far more likely to be someone that we've invited in. Try and think when you last wore those earrings. I'm trying to think when I last had my lighter and cutter."

"You definitely had them on James' birthday, because I remember seeing you use them," said Annabelle quickly. "Have you had them since then?"

Peter replied that he wasn't certain and asked Annabelle if she could remember when she last wore the earrings. She wasn't quite sure, but at the back of her mind, thought she had taken them out downstairs, and put them in a dish on the sideboard for safety. If they were missing, the couple agreed that it seemed likely that the person who had stolen Peter's cigar accessories had also had Annabelle's earrings.

Next, they cast their minds back to who had been in the house since James' birthday. Of course, all the family had and also Mrs Baxter.

"And Mrs Baxter's daughter," said Annabelle. "I had a lot of things that I wanted doing and when I asked Mrs B if she could give me some extra hours, she said she'd bring her daughter with her to help. Surely you don't think Mary would have taken anything?"

"I just don't know what to think," Peter replied. "Of course we can't go around accusing anyone. Before we can even think of doing anything, we need to be one hundred per cent certain that these things are actually missing. We need to go through the house with a fine toothed comb."

Annabelle was relieved how well Peter appeared to be taking the loss of the earrings. They had belonged to his mother and were worth tens of thousands of pounds. More importantly, though, they were stunningly beautiful. She had another sudden thought, which she didn't mention.

Stephen and Maria Somerville had also been visitors to their house on the last occasion they could remember Peter having his cigar cutter and lighter. Surely it couldn't be one of them? She really couldn't think of anyone else having called round. Grace and Jenny had both stayed. The more Annabelle thought, the worse it all became. And then there was Simon.

CHAPTER 31

Clearing customs at St Peter Port, Simon breathed a sigh of relief. He had got away with it! He'd chosen the ferry rather than flying as he felt there would be less scrutiny of his passport, or rather Greg's passport. It was fortunate they were very alike to look at and the same height. The only difference was their eyes. His were green and Greg's were blue, but fortunately no-one had noticed.

Had he flown, he would really have needed to hire a car or use buses. As he didn't have Greg's driving licence, hiring a car wouldn't have been possible. As it was, he could walk up into the town. Simon patted his pocket to reassure himself that the things he wished to sell were where they should be.

While he walked towards the town, he was thinking of the story he would tell prospective buyers. A pair of earrings and a cigar-cutter and lighter were a curious mix, after all. Perhaps he would do better to sell them separately. Definitely he daren't try and sell them in England and as the Channel Islands had wealthy inhabitants, they had seemed the obvious choice.

He was starting with Guernsey and taking it from there. It was very lucky that Greg had left his passport in a place where he had been able to find it. Simon planned on staying away for two or three days before returning to the room he had rented in a house in Bicester. When he had left Cholsey, he had wanted to put a few miles between himself and his brother and had seen an ad in *The Oxford Times* where the room was available immediately, which was how he had ended up in Bicester. How long he would stay, he didn't know. His immediate concern was to sell the items in his pocket.

Turning into The Pollet, Simon walked up to N St J Paint Jewellers. He was going to try the gold items here. They had a couple of beautiful gold pint tankards in the window that were second hand, so he felt very optimistic. Having been admitted to the shop after pressing the buzzer, he was greeted by a young man who enquired as to how he could help him. Simon showed him the cigar cutter and the lighter, explaining that they had been left to him by his father and that he had no use for them, so was interested in selling. The sales assistant said that he would have to get his boss as he wasn't allowed to make a decision on such fine pieces. Simon liked the words 'fine pieces' and felt more optimistic still.

After a couple of minutes, a portly gentleman emerged and greeted

Simon pleasantly. He agreed with his assistant that the cigar cutter and lighter were very fine indeed and were of interest, even though lighters were not that popular nowadays. However, having the matching cigar cutter made the lighter much more desirable. He carefully scrutinised the hallmarks and said that Aspreys made very fine, high quality pieces and then popped them on to his scales.

After scribbling some figures on a sheet of paper, he turned to Simon and asked him what he was hoping to sell the items for. Simon smiled his best smile, saying he believed that gold was at an all-time high and as they were quite heavy, he felt the scrap value alone would be substantial. The older man nodded his head, agreeing that they were heavy for what they were, but that they were also small. He then offered Simon £1,200 for the two. Simon didn't know whether this was good or bad, but decided that as it was £1,200 for nothing, he would take it and get out of the shop before any awkward questions could be asked.

He was surprised, however, when the gentleman he presumed to be the shop owner asked for his name so that he could write him out a cheque. He was going to have to tell the truth here, otherwise he wouldn't be able to bank the bloody thing. Sod it! Smiling again, Simon asked for the cheque to be made out to S Somerville. That way, his dad could also be implicated if need be.

Feeling relatively pleased, Simon left N St J Paint and headed downhill to Mappin & Webb. He thought that the earrings must be worth a few thousand, so he'd have to play his cards carefully this time. He decided not to accept a penny less than two grand.

Smiling again, he was admitted to Mappin & Webb, where he asked to see someone who had authority to purchase. The young girl raised her eyebrows at this, but returned with a much older woman, who asked Simon if she could help him. He carefully unrolled his tissue and showed the pair of them the earrings. The young girl positively gawped as the earrings sparkled magnificently under the shop lights. The older woman said that they were beautiful and started fiddling with some sort of gauge. Simon realised that she was assessing the weight of the carats. She then peered at the jewels through an eye glass to see the exact cut of the various stones.

The woman then asked Simon how he had come by the earrings, to which he replied with a wobble in his voice that his mother had passed away recently and as he had had to give up work to look after her, reluctantly he had to sell them because he needed the money. The two women looked at him sympathetically.

The older one then suggested he leave the earrings with her for a couple of hours so that she could work out an exact valuation. That wasn't what Simon wanted to hear, as he didn't want the earrings out of his possession, but he had the sense to realise that he had no choice. He replied that he would come back at 4.30 pm if that was suitable. The woman said that it was.

What should he do next? He was going to need to stay on Guernsey for tonight at the very least. Perhaps he should sort that out before he did anything else. To his horror, Simon discovered that anywhere within walking distance wanted between £125 and £230 per night. He couldn't find a single bed and breakfast that had a vacancy; it was only the posh hotels. To leave St Peter Port he would have to catch a bus, but where to, and would there be any vacancies when he got there?

He trudged round some more, eventually ending up back at The Old Government House, which seemed to be the only place in town that had a room left, at what Simon considered to be an extortionate £270 for bed and breakfast. He had to show his passport, so checked in as Greg, giving his address in Cholsey.

Having left his holdall in his extremely luxurious room, he set back off to Mappin & Webb. The same, somewhat grim looking, woman invited him to step into an office where she indicated a chair.

"These are exceptionally beautiful earrings, with quite a bit of age to them," she said. "They are most certainly Victorian with a centre drop stone which is marquise cut and is 1.2 carats..."

Simon stopped listening. He wasn't interested in the weight and cut of the stones. All he was interested in was how much he could flog them for. Suddenly, he pricked up his ears. He could sense the old bat was coming to the end of her speech.

"All set in platinum. We would be prepared to offer you £5,750."

Simon almost fell off the chair. Christ, they were worth some dosh if Mappin & Webb would pay him that. He'd best take the money and run. Perhaps he'd dine at Government House after all, rather than some caff. Mustn't appear too keen though.

With downcast eyes, Simon muttered his thanks and said it would be sad to part with them, as he felt they'd been in his family for some time, but then he did really need the money and wondered if it might be possible to have any of it in cash? He crossed his fingers hard as he said this, but he had no way of getting any cash out of the hole in the wall as he didn't have a card and he couldn't afford to run out of cash over here.

The only way he could get cash was to pitch up at the bank in Oxford, which he would do as soon as he got home. The woman raised her eyebrows at this and said that was not Mappin & Webb's normal procedure. They would normally transfer the money into his bank account, but perhaps in the circumstances she could arrange for the odd £250 to be in cash. Simon thanked her profusely.

To his amazement, the damn woman not only asked for his bank details, which were easy, but for sight of his passport too. Smiling at him, she explained that she couldn't just hand out £5,750 to someone without knowing who he was.

Simon smiled back and said that his passport was at Old Government House, where he was staying. That should impress you, you old bag, he thought to himself. Unfortunately, however, it didn't. He was told that he would have to return the next day with his passport, as it was now past closing time. A receipt was written out for the earrings as the woman said she was sure Simon would feel happier with them in Mappin & Webb's safe than in whatever facility Government House might offer.

Once again, he forced himself to smile and said that he would return the next morning, complete with his passport. This was turning out to be not quite as simple as he had imagined. Simon walked back to Government House where he sat by the swimming pool and ordered a pint of lager.

CHAPTER 32

There was a deadly silence in David's office. Eventually, James spoke and asked him what he meant by a substantial withdrawal. David shuffled the papers on his desk and replied that it was £50,000 and he was surprised that James hadn't consulted him about it. James gasped before saying that was because he hadn't made the bloody withdrawal. Immediately, his mind went to Simon. As the damn man appeared to have stolen his mother's dwarfs, could he also have managed to somehow get money out of his investment portfolio?

"How would someone make this withdrawal?" James asked David.

"Normally in writing," came the reply, "and either a direct credit would be made to your bank account or occasionally you might receive a cheque. When did you last get a balance on your account? This says the withdrawal was made on 3 June. Might be worth calling them now."

With a sinking heart, James made the call. As he suspected, there hadn't been a deposit of £50,000. He asked David what they should do.

"Not panic. That's the first thing," but before David could continue, James blurted out that he thought he needed to tell him something, which was all to do with why he had run out on Greg two evenings previously.

He started at the beginning, telling how Simon had arrived from Thailand, having been mugged and having had all his possessions stolen. James went on to say how Simon appeared to have gone out of his way to be helpful - shopping, working in the Lamb Arcade, doing jobs for his parents. Then things had started going missing from the Arcade, but nothing had gone from either Greg's shop or his mother's, until his mother lost a small piece of silver and then, finally, a pair of Derby Mansion House dwarfs. What was worse, two days ago, the dwarfs had been found in the garden shed, at home in Cholsey. At that point, he had walked out, even wondering if Greg was in some way implicated in their theft. David asked him why he thought that and James replied that Greg clearly knew that the dwarfs were there.

David was taken aback by these revelations. The night of James' birthday dinner was the one and only time he had met Simon, and he had sensed a bit of an undercurrent between him and his father, but not paid particular attention. Was the man a villain?

Certainly Annabelle's dwarfs would take some explaining away if they were found in Greg's garden shed. He sincerely hoped that Greg wasn't involved in anything and taking James for a ride at the same time. He liked

Susie's brother very much. Despite the fact that he had both inherited money and won even more on the lottery, James was a genuinely likeable bloke, if somewhat financially unaware. David felt concerned for him.

"Go for a walk for an hour, James, and leave it with me," he said. "With a bit of luck, I'll get to the bottom of this in your absence. If someone has withdrawn money from your account fraudulently they will have to have opened a bank account in your name somewhere, been money laundered, and by that I mean given proof of their identity, then notified Parmenion of the new details. What's more, Parmenion would normally only take instructions from a financial intermediary, so I really wouldn't worry at this stage."

James nodded his head and left the offices of George Timmins and Son without even a glance at his sister.

That annoyed Susie. She flounced into David's office demanding to know what was going on with James. He asked her to close the door and sit down, then explained that he couldn't discuss James' business with her, but he did have to point out to her that she had been rude to James on his arrival and that that wasn't acceptable office behaviour.

"You sound just like that old cow Miss Jennings at Woodstock School," Susie said. "She told me that my behaviour wasn't acceptable just before I walked out."

David replied that it probably wasn't then and that it certainly wasn't now, which was what concerned him. All clients had to be treated with respect.

"Just listen to yourself," his fiancée replied. "James is my brother for God's sake. What's with all this client nonsense? Don't be so pompous, David."

"He may well be your brother," David replied, "but when he's in these offices he's a valued client and you will treat him as such. Please remember that."

Susie pulled a face at her husband-to-be and flounced back out again. What the hell was the matter with people?

***

After a delicious dinner, Simon slept very well indeed and didn't wake until almost 8 o'clock. Getting out of bed, he headed for the lavish bathroom and filled the corner bath to the brim. That took almost twenty minutes, so he thought it would be a good idea to have his breakfast in his room. He ordered it while his bath was running, asking for it to arrive in half an hour's time. He had only just wrapped himself in the super soft bath robe when there was a knock on his door.

A pretty girl brought in his breakfast and set it out for him on the table by the window. Simon thanked her, then ate with great enthusiasm. He needed to fortify himself before he returned to Mappin & Webb. You certainly couldn't fault the nosh in this place. He grinned to himself.

In January, he had been in the Scrubs and now here he was in June in a posh hotel in Guernsey, with a few thousand in his bank account and the prospect of a few more in about an hour's time. Thank God Greg's middle name was Stephen. That should solve the problem that his bank account was S Somerville.

Simon got dressed, checked out of the hotel and made his way back to Mappin & Webb. The same woman as the previous day was there. He showed her Greg's passport, and as anticipated she looked surprised at the name on his bank account, but Simon smoothly told her that he had never liked the name Greg and had never used it and had managed not to have it on his bank account. He wondered for a moment if she looked suspicious, but despite whatever he thought, the woman disappeared to her office once more and returned saying she had transferred the money to Mr Somerville's account and that all was in order.

"What about the cash?" Simon asked. He was very relieved when £250 in crisp Guernsey ten and twenty pound notes was handed to him. Thanking the woman, he left the shop and walked slowly towards the ferry port, deep in thought.

When he got there, Simon was disappointed to find that he had missed the ferry for that day, but he was able to book on the next morning at 9 am, which he did. Now, of course, he had to find a room for the night again.

Although travelling light, Simon was fed up with lugging his travel bag around. He didn't want to go back to Old Government House as he had only checked out a couple of hours ago, so this time he tried the Duke of Richmond. They had one suite left, costing £300 for the night. Christ! This was proving to be a much dearer trip than he had bargained for. He couldn't even enjoy a swim as he had no swimming gear and everything in the shops was so expensive that he didn't want to buy anything. Dumping his bag, Simon decided that a pub crawl might cheer him up and help pass the day.

***

Sitting in his office in the bank, Stephen was horrified to see that two deposits totalling £6,700 had been paid into Simon's account, from Guernsey of all places. Whatever was his son up to? This confirmed to him that, whatever it was, it wasn't right.

On further investigating the transaction, Stephen discovered that £5,500 had come from Mappin & Webb and the other £1,200 from N St J Paint - whoever they were. Alarm bells were ringing loudly in his head. Simon must have stolen some jewellery and taken it to Guernsey to sell. He couldn't have taken anything in that jewellery raid he went to prison for, because the jewellers themselves had confirmed that nothing had been stolen, so where in God's name had he been stealing from?

Whilst Stephen was puzzling over what his youngest son could have been doing, a junior clerk came in to tell him that his 3 pm appointment had arrived. Absentmindedly, he thanked her and asked her to show the people in.

***

Peter and Annabelle had searched high and low for the missing earrings and cigar accoutrements, but to no avail. Annabelle asked her husband what they should do next. He said that he would notify the insurance company to try and make a claim, but that they would have to tell the police first, as the insurance company would want a crime number. Annabelle left him to it.

A while later, Peter emerged from his study to say that a Police Officer was on his way to take statements from them, as there was the possibility that the things could have been stolen by someone who had been invited into the house. He continued to say that they had been asked to make a list of anyone they could think of who might have had the opportunity to steal their items.

Whilst Peter and Annabelle were discussing who to put on the list, the doorbell rang, and who should Peter find standing outside but Sergeant Green, who had been to see them the previous year when Major Williamson had been robbed and murdered. Peter showed the sergeant through to his study, where Annabelle was frowning over a sheet of paper. She got to her feet and said that she would make some tea whilst Peter gave Sergeant Green some background information.

When she came back with the tea tray, Sergeant Green was scribbling away in his notebook.

"Your husband tells me that the last time he remembers using his cigar cutter and lighter was on 20 May, when you had a dinner party for your son's birthday. Is that the last time you wore your earrings, Madam?" he asked.

Annabelle apologised and said that she wasn't certain, but that she could remember taking them out and putting them in a dish on the sideboard, because one of them was irritating her.

Sergeant Green went on to say that Peter had furnished him with a list of all the people who were present at the dinner on 20 May and had also given him the address of their cleaning lady, Mrs Baxter, but wasn't sure whether or not Mrs Baxter's daughter lived with her. He went on to ask Annabelle if she could think of anyone else who had been in the house and would have had access to both the dining room and Peter's study. She said that she couldn't.

Sergeant Green closed his notebook and said that he would have a word with the dinner guests, and Mrs Baxter and her daughter, as it did seem that the items had been stolen. Annabelle looked at him aghast and said that he surely couldn't think any of her family could be involved? The sergeant replied that it was purely routine.

CHAPTER 33

After wandering aimlessly round Chipping Norton for about an hour, James went back to see David. Susie was dripping sarcasm this time.

"Good afternoon, James. How lovely to see you again so soon," she said. "Do please take a seat and I'll see if David is free."

James glared at her and sat down. It wasn't many minutes before he was in David's office, where the IFA was quick to reassure him that all was well. It appeared that when Susie had phoned for the valuation there had been some mix-up and she had got incorrect information. No withdrawal had been made. James let out a sigh of relief. He hadn't lost any money, but had in fact made just over £6,000 and was well placed to consider property purchase, either on his own or with Greg. David repeated his warning not to put more money into a property than Greg. James nodded his head, saying that he wasn't going to make any immediate decisions, but that he wanted to know where he stood.

Feeling much better James set off back to Cholsey, wondering how his reunion with Greg would be. He appreciated the fact that his lover had ousted his brother, but there was still the matter of the dwarfs in the shed. Greg had clearly known they were there, so if he hadn't been involved in their theft, which James was sure he hadn't been, or maybe rather hoped he hadn't been, why had he protected Simon? Was blood really thicker than water?

James had to go via Wallingford to get back to Cholsey and wondered whether he should call in at The Lamb. He hadn't been there for a couple of days, but thinking it through, he felt that Greg would have told his mother some story to account for his not being there, and not knowing what that story was, it was probably better not to visit until he had seen Greg.

Going straight to Cholsey, James realised that he would be the first one home. Should he do something about dinner? He was no cook though, so maybe not. He would wait for Greg. Letting himself into the house James was surprised to see that the dining table was beautifully laid for two. On further investigation he found a bottle of champagne in the fridge. It appeared that Greg had plans for the evening!

***

Greg's day had been tiresome to say the least. He had got up early to lay the dining table ready for James' homecoming. The previous evening he had gone shopping after speaking with James and had bought a couple of bottles of champagne and some excellent fillet steaks. He intended to make it a night to remember.

He had sensed all day that Annabelle thought that something was wrong between him and James, when finally, near the end of the day, she came out with it and asked him what was going on.

"What do you mean, what's going on?" Greg asked.

"There has been no sign of either Simon or James for the last two days, which is very odd, to say the least," she replied. "Where are they? Have they gone off somewhere together? I think Peter was expecting Simon to come round and do some gardening yesterday and he never turned up. I also think there's something that you're not telling me."

Shit, thought Greg. He was going to have to admit that Simon had moved out. He turned his most charming smile on Annabelle.

"Simon suddenly got bitten by the travelling bug again and decided to leave," he said. "I'm so sorry if in the process he let you and Peter down. You must have completely slipped his mind in the excitement of being contacted by an old friend who was planning a walking expedition. Simon couldn't leave Cholsey to move in with this chap fast enough. As for James, he's combining a buying trip with seeing a couple of old college friends who live on the south coast."

Annabelle couldn't remember James ever mentioning any college friends on the south coast and said so. She also considered Simon's departure to be somewhat strange, but said nothing about that. Greg shrugged his shoulders, smiled again, and said that no doubt there were other things that James hadn't told her. She looked somewhat cross at this and told Greg in no uncertain terms that they were a very close family indeed, and didn't tend to keep secrets. Greg felt she was being unnecessarily dramatic, but managed not to say so. He really didn't need Annabelle on his back today of all days. He already had to think about how he was going to reassure James this evening and wanted to be on top of his game, not feeling drained by James' bloody mother. He wanted the evening to be just perfect. However Greg knew that he couldn't possibly fall out with Annabelle. She was his lover's mother and a work colleague to boot.

"I'm expecting James back tonight," he said. "Would you like me to ask him to call you?"

Annabelle thawed a bit at this. "There's no need, thanks, Greg. If I needed to speak to James, I could make the effort and call him myself. It just seemed a bit strange that both he and Simon seemed to have gone missing at the same time. I'm probably being silly and over-imaginative. It must be the strain of Susie's wedding taking me over."

Greg smiled again. "I'm sure it's a very demanding time for you

Annabelle," he said. "Please don't be afraid to ask me if there's anything I can do to help. James and I can easily cover your shop to save you having to come in here."

They finally parted on good terms at the end of the day and Greg hurried home to Cholsey. He was both pleased and disappointed to see James' Mini already parked outside. Part of him wanted to have the dinner nearly ready, the other part of him was delighted that James was back.

James didn't go to the door to greet his partner, as he was still feeling extremely hurt by what had gone on. Instead he remained sitting on the sofa, waiting for Greg and Zizi to come in. Zizi bounded over to James and hurled herself on to his lap, which helped to break the underlying tension between the two men.

"Are you pleased to see me, pretty girl?" James asked the terrier.

"We both are," came the reply. "Now come here and give me a hug and tell me what you've been doing."

James did as instructed, but with a hint of reservation, which Greg picked up on immediately. Releasing James, he went to the fridge, pulled out the bottle of champagne and popped the cork.

"Here, tell me all over a glass of bubbly," he said.

James replied that there wasn't really that much to tell – that he had been and stayed in Church Enstone, as Greg already knew, and that he and Susie weren't really on the best of terms. Greg nodded his head and said that he thought that the wedding was also getting to James' mum, as she had seemed a bit out of sorts today. He went on to say that she had also been enquiring as to James' whereabouts and that he had told her that he had been on a buying spree to the south coast, where he had also looked up a couple of college friends.

"But I don't have any friends on the south coast," said James.

"That's what your mother said," was the dry reply.

"Anyway," James went on, "I think you owe me an explanation as to what my mother's Derby dwarfs were doing hidden in the back of the shed. You obviously knew that they were there, but hadn't told me. That means you were up to no good. Please tell me that you didn't steal them from her shop. I can't believe that you're a thief."

"Of course I'm not a thief," Greg replied. "Zizi dug the bloody dwarfs up out of the garden. They were where the magnolia tree was originally, which made me wonder if Simon could somehow be involved with them, as he was the one who put the magnolia tree in the garden in the first place. That suggested to me that he needed the tree as a marker to know where he had buried the dwarfs. I'm quite sure that he stole them from your mother, although of course he denied it. I shoved them to the back of the shed as I didn't know what to do about them. I didn't know whether to tell you I'd found them, tell your mum, or what the hell to do. Anyway I had a bust-up with Simon, and threw him out. I can't tell you how shocked I was when you walked out the other night. I was frightened that I might have lost you for good. That meant that Simon had to go."

James was relieved that he appeared to be more important to Greg than Simon. He then explained to Greg that he had been made to feel like an outsider in the house in Cholsey. Everything in the house belonged to Greg, and then to top it all, Greg's brother arrived. And finally the dwarfs were discovered, which the two brothers knew about, and once again, he, James, was the odd one out, knowing nothing. That was why he had left.

Greg edged up closer to James and put his arm round him.

"I didn't know that Simon's presence was having such an effect on you," he said. "I thought the two of you were getting along rather well."

"We were until the dwarf incident," said James, "and then suddenly I became the outsider. I panicked and ran. I'm back now, though, and we need to decide what we are going to do about the bloody things. Sure as hell they're my mother's and sure as hell your brother stole them. The question is do we come clean or bury them in the garden again?"

***

When she got home that evening Annabelle told Peter that Simon had gone travelling again and that she hadn't seen James for a couple of days. She went on to say that Greg had said that James had gone antique hunting on the south coast and was catching up with a couple of college friends who lived down there. Peter replied that he had told her that he had never taken to Simon so his disappearance didn't surprise him at all and did it really matter where James was? He was a grown man after all and not tied to Annabelle's apron strings.

"Perhaps I am being a bit over-imaginative," she said, "and letting things get on top of me. The Susie/Grace fiasco hasn't really helped. Those two had been friends since children, and now I'm not even sure if Grace will come to Susie's wedding. Such a shame."

Peter sensed that his wife was feeling down. "Tell you what, darling, why don't we take the plane and go somewhere for the weekend? I think a break would do you good. I'll fly us out on Friday afternoon and we can come home on Sunday afternoon. I'm sure the boys would look after Allsort for us. What do you say?"

Annabelle replied that she would like that very much. Peter headed off to his study to sort out a hotel.

CHAPTER 34

Jonathan had struggled a bit to get a character reference, but had finally coaxed something out of the bank manager which he hoped would suit Eileen Shaw's requirements.

It must have done, because a couple of days later he received a letter from her, enclosing his job description, terms and conditions, and an agreement that would allow him to live in the flat. Jonathan noticed that Mrs Shaw was no pushover and expected a thirty-five hour working week from him, even though the advertisement had referred to some part-time work in exchange for a reduced rent. Well, he had two choices, so he wrote a letter of acceptance and walked across to the Post Office and posted it off.

After some to-ing and fro-ing, it was agreed that Jonathan would move to Enstone on 1 July. He now had to tell Angela that he would be vacating the Kirtlington house. He also had to think how he would move his personal possessions and discuss with Angela what would happen to the remainder of the house contents. The best way to sort it all out would be face to face. Jonathan picked up the phone and dialled Angela. Annoyingly, the call went to voicemail, so he left a message asking if they could meet up, but not saying why.

"That's interesting," Angela said to Alex. "I've had a message from Jonathan asking if we could meet up, but he hasn't said why. I wonder what he's up to?"

Alex replied that he didn't know and asked her what she was going to do.

"Ring him back eventually and find out what he wants," Angela replied, "but meanwhile, we've got a wedding to arrange. I know you've sorted out your kilt, but I haven't chosen my dress or bought anything for the girls. I don't know whether I could pick up the colours of your tartan in their outfits."

"Aren't red and green a bit wintry?" enquired her husband to be.

"Probably," she replied, "but just leave that with me."

Alex smiled at her fondly. In his eyes, Angela was a marvellous home-marker who also had excellent taste. He knew that she would never dress flashily, but would always be extremely tasteful and that would be reflected in how Alice and Emily were also dressed. He was very much looking forward to their wedding day in a few weeks' time.

Most of the preparations were in place. St Hilda's Chapel had been booked and they were having a very small marquee erected on the South Lawn. There wouldn't be many guests – about twenty in all – but everything would be perfect. Alex had ordered the wines and champagne and they had selected their menu, which would be simple but delightful. A cake had been ordered from the shop in the covered market and flowers had also been organised. Invitations had gone out and all that was left was for Angela to choose dresses for herself and her daughters.

She was planning a shopping trip on Friday to do that very thing. The honeymoon would be more of a family holiday as they had no intention of leaving Alice and Emily behind. Once again, Alex counted his blessings. He had had a wonderful marriage to Elizabeth, but sadly they had not been able to have children, and here he was about to be married again, and his lovely new wife was bringing him two daughters. What more could any man ask for?

Jonathan was a small fly in the ointment. However, he had not been particularly difficult over Angela's divorce, and Alex could only wonder what on earth he could want now.

It didn't take too long to find out. Angela decided to ring Jonathan back sooner rather than later. She came off the phone and told Alex that he wanted to meet with her as he was planning to move out of the house and wished to sort out some bits and pieces. Angela went on to say that she had arranged to meet him at the house on the coming Saturday and would know a lot more after that.

"I want to leave some furniture in the house as it will be much easier to sell if it looks like a home rather than an empty shell," she said. "However, I can't imagine that Jonathan will be going anywhere that can accommodate much of the furniture. We shall see though."

"Whilst we're talking about exes, how would you feel about having Peter and Annabelle Rowlands at our wedding?" Alex asked. "I know their daughter had a fling with Jonathan, but if she hadn't, maybe we wouldn't be sitting here organising our wedding. It's hardly Peter and Annabelle's fault, either, is it? It's just that I don't have that many friends around Oxford and bumping into Rowlands at Buck House seems rather like fate. Would you mind awfully, Angela darling?"

Angela considered for a moment. What Alex was saying was quite true. It wasn't the parents' fault how their daughter had behaved, and without Susie's bad behaviour, would she have ever left Jonathan? Certainly not while the twins were small. She could afford to be gracious. After all, Alex was such a very dear man and he never asked for anything. She turned to him and smiled and said that she would have no problem with that. Alex smiled back and kissed Angela's cheek and once again reminded himself what a lucky chap he was.

****

Weddings were very much in the forefront of people's minds. Susie had finally got her wedding stationery and Annabelle was busy sending out the invitations. It was going to be on a very different scale to that of Angela and Alex. Peter was spending as much time as possible out of the way and was delighted when Alex Drummond rang him up suggesting they go out for a bite to eat.

"Just had a call from old Drummond, darling, suggesting we have a bite to eat. There's nothing I can do to help you here, so I've accepted. See you later, Belle," he said, looking at the dining table, which was covered with invitations, lists, and goodness knew what else.

Annabelle nodded her head absently. Peter was quite right. He really was no help at all. All she had to do was address envelopes because the invitations had all been printed with the guests' names, but nevertheless it was very time consuming and tedious. She was pleased when she heard a knock at the door, but very surprised when she saw Mrs Baxter standing there.

"Hello, Mrs Baxter, we don't normally see you on a Thursday," she said. "Is something the matter?"

"I'll say it is," replied the cleaning lady in a huff. "I've just had the police round, questioning me and my Mary regarding things that have gone missing from here. How dare you accuse me, Mrs Rowlands, after all the years that I've worked for you?"

Annabelle sighed inwardly and invited Mrs Baxter in. "Go and sit in the conservatory and I'll make us a nice cup of coffee," she suggested.

"You can stick your coffee where you can stick your job," came the swift reply. "Me and my Mary have never been so insulted in all our lives as when that bobby came round asking questions."

"Please come through and let me explain," said Annabelle. "Of course no-one's accusing either you or Mary of stealing anything. The police asked us when we had last seen the missing items and who had been in the house. That included our children, Greg's brother and parents and you and Mary. Can't you understand that?"

"Huh," was the reply. "I've never stolen anything in my life and neither has my Mary."

"I'm quite sure you haven't, Mrs Baxter," said Annabelle, in what she hoped was a soothing tone. "The police would be seeing you just as a matter of routine, and they will be doing the same with all my family and the other guests, although you do have to admit it odd that both Peter and I have had something stolen, without the house being broken into."

"That's as may be, Mrs Rowlands, but you need to know that neither me nor my Mary had anything to do with it. In view of what's happened, it's best that I give in my notice as things can never be the same again."

This was all Annabelle needed. She had an antique shop to run, and a wedding to organise, and she most certainly couldn't be without a cleaner. Smiling again, she asked Mrs Baxter to reconsider, saying that she would be sadly missed.

Mrs Baxter looked slightly mollified at this, but said she would have to discuss it with her husband. With that, she said goodbye, leaving an unhappy Annabelle to her wedding invitations.

She was still sitting at the dining table when Peter returned, full of the joys of spring. He had enjoyed a good lunch with his old friend and furthermore had been invited to his forthcoming wedding. Peter felt that this might be a bit awkward as far as Annabelle was concerned, so chose his words carefully when he told her about it.

"Go to their wedding?" said Annabelle in amazement. "He's actually invited us after the way Susie behaved? Whatever does Angela think about that, I wonder?"

Peter replied that Angela must be happy otherwise Alex wouldn't have invited them. "Perhaps he's grateful to Susie for causing the break-up between Angela and her husband," he suggested. "Maybe he's thinking that without Susie this wedding wouldn't be happening."

"That's all well and good," replied his wife, "but I gave Angela something of a dressing-down that day in the Ladies' cloakroom in the Ritz. I went in and she was clearly telling Susie off, so I said a few things to her along the lines that had she been a proper wife, perhaps her husband wouldn't have felt the need to stray. Were you thinking of accepting the invitation, by the way?"

"Why not, if we're not doing anything else?" said Peter casually. "We haven't even received the thing yet. Maybe Drummond hasn't consulted with his wife-to-be. Maybe we won't even get an invitation. Who knows? Anyway, how are you getting on with the invitations? You don't look as though you've finished yet."

Annabelle replied that she hadn't as she had been interrupted by an extremely disgruntled Mrs Baxter, who had been visited by the police and subsequently had resigned. She went on to say that she had asked the woman to reconsider, but that it now appeared that they were in the hands of Mr Baxter, who was going to have the final say in the matter. Peter laughed at this and asked if it mattered if Mrs B did resign? Annabelle had a hissy fit and told him in no uncertain terms that it most certainly did as she somehow felt he wouldn't be doing much cleaning and that, as usual, everything would fall to her.

Peter told her to calm down and remember that they were going away the following day. When she asked where, he refused to say, saying that it was a secret and that all she had to do was pack a bag and be ready for 10 am.

"Oh well, by that time I'll have discovered if Mrs Baxter has come to work," was all she said.

CHAPTER 35

Simon's return to the UK was uneventful. He caught the ferry on the Friday morning and was back in his new place in Bicester by bedtime. He had a room in a house with two other guys near to the centre of town. It was a three-bedroomed terraced house and his room was a decent size. It also made walking into the town a two-minute affair, where there was a good bus service, supermarkets and plenty of restaurants.

Getting off the bus, he had gone into Dean's Diner where he had enjoyed a hearty burger and chips before going back to his new home. The other two were in, watching TV and having a beer. Simon just said hi to them and then went up to his room. He was feeling very pleased with his trip. Greg's passport had been pure brilliance on his part. It was very useful that they were so close in age and looked so alike. It might be wise not to use it again though, which begged the question as to whether or not he should dispose of it? If so, where?

Deciding that the passport didn't need sorting out immediately, Simon went back downstairs and made himself a cup of tea. The weekend stretched ahead invitingly. After that, he really needed to think about finding some work. His recently acquired capital wouldn't last forever. He needed to keep topping it up. Besides, it would be good to have a place of his own, rather than sharing.

First thing tomorrow, he'd buy the papers. He could look at jobs and flats and see what was around. Another thought crossed his mind, that it would be good to have a girlfriend again – not that he'd want to bring one back to a shared house. He was too old for that game, and he wouldn't want any girl being put off by his circumstances. It would be hard enough that he didn't have a glam job, but if he had somewhere decent to live he could probably gloss over the rest.

After all, he could always say that he was a wheeler dealer in antiques. He had learned a few things during those few months with Greg and James at the Lamb and he could bullshit the rest. That was his plan – in antiques. Thinking about sex with a good-looking girl in a new flat, Simon went to bed and was soon asleep.

***

Mrs Baxter decided to let Annabelle sweat and was purposely fifteen minutes late on the Friday morning. She knew that Mrs Rowlands was not really in a position to give her a dressing down, and when she had reflected on the visit by the police, Mrs Baxter realised that it probably was only a matter of routine. Besides which, her Ron had told her not to be a silly cow and to get herself down to the Rowlands. Where else would she earn £15 an hour and get posh Christmas and birthday presents? In her heart of hearts, Mrs Baxter knew that her husband was right, but it still didn't hurt to make Mrs High and Mighty wonder whether or not she was going to turn up.

Annabelle's greeting was pleasant, but she had no intention of going over the top. Equally, the devil you knew was far better than the devil you didn't. All in all, she was feeling quite happy as she handed Peter her suitcase.

"I said pack a bag, Belle, not half your wardrobe," he remonstrated.

She smiled at him. "As you won't tell me where we're going I have had to pack for most events," was the reply. "If you'd like to change your mind, I can soon re-pack in something smaller." Peter groaned. It was far easier to take the proffered suitcase than to hang around whilst his wife dithered and wondered what she should take with her. Besides, he had a flight plan and timings to comply with.

It wasn't long before they were at the airport and boarding the Cessna en route for – Annabelle had no idea where… She wriggled down comfortably in her seat before clamping on the headphones. She always liked to feel part of Peter's flying. After all, how many women were as lucky as she was to have a retired RAF pilot for a husband, who also had a share in a light aircraft?

It would be good to have a weekend away. Peter was right, Susie's wedding was beginning to get to her, but at least she had managed to post all the damn invitations the previous evening, so that was another job ticked off her long list. Maybe she would find her outfit wherever they were going.

Perhaps it would be Paris. Wherever it was, it would be far less stressful than shopping with Susie. Peter could go and have a drink somewhere whilst she hit the shops.

***

The forthcoming wedding was also taking its toll on David. Susie was being a real prima donna and behaving in ways he didn't like in the least. She had been a very spoiled and demanding girl when he had first met her, but over the months had calmed down and become a beautiful person with a lovely personality.

However, the tide seemed to be turning and she was beginning to be more and more like her old self. He was glad to be going off to Silverstone with his mates on Saturday to get away from her for a bit.

The way she had spoken to James in the office the other day had shocked David. To make matters worse, his dad had also heard and although he hadn't said anything to Susie about it, he had plenty to say to David. Being a loyal soul, David had defended his bride-to-be, but in his heart, he knew his father to be right.

What was worse, David was beginning to wonder whether he could spend the rest of his life with someone who had tantrums as soon as everything wasn't going exactly her way. He told himself it was probably pre-wedding nerves and to get a grip. Susie was the woman of his dreams and he was very fortunate that she had agreed to marry him. Their wedding day would be wonderful and their life together more than wonderful. Why then, was he having these feelings of anxiety? A day's motor racing the next day would sort everything out.

As he was pondering over a cup of coffee, the person he had been thinking about appeared. Even dressed for the office, Susie took his breath away. This morning she was wearing a navy suit with a crisp white blouse. She had certainly embraced the dress code and ethics of an IFA practice and bought a couple of more conservative, smarter outfits. Smiling, David told her how smart she looked.

"Smart?" she said, wrinkling her face up. "Smart's for old people. I want to look glamorous and sexy, but I don't suppose that would be appropriate in your office."

David replied that she always looked glamorous and sexy, but looking at Susie's face, she wasn't going to be easily pacified. He tried another tack.

"Do you fancy going out for the day somewhere on Sunday? Perhaps to the seaside?" he enquired.

"If you're not too tired by your boys' day out tomorrow that would be very nice," Susie replied, unable to resist the sting in the tail.

David decided to ignore that remark and got himself ready for the office. Susie Rowlands could be a very demanding woman at times.

***

Making up and getting back together again had been very pleasurable for Greg and James. James had broached the subject of the pair of them buying a house together, which had pleased Greg. He loved James, but also loved James' money and the lifestyle it could provide. He had been shocked when James had run out a few nights previously, but was delighted that he now seemed to want to make their relationship more permanent still.

With half his mind, Greg thought of Simon, wondering where he had gone. It was whilst he was thinking about his brother that his dad called up, sounding extremely agitated, saying that he must speak to Greg in private.

Luckily, James had volunteered to open the shop that morning, so it wasn't long before Greg had the opportunity to return his dad's call. He was surprised how tense his dad sounded. Hoping that nothing had happened to his mother, Greg asked him if everything was OK.

Sitting in his office in the bank, Stephen Somerville told his son that things certainly weren't OK. What he had to say shook Greg to the core and it was a very worried man who finally drove to Wallingford that morning. What he had learned from his father, coupled with what he already knew, was cause for serious concern. This wasn't for sharing with anyone, particularly James. Putting a smile on his face, Greg sauntered into the Lamb, looking as though he was on top of the world.

CHAPTER 36

Once they had cleared Customs and collected their hire car, Peter and Annabelle headed out to their hotel. Although she now knew what country she was in, Annabelle still didn't know where she was staying and was pleasantly surprised when they reached Le Manoir. She had never stayed there before, but had always wanted to.

After they had unpacked, Peter suggested they drove the short distance to the town centre where they could get something to eat and then have a look round the shops. They parked on the harbour car park and started to walk towards the town, stopping on their way for plates of seafood washed down with a bottle of Sancerre. Annabelle insisted that she should have the lion's share, as Peter was driving.

They meandered happily along the streets, arm in arm, chatting away about previous visits and the things they had done. Suddenly, Peter turned to his wife and told her that he was hoping he could surprise her again and steered her towards a particular shop, telling her that it wasn't long to her birthday and their wedding anniversary, and he knew what he would like to buy her. Seeing where she was going, Annabelle became very excited indeed.

She tried on several things, but nothing seemed quite right. They were preparing to leave when the assistant suggested that maybe they would like something that had only just come in. Excusing herself, the woman disappeared through a door. A few moments later she returned, carrying a small box. When she displayed its contents, Peter and Annabelle looked at each other, momentarily unsure of what to do. Calmly, Peter asked the price. He nodded his head when told, saying he and his wife would take a walk and discuss whether they wished to spend so much money. The assistant replied that she completely understood, as the price was indeed significant.

Leaving the building, Peter and Annabelle walked in silence for several minutes. He then turned to her and asked her what she thought. His wife replied that she was positive and asked him what they should do next? Peter suggested various courses of action, saying they should go back to the hotel and thrash out the options. They would need to have made their decision before the shop closed the following day, but until then there was no rush.

Annabelle was very preoccupied on the journey back to the hotel. Could she have made a mistake? Could they both have? Surely not, but how in the world could this have happened? What should they do? As ever, she would be guided by Peter.

Once back in the hotel, her husband headed for the bar at high speed and ordered a large gin and tonic for himself, then asked Annabelle what she would like. She chose a large glass of Chablis. They went and sat at a quiet table, whereupon Annabelle looked at Peter and asked what they should do.

He replied that he had a mind to fly back to England the following day and search for photos, as they were bound to have some, and then come back on Monday and return to the shop. Annabelle felt they couldn't take that chance in case the goods had been sold. Peter sighed and said she was probably right. Should they go back and make a purchase or what?

After lots of thought, Peter went and phoned James, who said he would call back after he had had a good hunt.

***

"That was Dad on the phone," James said to Greg. "I need to go to Riverside House and look for something for him. I won't be long."

Greg took the hint that he wasn't being asked along, so said that he would take Zizi and Allsort (who was staying with James and Greg whilst Peter and Annabelle were away) for a walk and sort out dinner. James jumped into his Mini and headed out to Moulsford, wondering why his dad had asked him to find a couple of particular photos.

After about half an hour of searching, James phoned Peter and told him what he had found. His dad wasn't sure if they were what he wanted and asked James if he could scan them and e-mail them over. Apparently they weren't, so James had to go and look again. Time was getting on, so he phoned Greg and said he would be longer than he had at first thought. Poor James could feel the bad vibes coming down the line as a sulky voice told him that supper was ready and he would have to keep it warm. James apologised and said that what he was doing was really important and that he'd eventually be able to tell Greg all about it.

Finally, James found what Peter was looking for, and having sent it to him returned to Cholsey and a rather unhappy lover.

Meanwhile, Peter and Annabelle were delighted with what their son had found. Peter made yet another phone call to England. His last words, before hanging up, were, "Don't worry, we can do that. Speak again soon."

He and Annabelle had a relaxed dinner, planning exactly what they would do the next day...

***

The sales assistant smiled when she saw Peter and Annabelle the next morning and greeted them warmly. "You couldn't resist them, then, sir?"

she enquired. "I think your wife will look absolutely divine wearing them. I'll just go and get them."

Once again the assistant returned, carrying the little box. After she had placed it on the counter, Peter took his phone out of his pocket and scrolled to the photo that James had sent him the night before. It was a headshot of Annabelle.

The assistant looked very puzzled when he showed it to her, saying that the earrings looked identical to the pair that she was offering for sale. Annabelle explained that the pair she had been wearing in the photo had recently been stolen from their home and she was positive that the earrings in the shop were the missing pair. Peter went on to say that it was particularly relevant that this pair of earrings had only recently come in.

"Yes, yes," replied the salesperson. "I dealt with the young man myself. He said that his mother had died recently and he wished to sell them."

"That's good that you can recall those details," said Peter. "It will certainly help the police. I spoke to our local force last night and was asked to call them today once I was positive that those were, in fact, my wife's earrings."

The assistant nodded and took the couple through to a private office. Peter then phoned Sergeant Green who said that he would contact the Guernsey Police personally, who would then come and take statements from the relevant parties.

The sales assistant brought a tray of coffee whilst they waited for the police's arrival. She also informed the manager as to what had happened. He came and joined the Rowlands. Peter showed him the photograph of Annabelle wearing the earrings. The poor man was extremely apologetic, saying it was not Mappin & Webb's policy to purchase stolen goods!

A couple of hours later, statements had been taken, the photograph on Peter's phone had been printed off for evidence, and the earrings had been seized by the Guernsey Police who had told the Rowlands that Mappin & Webb had produced a copy of the suspect's passport. They went on to ask Peter and Annabelle if a Gregory Stephen Somerville was known to them. The pair exchanged a horrified glance before Peter told the police that Greg had a shop in the same antiques arcade as Annabelle. As the question wasn't asked, he didn't volunteer the information that Greg lived with their son and that he was a frequent visitor to Riverside House.

Driving back to the hotel, Annabelle was oblivious to the sunshine and the sparkling sea. All she could think about was James and the heartache he was about to endure. "How are we going to tell poor James?" she asked Peter. "I just can't believe this is happening. Do you think he will have warned Greg about the earrings, saying why you wanted that photo of me?"

"No," said Peter. "James doesn't know why I wanted that photo, because I didn't tell him. You know how secretive I can be. The question has to be whether we go home today and tell James what's going on?"

"How quickly will Thames Valley Police move?" Annabelle asked. "It's turned midday now. Even if we checked out immediately when we got back to the hotel you would still have to file a flight plan and get clearance to take off. We probably wouldn't be home much before this evening, which gives the police a good start. I can't believe this of Greg, I really can't. James has been living with him for the best part of a year now and I'd known him for a few months before that. He's James' first love. Oh Peter, this is absolutely dreadful."

"I know, sweetie, I know," replied her husband, "and this weekend was supposed to relax you after all the hassle that you've had from Susie regarding her wedding. Fat lot of good it's done you. You're going home more stressed than when you came away."

"It's not your fault, Peter darling," Annabelle replied. "You brought me to an island we both love which holds many happy memories and you tried to buy me a pair of earrings to replace your mother's, and look what happens! However, it's the knock-on effects that concern me most."

CHAPTER 37

Late on Saturday morning, Susie walked to Enstone Stores to buy some odds and ends. She had all day in front of her as David had gone racing with his friends, so had started her weekend with a long lie-in, followed by a luxurious soak in the bath. All stuff she didn't normally have time for during the working week.

She felt that she had been a bit mean to David recently, so was planning to cook a special meal for his return that evening. It didn't take long for Susie's good intentions to go out of the window. She had become quite friendly with Michelle, who was one of the store assistants, and was soon leaning on the counter listening to the gossip about the chap Mrs Shaw had taken on to manage the business, who would be moving into the flat at the end of the month. Susie wasn't really that interested, but talking to Michelle was more fun than doing housework, or fiddling around cooking a meal for David.

Part of Susie was still miffed that David had gone off with his friends when she was busy planning a wedding, and a honeymoon too for that matter. When she got back to Mill Lane, who should she bump into, but old Alf walking across the pub car park.

"Hello, Susie love. How are you?" he called out. "How're the plans for the wedding of the year coming along?"

"OK, I suppose," was the reply, "but I'm feeling sorry for myself today. David's abandoned me to go to Silverstone. I was going to cook him a nice dinner, but I got chatting to Michelle in The Stores and now I can't be bothered. I don't much feel like cleaning either. After all, I'm not some sort of skivvy."

Alf smiled and said she'd better come in and he'd treat her to a drink to cheer her up. Susie brightened up at this. If there was one thing that appealed to her, that was being spoiled and the centre of attention. She quickly put her few bits of shopping inside the cottage, then went round to the pub where she found a large glass of wine waiting for her. The wine was so good that Susie bought herself another and before she knew it she was feeling a bit wobbly. Oh hell, and she still had David's dinner to worry about.

"What's Phillip's special tonight?" she asked Alf, and was very disappointed when he told her it was pan-fried pork medallions in some sauce or other. She couldn't take two portions of that home and pretend that she'd been slaving all day, as it needed to be cooked there and then, and probably wouldn't respond well to her best efforts with the microwave.

She'd better book them a table at the pub instead and make it her treat. Not being sure as to what time David would be back, Susie asked for a table at 8.30 pm, to be told by Alf that she must be joking as it was Saturday and he was full. Shit! She'd have to sober up and walk back to the shop. She would be able to buy the ingredients for something basic like spag bol. Saying a cheery "See you later" to Alf, Susie wandered home to have a little rest before she went back to her shopping.

She'd just lie on the sofa and give George, her beautiful ginger cat, a cuddle for ten minutes and then she'd get organised. Unfortunately though, the wine had been too good and Susie was soon fast asleep, with George snuggled up beside her. She awoke to hear a key turning in the front door lock and her husband-to-be coming through the front door.

David had had a good day at Silverstone. There had been four of them and coincidentally they happened to be his best man and two ushers. The wedding, however, had not been their main topic of conversation. Lap times and grid positions had been far more interesting. The fresh air had made David hungry and he was looking forward to his supper. He felt sure that as Susie had been home alone all day she would have had the time to do something special.

He was very disappointed therefore when he walked through the door of the cottage to find Susie and George curled up together on the sofa, with the former attempting to wake up. There was no sign or smell of anything to eat.

"Hello David, I must have dozed off," she said sleepily. "Have you had a good day watching the cars going round?"

"Yes, thank you," he replied. "The fresh air has made me really hungry though. What's for dinner?"

Shit, shit and more shit, Susie thought to herself. David would be hungry and she hadn't a clue what she was going to cook. She gave him her best smile, trying to look seductive and sexy, which didn't work too well as her hair was ruffled from sleeping and the shorts and tee shirt that she'd been wearing all day were all creased.

"I've missed you, you handsome beast," she said, going towards him and turning her face up to be kissed. "Do you fancy a horse's doofer upstairs, love of my life?"

David leaned towards her and was almost knocked over by the smell of stale alcohol. Looking round the room he could see that Susie hadn't lifted a finger to do any cleaning or tidying up in his absence. Nor was there any dinner. He began to feel very cross indeed. He hardly ever went out with his friends on a Saturday and the one time that he did, he came home to mayhem and a fiancée who stank of booze.

Pulling back from Susie, he asked her somewhat sharply what she'd been playing at, as she reeked of alcohol and the house was in the same state that it had been in when he left that morning.

"Why should I do housework and turn myself into a skivvy when you're out having a ball with your friends?" she asked petulantly. "I bumped into Alf and he invited me for a drink, so go and blame him if you don't like things here. For your information, I was planning on taking you next door for dinner tonight, but the bloody place is fully booked. You can't blame me for that."

To bump into Alf, Susie would have had to have been passing the pub. Unless, of course, she had gone in to book a table, but her own sense should have told her that the place was always fully booked at the weekends, so had she wanted a table for tonight, Susie should have thought about it a week ago. Still, he couldn't knock her for trying to be spontaneous.

"I'm not blaming you for anything, darling," he said, "it's just that I expected you to have tidied the place up, and once you knew that you couldn't get a table next door, I would have expected you to sort out supper for us. However, it appears that Alf's wine was irresistible. I'm a bit disappointed, that's all, Susie."

"I sincerely hope that's not how my life's going to be from now on," she shouted. "You going out and expecting to come home to a sparkling house and a casserole in the oven. I'm not that type of girl."

David knew only too well that Susie wasn't that kind of girl, she was glamorous and beautiful and un-domesticated. However, she could make an effort and certainly had many times in the past, but that was when they were first going out together and she had lived in Rose Cottage. He'd been sorting out her finances then, which had been in a very sorry state indeed. And then when Amanda had been knocked off her bicycle and killed, he had got Susie a job in the practice.

She had blossomed from the surly, aggressive girl that he had first known, into a beautiful young woman, whereupon David had asked her to marry him. They had decided to live in his cottage for a while and let out Susie's. Initially, he had never been happier, but recently Susie had started behaving badly again and David was beginning to wonder just what he was letting himself in for. No good worrying about that now. The most important thing was supper! He went into the kitchen and decided that the best he could rustle up would be cheese omelettes with salad.

***

The Lamb Arcade had a busy Saturday, although James' mind hadn't always been completely on the job. He had spent much of the time wondering why his dad had wanted a certain photo of his mum so urgently that he had rung him from Guernsey.

He still hadn't told Greg exactly why he had gone to Riverside House the previous evening, as something had told him not to. Much as James loved Greg, and was considering buying a house with him, the dwarfs had unsettled him and he did wonder if things would ever be quite the same. He was somewhat troubled, but didn't really know where to turn. Definitely not to Susie; she had made that quite obvious earlier in the week. After all he had done for her last year, he felt really let down by his sister.

James had just finishing cashing up in both shops, Greg having left a bit early in order to sort out food and walk the dogs, when he saw two chaps walking towards him.

"I'm sorry, but the Arcade has just closed. I'm afraid you'll have to come back tomorrow," he started to say, when one of the men pulled a warrant card out of his pocket and said that he was Detective Constable Dickinson and his companion was Detective Constable Jones, both from Thames Valley Police.

He then asked James if he were Gregory Stephen Somerville. Heart in his mouth, James replied that he wasn't, but that Greg was his partner, and had something awful happened? The detectives merely asked where they might find Mr Somerville and left James to finish what he was doing. It didn't take James long to finish counting the money. He then drove back to Cholsey as quickly as was safe.

There was a car he didn't recognise parked across the road from the cottage. Inside it were the two police officers who told James that Greg wasn't in and asked if he had any idea exactly where he might be. Before James could answer, the tall blond figure of Greg appeared, accompanied by the dogs.

CHAPTER 38

As he rounded the corner, Greg was surprised to see James talking to two chaps just outside the house. He was more surprised still when one approached him, showing a police warrant card and asking if they could go inside.

Events then moved forward at whirlwind pace. Greg was cautioned regarding the theft of Annabelle's earrings and the sale of them to Mappin & Webb in Guernsey whereupon he tried to tell the officers that he had already made a statement to one of their colleagues, as had everybody who had been to James' birthday dinner. And what was more, he hadn't stolen them!

James felt physically sick, realising now why his dad had wanted that particular photo of his mum. Surely Greg hadn't stolen the earrings. DC Jones went on to tell Greg that he was being arrested on suspicion of the theft of Annabelle's earrings.

"You do not have to say anything but it may harm your defence if you do not mention now, something which you later rely on in court. Anything you do say may be given in evidence." The police officer continued by saying that they were going to search the property and that James and Greg could remain present during the search.

They would also be seizing Greg's passport and asked him where he kept it. Greg pointed to the small cabinet in the corner of the room and said that his passport was kept in the top drawer. Only it wasn't there...

Greg was told he would have to accompany the officers to Oxford Police Station. He was then led away.

James didn't know what to do. He was distraught. Surely Greg hadn't stolen his mother's earrings? Then there was also the matter of the dwarfs. What should he do? The only thing he could think to do was ring his dad, who surely must be involved in some way. How had he known where to go to find the earrings in the first place? A very unhappy son phoned his father. He got the answer phone, so left a garbled message to the effect that Greg had been arrested for stealing his mum's earrings, which his dad must have known all about, and he didn't know what to do. The police had also told James that they would be wanting another statement from him.

Susie would be no help, but perhaps David would. Of course, James couldn't know that David and his sister were having an argumentative evening and that his phone call wasn't made at the best time. Susie answered the phone and seemed surprised when James wanted to speak with David, who was busy in the kitchen making omelettes. She told James this and said that David would call him back in an hour or so.

Time dragged on for James. Finally, his dad phoned him. James was feeling quite hostile as he felt his parents could have told him that Greg was implicated in the theft of his mother's earrings. Annabelle eventually took the phone from her husband and explained to James that they couldn't let him know about Greg because of the family link. For instance, if Greg had disappeared and they had told James that the police were on their way to arrest him, they could all have been accused of trying to pervert the course of justice.

Peter came back on the phone and told James the best thing he could do would be to get Greg a good solicitor, although that wouldn't be easy gone 10 pm on a Saturday night. He told his son to try not to worry, going on to say that he and Annabelle would be home the following day and that they could talk more then. He reassured James that they hadn't gone to Guernsey to look for his mother's earrings, but had come across them quite by chance. Then, when they had found them, he had rung James and asked him to look for the photo and send it over as proof.

Shortly after that conversation, David phoned. Once he had listened to James' tale of woe from beginning to end, he asked what he could do to help. James replied that he didn't know, just that he needed someone to talk to and that David knew all about the dwarfs.

"Please tell me that Greg isn't a thief and there's some perfectly logical explanation," he begged.

David replied that he wished that he could.

***

On arrival at Oxford Police Station, Greg was processed, searched and given his rights. Not knowing any solicitors and feeling that he had nothing to fear as he had done nothing wrong, Greg had refused the offer of one. He had, however, accepted the offer of a phone call.

He had rung his father and told him that he had been arrested for the theft of Annabelle Rowlands' earrings, which had subsequently been sold to Mappin & Webb in Guernsey. The police had shown him a copy of his passport, which the thief who sold the earrings had been travelling on, and which the sales assistant who bought the earrings had taken. Greg went on to say that his passport was now missing and only one person could possibly have taken it and used it. At the other end of the phone, Stephen's mouth went very dry indeed.

"You've got to help me, Dad," Greg said. "We both know that the only person who could possibly have travelled on my passport is Simon as we look so alike, apart from the colour of our eyes. He and James are also the only people who could have had access to it. I'm going to have to tell the police about Simon and you are going to have to tell them about the bank deposits.

"As you know from the previous police contact, not only were Annabelle's earrings stolen, but also Peter's cigar piercer or whatever it was and his lighter. The proceeds of the sale of those must be the other deposit into Simon's bank account. I'd give anything to know where the little shit is so that I could shop him, but at least I can tell the police that he's been in jail before and that he was staying with me so had access to my passport. If it gets to court, you can then produce the bank statements."

Stephen reassured Greg that he would do everything he could to help him, and could be at Oxford Police Station that night should he be needed. With that, the conversation ended.

Following a police interview, Greg was bailed under section 47(3) to re-attend the police station in a month's time. Prior to his release, he was further humiliated by being photographed, fingerprinted and having a DNA sample taken.

It was 1 am the next day when Greg rang James and asked him to collect him from Oxford, explaining that he had been bailed. James had just drifted off into a restless sleep, so was not best pleased at being woken. However, he did as requested. The two men travelled back to Cholsey in silence.

Once inside the house, James uttered the one word. "Well?"

"For Christ's sake, let me have a drink before you start cross-questioning me," snapped Greg. "Have you no idea what I've been through these last few hours?"

"Never having been arrested for anything, I guess I haven't," was the reply, "but once I've made us some coffee, I'm sure that you'll tell me."

James was desperately upset and trying very hard not to show it. What a week it had been. First the dwarfs and now his mum's earrings. It also begged the question as to whether Greg had also taken his dad's cigar cutter and lighter. He had no-one to turn to.

Susie was totally uninterested in his life, as all she could think about was her wedding, and his mum was wrapped up in that too. That really left his dad and David. Only a few months ago, James had believed his life to be perfect - he had inherited a large sum when he was twenty-one, moved in with the perfect man, won substantial money on the lottery and had a wonderful holiday in Kenya. Now this week, it appeared that he was living a lie, with a thief and a cheat.

He put two mugs of coffee on the table and prepared to listen to Greg's story.

Greg started at the very beginning telling how Simon got involved with the wrong crowd and was sent to jail for using a pretend firearm to hold up a jeweller's shop, then when he was released from prison their parents didn't want to know and how he had come home to find that Simon had broken into the house, so he had made up the travelling story, as he didn't want to admit that his brother was an ex-con.

Greg had been worried when things started to disappear from the Arcade and had made up the toothache story so that he could follow Simon to Oxford to see if he were selling stolen goods, but that he had lost him. He knew now, thanks to his dad, that Simon had been depositing money in the bank, so he must have sold the stolen goods before Greg caught up with him.

"And you didn't think to tell me, and you let him go to my parents' house and steal from them," said James. "I can't believe this, Greg. I feel so used, both by you and your brother. I really thought you loved me and then all this happens."

"You're not the one who's been arrested for theft and whose passport has gone missing," yelled Greg. "You're not the one who has to prove he isn't a thief. Stop being dramatic, James, and stop thinking about yourself. I'm the one who needs help and understanding. Not you or your wealthy parents."

James was shaken to the core by Greg's reference to his wealthy parents. Was Greg after his money? He had been very keen on a seriously expensive holiday just after James' lottery win. He could feel his world collapsing and the feeling of being a guest in Greg's house was washing over him again. Should he drive off to Moulsford and spend the remainder of the night there, waiting for his parents to return, or should he stay put and try to believe what Greg was telling him?

"So what you're trying to tell me is that Simon has done all the stealing, including your passport? He has then travelled to Guernsey on it, where he sold my mum's earrings to Mappin & Webb and possibly sold my dad's cigar cutter and lighter too?"

"That's about it," replied Greg. "Think how alike the two of us look and how close we are in age. It would be an easy deception. The thing now is to find the little rat and bring him to justice yet again."

CHAPTER 39

The aircraft taxied down the runway and came to a stop. Peter and Annabelle took off their headphones and seat belts and climbed out of the plane in silence. They were both worrying about James. Should they visit him at his home or should they invite him over to Moulsford? Should they invite Greg to come too? Annabelle was more concerned than her husband. James was sensitive and Greg was his first love. She couldn't imagine how dreadful her son must be feeling.

Their dilemma was solved. As Peter swung the BMW through their gates they could see James' Mini parked up against the garage where Annabelle kept her car. He came out of the house to meet them.

"Need any help with the luggage, Dad?" he called.

"Despite your mother's best efforts, I can manage, thanks," replied his father.

The three of them walked into the house together.

"I've got so much to tell you and I don't know what I'm going to do," said James. They told him to start at the beginning.

***

Once James had left the house, taking Allsort with him and making it quite clear that he didn't want Greg's company, Greg decided to ring his dad, who suggested that he should drive up to London to see them. He went on to say that Greg could stay with them for as long as he needed. Greg thanked his dad very much, but said he had a feeling that the police might be back to speak with him again. He also needed to try and save his relationship with James, so staying with his parents wasn't really an option.

Greg hardly ever visited his parents' house in Edgware. As he walked through the front door, he remembered why. He found his mother's pristine home quite claustrophobic and her desire to please irritating at best. Pushing aside his feelings, Greg perched on the end of the sofa where he could see the neat little garden and started to tell his story from the beginning again, just as he had told James in the early hours of the morning. By the end of it, Maria had tears running down her face and Stephen was pacing up and down the small sitting room.

Stephen then went into detail about the bank deposits, saying that he would find out more about the latest two from Guernsey and then pass all the information to the Oxford police. He asked Greg if he had any idea where his youngest son could have gone. Greg shook his head, replying that he hadn't had much to do with Simon since he went to the London School of Art, as Simon had considered his choice of career to be poofy.

Stephen winced at this. He wasn't overjoyed by his eldest son's sexual preference, but Maria had convinced him that he had to accept Greg's choice, even if he didn't like it or approve. That afternoon, Stephen knew that Greg needed their help and support more than ever. He hoped that the police would find Simon and find him quickly.

***

David and Susie were discussing James and his predicament. Susie wondered whether Greg might have been after James' money all along and whether or not he really was a thief. She did, however, have to agree with David that the two brothers looked remarkably alike.

"It's funny that James told you his problems and not me," she said, moving her chair so that she got more sun on her face.

"Not really," was the reply. "If you remember, when he came to Church Enstone after he'd run out on Greg, you didn't want to listen. You were too wrapped up in your wedding invitations and had no time for him. He came to me to talk about his investments, and due to a mistake on your part, we thought someone had withdrawn a chunk of money from his portfolio and in a panic, he told me the story of the dwarfs. Once I knew that, he phoned me when Greg was arrested and told me about your mum's earrings."

"Oh, I should have known it'd be my fault," said Susie, a little too loudly for David's liking, as he was aware that the couple next to them on the beach was now listening to their conversation. "Most things are. The Grace affair and now James too. I'm sick of being picked on."

"No-one's picking on you, Susie. I'm stating facts. That's all," replied David. "You didn't have time for your brother, your parents were away for the weekend, so he came to me."

"You're such a good person, aren't you, David?" was the reply. "I'm so grateful that you can love someone as bad as me." With that, Susie jumped to her feet and walked towards the sea, leaving David with an all too familiar feeling of disappointment.

Their eventual journey home was not particularly comfortable.

***

Peter and Annabelle did their best to comfort James, although Annabelle was not best pleased when the tale of the dwarfs came to light and asked James why he hadn't told her about them. Her son replied that he just hadn't known what to do as he had been so upset himself by their discovery. He told her of his flight to Church Enstone to seek help and advice from Susie.

That made his father laugh out loud and say that he doubted much was forthcoming. Annabelle realised that tied in with Greg's story about James' visit to Brighton, as he had obviously not wanted her to know that anything was amiss.

After several hours of talking, Peter turned to his son and asked him what he was going to do. Whether he was going to stay the night in Moulsford or go home to Greg. James replied that he still didn't know what to do and was told that at the end of the day, only he could decide.

Eventually, he made the decision to go back to Cholsey, where he found an empty house.

***

Similar conversations had taken place all afternoon in Edgware. The main difference being that the Somervilles' concern was to the whereabouts of Simon. Little did they know that he had spent a large part of the day visiting estate agents in Bicester looking for a property to rent and had found a two bedroom house that was very much to his liking, which he was going to view in a couple of days' time.

Greg, like James, decided to go home to Cholsey and wait to see what his dad could uncover the following day. As he joined the M40 heading north, Greg felt a little more settled. Although he wasn't keen on visiting, his parents had been wonderfully supportive.

He found James listening to Il Divo, with a can of Fosters in his hand, looking as though he had all the cares of the world on his shoulders. Greg poured himself a large glass of Merlot and sat on the opposite sofa. Zizi had gone and snuggled up to James.

Taking a large slug of his drink, Greg started to tell James about his visit to his parents and that they too were convinced that Simon had stolen Greg's passport. He then went on to the bank deposits that his father had discovered by chance, as his father and Simon had the same initials, and for some reason how Simon's bank statement had gone to Stephen. He said he hoped to know more the following day after his father had done some digging, and that once his father had found out all that he could, he would be making a voluntary statement to Oxford CID.

James felt very relieved. Perhaps this nightmare would sort itself out. He needed, and wanted, to trust Greg. Pulling the little terrier closer, James slowly began to relax. Sensing this, Greg got up and went to sit beside James. Tentatively, he stroked James' leg. He was very relieved when he wasn't pushed away. Draining his glass, Greg suggested they went to bed.

CHAPTER 40

The day for Jonathan's move soon came around. He had hired a van and a driver to take his few possessions to Enstone and had arranged to meet Eileen Shaw at 2 pm. Angela had asked him to push the keys through the letterbox after he had locked up, which he duly did. He wasn't sure what he felt when he was driven out of the Mews for the last time. He had lived there for quite a few years and that was the house Angela had brought his babies home to.

Still, this was going to be a new start for him. He had somewhere to live for a small rent, but in return he had to work in a damn shop. Well, needs must. Once he had his driving licence back, more doors would open for him, but that was not for another six months plus. In the meantime, his sights were set on Susie Rowlands. He was sure that he could get her back and move in with her.

Mid-afternoon saw him installed in his new home. He had met with Eileen Shaw, who had explained to him how the alarm system worked and given him a list of the staff and the hours that they worked. She hoped it wouldn't be long before Jonathan was able to oversee them, as she wished to do less in the business. She would arrange a staff meeting in a couple of weeks' time, once Jonathan had found his feet. He noticed that his name was also on the staff rota and that he seemed to have to work a lot of hours.

After he had unpacked, Jonathan went downstairs to The Stores and did some shopping. He thought to himself that Mrs Shaw certainly knew how to charge and that he would have to take a bus or a taxi to Chippy in order to stock up properly.

It was a fine evening, so after he had an early supper, Jonathan decided that he would take a stroll to The Crown. There was always the possibility that he might bump into Susie. It was a pleasant walk to the pub. Jonathan found himself relaxing for the first time in months. It wasn't long before he was walking through the pub door and into the bar, where he was greeted by Alf. Nothing changed!

"How do, Jonathan? What can I get you?" Alf asked cheerfully.

"A pint of your finest, landlord, please," was the reply. Jonathan went on to tell Alf that he had moved into the flat above The Stores. Alf already knew that, because Joan and Eileen Shaw were quite friendly and Eileen had asked Joan what, if anything, she knew about Jonathan Browne.

Joan had not been able to be much help on that front, as Jonathan was merely someone she had seen in the bar from time to time, usually at lunchtime. Much as she liked Eileen though, she would not have told her anything to Jonathan's detriment. What she heard in the pub, stayed in the pub - a policy that both the Hursts emphasised to their staff.

Whilst he was telling Alf that he would also be working at The Stores, who should come rushing in to the bar but Susie Rowlands? It used to be her stomach that lurched when she saw Jonathan. This time the roles were reversed.

"Hi Susie. How lovely to see you," Jonathan said calmly, delighted that, so far, she appeared to be on her own, and at the same time wondering why. "May I buy you a drink? What would you like?"

Jesus, Susie thought to herself. Jonathan Browne, no less. What was he doing here looking as devastatingly handsome as ever? She knew that she shouldn't, but after all, it must be about a year since he had dumped her, and David was away at some boring IFA Conference or other...

"Hello, Jonathan. This is a surprise," she said. "I came in to buy some wine for supper, but a glass would be lovely now. Thank you."

Half an hour of Jonathan's company would be better than sitting with George. She could rely on old Alf's discretion, so David would never know, and even if he did, so what? Much as she loved him he could be a bit boring and straight-laced at times. It wasn't as though she was going to have sex with the man, for God's sake. Anyway, it would do Jonathan good to see exactly who he had dumped.

Jonathan was delighted. Not only had he found Susie without trying, but here she was agreeing to have a drink with him. He suggested she find a table and said he would join her with the drinks in a minute. Susie went and sat as far away from the bar as possible. Alf might be discreet, but then again, he didn't need to hear anything that didn't concern him.

Jonathan was soon over with a bottle of New Zealand Sauvignon Blanc and two glasses. He poured them one each and then raised his glass to her, telling her she was as beautiful as he remembered. Susie preened at this, picking up her glass of wine with her left hand so that Jonathan would be sure to clock her beautiful engagement ring. She knew he was keen to get back with her, courtesy of the flowers he had sent a few months back, so she was now going to play the bastard for all he was worth.

Smiling, she asked him what or who he had been up to since he dumped her. Jonathan didn't miss the innuendo; neither did he rise to it. He told her that he and Angela had decided to divorce, as a result of which he had been caught for drink driving, so had had no choice but to resign from Lotus.

He was doing various freelance consultancy work, no mention being made of the dating agency and his brush with Miss Jennings, and had come to live in Enstone, as he'd always liked the village. However, he decided against telling her where, or about his involvement with The Stores.

Time to turn the tables, Jonathan thought, so he asked Susie what was happening in her life. She gave him another dazzling smile and told him that she was engaged to the man he had met briefly when he barged his way into her cottage, which she thought was most likely the night he got done for drink driving. She no longer worked at Woodstock Academy, but instead worked for her fiancé and his father in Chipping Norton.

"So you see Jonathan, that although you broke my heart at the time, you actually did me a great favour."

Yes, but you're still sitting here having a drink with me, he thought to himself. Where was wonder boy? Best way to find out would be to ask.

"Oh, he's away for a couple of nights at some boring old IFA Conference," said Susie tossing her head, "so I popped round to get a bottle of wine to jazz up my solitary supper."

"Such a shame I've already eaten," said Jonathan smoothly. "Perhaps I could buy you dinner tomorrow by way of an apology for the shameful way I treated you?" He reached across the table and covered her hand with his. Good. She hadn't pulled away.

Without a moment's hesitation, Susie agreed. As Jonathan had hoped, the wine on an empty stomach was certainly doing the trick. Why should she fiddle about if she could be treated to one of Phillip's delicious dinners? David would no doubt be having something sumptuous as he was staying in a top London hotel. Anyway, everything was completely above board. If she were up to no good, she would hardly be playing around on her own doorstep now, would she?

Arrangements made to meet the following evening, Jonathan drained his glass and said he would have to be going. He walked back to The Stores with a definite spring in his step. Not only had he met Susie without even trying, she was not hostile towards him and had told him where she lived to boot.

Susie was feeling equally pleased with herself as she finished the wine. Jonathan quite clearly still had the hots for her and, oh boy, she planned to make him suffer. She took the empty bottle and glasses back to the bar, where she decided she would have another glass of wine and a natter to Alf. The remains of last night's cottage pie could wait a little longer to be microwaved.

When he phoned her later that evening, David was relieved that Susie sounded a lot more cheerful. She had been difficult to live with lately. Maybe the wedding arrangements were all coming together and she felt more relaxed.

He knew that Annabelle was busy collating the replies and that the next hurdle would be the seating plan. Still, they did have a wedding planner at The Swan. She would be sure to have some helpful suggestions. Telling Susie how much he missed her and that he was looking forward to seeing her the day after tomorrow, David hung up and got ready for bed.

At Enstone Stores, a competitor he didn't know he had, was also looking forward to seeing Susie.

CHAPTER 41

The next day whizzed by for Susie. She was thinking about her dinner with Jonathan, or rather, if she was honest, she was looking forward to it. Her fingers flew as she typed spreadsheets, she was especially charming when booking client appointments and couldn't do enough to help George. This was something of a relief to him as her behaviour recently had concerned him, particularly the way in which she had spoken to James. He had also felt that David was a bit worried, but Julia had assured him that it was most probably pre-wedding nerves.

They would both be pleased to see their son settle down. On first meeting Susie, they had found her quite charming. She had also proved to be a good worker in the practice, with the clients liking her easy manner. Snobby as it might sound, it made them happy that Susie came from a good family. They had been to Riverside House, where they had been lavishly entertained and liked the Rowlands very much. Jenny had been friends with James when they had been at university together, so it really did seem to be a family affair. They were also glad that the couple wouldn't be moving away, as both were valuable assets to George's business.

5 pm soon came. Bidding George a cheery goodbye and sending her love to Julia, Susie was soon driving home to Church Enstone and the feline with the same name as her future father-in-law. As ever, he was delighted to see her, and his food too, of course! What Susie didn't know was that he'd paid a lunchtime visit to The Crown, where Alf had treated him to a bit of salmon.

George popped round on a regular basis. He knew that by giving Alf a pathetic look, he was bound to get a delicious morsel or two of one kind or another. The old boy had a soft spot for animals which George used to his advantage.

George fed and watered, Susie ran herself a bath and lobbed in a generous helping of Chanel no 5 bath oil. This was a new perfume for her. George and Julia had given her the eau de parfum and matching bath oil for Christmas. It was more sophisticated than she would have chosen for herself, but Susie liked it nevertheless. She felt sure it would impress Jonathan, whose duty-free gifts she sadly missed.

Wrapping herself in a bath towel, Susie went into her bedroom where she contemplated her wardrobe. What should she wear? She wanted to wow Jonathan, but did not want to attract the attention of any of The Crown's staff by looking super glam.

Eventually, she chose a very short, white linen skirt and a bright red top, teamed with red pumps and a little red clutch bag as she only needed to carry her phone and her house keys. She then layered a variety of necklaces around her long, slim neck, pushed a selection of bangles up her arm, added her watch and engagement ring and was good to go.

In the neighbouring village of Enstone, Jonathan Browne had also taken time with his appearance. He viewed the evening as the start of winning Susie back. This time he was the free one and she would be the one being duplicitous, if things worked out as he intended, which of course, Jonathan being Jonathan, he was sure that they would.

He was determined that he would be in the pub before Susie, so that he could decide where to sit. As he walked briskly up the road, Jonathan wondered whether champagne would be too showy, too expensive, or both. Sod showy, he thought to himself and sod expensive as well. He had to regard this as an investment.

The Crown was quiet when he arrived. Unusually, Joan, Alf's wife, was behind the bar. She greeted Jonathan pleasantly enough and called one of the waitresses to show him to his table. Jonathan chose the seat looking into the room and left the one overlooking the garden for Susie. He felt that without other people to distract her, she would have to pay more attention to him. Jonathan then signalled to the waitress and asked for a wine list. When Susie arrived, she was both surprised and delighted to see a bottle of champagne chilling beside their table.

She allowed Jonathan to kiss her cheek. After all, it was only polite, wasn't it? He poured her a glass of champagne, then sat looking at her, but not saying anything, which was rather unnerving. She started a conversation, to fill the silence, by asking Jonathan exactly what he was doing in the village. This was the question he had wanted to avoid and had managed to side step the previous evening.

"Never mind what I'm doing. Tell me about this wedding of yours," he replied smoothly.

Susie gabbled on at great speed - about her dress, how she had fallen out with Grace over David's silly sister, how she was getting married in Moulsford Church and having her reception at The Swan at Streatley which used to be owned by Danny la Rue, who her mother said used to be a great entertainer.

Jonathan muttered something under his breath. He was very relieved when a waitress came to take their order, as Susie's wedding was beginning to get on his nerves. He'd definitely asked the wrong question. Perhaps this wasn't going to be as easy as he thought. Maybe he'd need a second bottle of champagne to loosen her up.

From behind the bar, Joan was watching the pair of them with interest. She felt concerned that Susie was in the restaurant with the chap who used to work on the aerodrome for the racing team. She had never warmed to him, although Alf always accused her of imagining the worst and reading things into situations that weren't there. Despite that, when Alf made an appearance, Joan pointed out Susie and Jonathan and said she was sure they were up to no good. He rolled his eyes to heaven.

"His kids went to the school where Susie was a secretary," he explained to his wife. "She bumped into him in here last night and they're having a meal. Jonathan has moved to Enstone to live, so I'm hoping that he'll become a good customer. He can walk here, so that means he can drink. Suits me just fine."

With that he walked away to greet one of his locals. Joan continued to watch Susie and Jonathan out of the corner of her eye.

***

David's conference had gone well and had finished earlier than anticipated. It seemed pointless to him to spend another night in London when he could be at home. He decided that he would surprise Susie and not let her know his plans. He would either ring her as the train got near to Charlbury station and ask her to come and pick him up, or he would just get a cab. Thinking about it as he travelled along, complete with a vodka and tonic, David decided he would go for the surprise. Hopefully, she wouldn't have eaten, so they could go next door for something.

He got a cab quite easily as the train was unusually empty, with not many people getting off at Charlbury. He was soon back in Church Enstone. David was a bit surprised to find only George at home, but then Susie wasn't expecting him back. He did think she would have told him when he phoned her if she had been going out, but maybe it was a spur of the moment thing.

"Where's your mistress gone, George?" he asked the large ginger cat, who ignored him and carried on snoozing on the sofa. Smiling to himself, he went upstairs to get changed and sort out his overnight bag. There was a strong smell of Chanel no 5 in both the bedroom and the bathroom, which suggested to David that Susie had definitely gone out and probably wouldn't be home too early. That being the case, he might as well have a quick shower and get himself round to The Crown for some dinner. Half an hour later, he was walking through the pub's door.

"Evening Alf, I came home early to surprise Susie and she's the one that's surprised me by being out," he remarked as Alf went to pull him a pint, "so I thought I'd come and get something to eat here."

"Good idea, son," said Alf jovially, wondering if he could somehow avoid David's planned surprise for Susie turning into an almighty shock for the two of them. "What do you fancy? Can I recommend something perhaps?"

CHAPTER 42

Simon was pleased with the house that he had managed to rent. It hadn't been easy to find a property as he had no rental history, but he had done it! The house was on the London Road in Bicester, so he was still extremely convenient for the town centre. His next project was to find some work. There was a variety of pubs and restaurants - one of those might want a casual worker. He decided to walk round the town and have a look. There was also a couple of recruitment agencies, but they were going to want some form of credentials and references. Something he definitely couldn't provide.

The household names such as Prezzo weren't interested in him. They had a strict policy regarding employment. He needed somewhere that was privately owned, where the owner wouldn't be suspicious of him, and would be happy to pay cash in hand. He did need work, because renting the house didn't come cheap. It was a grand a month. His money wouldn't last long at that rate.

He wandered into a new Italian café-cum-restaurant and ordered a Latte. Simon then started listening in to the various conversations that were taking place around him. It soon became apparent that this café was looking for a waiter. He knew he could do that job. All he had to do was convince the proprietor. When the girl came to take away his empty cup, Simon asked for another and went on to ask her if it was right that the boss was looking for a waiter. She said that it was and enquired if he were interested.

"Does the Pope wear a silly hat?" he asked. She looked very puzzled by this, shrugged her shoulders and walked away. The penny suddenly dropped. The girl was probably Eastern European and didn't understand the expression.

Finishing his coffee, Simon walked up to the counter to pay. The girl had disappeared, to be replaced by an older chap. Simon tried his luck again and was delighted when it turned out that this man was the owner. He told Simon to come and see him at 9 am the following day if he wanted to apply for the job.

Feeling pleased with himself, Simon did his grocery shopping and walked back to his new home.

***

James and Greg were trying to pretend that all was right with their world, although quite clearly it wasn't. James was trying hard to believe that Simon was the thief who had both stolen from the Arcade and his parents, and had also nicked Greg's passport, which had certainly gone missing as the police had proved. Greg was feeling very injured by the whole business and uncomfortable around Annabelle, who was doing her best to pretend that nothing had happened.

In the end, it was she who took the bull by the horns. "We can't go around acting as though nothing has happened," she said. "Greg, you took in your brother and lied to us all regarding his circumstances. I understand that, up to a point, but I do think you could have shared your suspicions that it was Simon who was stealing from the shops here. As for my Derby dwarfs, words fail me. Why on earth didn't you tell me what had happened?"

Greg tried to explain that he really hadn't known what to do. If he had told Annabelle about the dwarfs, he would have been admitting to her that he knew his brother was a thief and he had introduced him to Peter and Annabelle. How did Annabelle think that would have made Greg feel? He went on to say that he hadn't known her earrings and Peter's lighter and cigar cutter had gone missing and what a shock it had been to him when the police had arrested him.

Why was life so complicated? Annabelle wondered to herself. Susie was shortly to be married, but she sensed that something wasn't quite right there. She felt it was because of Grace.

Grace getting up and going seemed to have once more brought out all Susie's insecurities. Annabelle was well aware that her daughter had always felt that she was in her brother's shadow, as James was the brighter one of the two, who had ended up at university. Also his win on the lottery had to have made Susie resentful, particularly when she was in such a financial mess herself at the time of his win.

Then there was James. He had come out of the closet about a year ago, was clearly besotted by Greg, who had been arrested for stealing from her. Annabelle's heart went out to both her children. Their lives certainly made her own seem simple! The question was, how could she sort it all out? Peter was oblivious; the only comment he would make was that he wasn't sure about the Somervilles.

**

Stephen Somerville felt that he needed to apologise to Peter and Annabelle regarding the behaviour of his younger son. He suggested to Maria that they should invite the Rowlands to lunch one Sunday so that they could explain everything. Maria turned pale at the very thought.

"How can we possibly invite them here?" she gasped. "Look at the way they entertained us - different wine with each course, delicious food cooked by Annabelle, and then to top it all, we stayed the night at their beautiful house on the banks of the Thames. I can hardly ask them to stay in our semi!"

Part of Stephen knew that she was right. He sighed and said that perhaps it would be better to take Peter and Annabelle out for Sunday lunch somewhere. Maria nodded enthusiastically at this and asked where exactly? Stephen thought for a moment, then said maybe it would be best to put the ball in the Rowlands' court and ask them to choose. He didn't mind if they had to drive to Moulsford. With all the things he needed to discuss and explain, he was more than happy not to have a drink.

Stephen made the phone call, which Peter answered as Annabelle was at the Lamb. He was surprised by Stephen's offer of lunch, but quite impressed, as the man must be feeling mightily embarrassed. Perhaps the chap did have balls?

He accepted graciously and suggested they should meet at The Home Sweet Home at Roke as it was reasonably near the Thame exit of the M40. The pair agreed a date and time and rang off amicably.

When Annabelle came home, she told Peter that she had been talking to Greg about Simon and that she had sort of indicated how let down she had felt by Greg. Peter stopped her in her tracks to tell her about Stephen's invitation to lunch.

"Have you accepted?" his wife enquired. "I feel this could be on a par with your friend Alex's wedding."

"What's wrong with you, Belle? I thought you'd be pleased that I'd agreed to listen to the Somervilles' side of things. Don't forget that our son lives with their son."

"As if I could," an exasperated Annabelle all but shouted. "I spend a fair portion of my time working with one or the other or both. If you think having lunch with Stephen and Maria will solve anything, that's fine by me. I'm concerned about James. This whole affair has hit him hard, and if we could help to lay everything to rest that would be wonderful. Whilst we're talking about our children, I'm also concerned about Susie. She seems to be very moody in the lead-up to her wedding."

Peter groaned. Operation W had been quite calm recently, but it appeared to be rearing its ugly head again. Not knowing what to say, he didn't say anything.

***

Greg had no idea about his dad's plan to talk to Peter and Annabelle. All he wanted was to try to get James back on side. He didn't like the underlying tension, although he did understand. He felt betrayed by Simon, which must be exactly how James was feeling about him. Tentatively, he broached the subject whilst they were sitting drinking coffee after supper.

"I think I know how you're feeling, darling," he said. "I imagine that you feel that I've betrayed you. That's just how I feel about Simon. I only let him stay here because he had nowhere else to go. Had I realised what I was letting myself in for, I would never have done that. You must believe me. I love you, James, and couldn't cope if I lost you. You must realise that."

James replied that he didn't really know what to think and that yes, he most certainly felt betrayed and very alone. Even his own sister hadn't been prepared to listen to his tale of woe. The kindest person had been Susie's fiancé, David. He did want to believe Greg, he really did, and could quite see how Simon could have stolen Greg's passport and got away with using it.

Could they put all this behind them? That was what Greg wanted to know, although he did understand that James had to be torn between him and his parents.

He was sorry that he hadn't gone to Annabelle immediately regarding the dwarfs, but he just hadn't known what to do. His objective had been to move Simon out, but James running away had kind of pre-empted that. However, they were back on their own and he really hoped they could forget about Simon and move on - perhaps literally? Greg knew that James had been talking to David about them buying a place together.

James replied that he would feel much better after Simon had been convicted, and asked Greg if he could understand that. His lover nodded his head.

Feeling that they had cleared the air, the couple snuggled up together on the sofa with Zizi spread across the two of them.

CHAPTER 43

Although he was enjoying his dinner, David couldn't help but wonder where Susie was. Finally, he decided to ring her, but her phone went straight to answer. Where could she be? It was unlike her to go out without telling him, as she didn't have that many local friends. Maybe she had gone into Oxford and had turned her phone off. After all, she wasn't expecting him home. Her car was there though, so someone must have picked her up. Curiouser and curiouser.

He came out of his reverie as he realised that the waitress was asking him if he'd like to see the dessert menu. David decided that he might as well have a pud, as Susie's cooking was not one of her best attributes. With a smile on his face, he took the menu that was offered to him. Sticky toffee pudding - that would go down well, and he'd finish off with coffee and brandy. Susie probably wouldn't be home for hours, so he might as well make the most of things.

Having finished his meal, David returned to the bar, so that he could chat with Alf. Both he and Susie were very fond of the outspoken Yorkshireman. Neither of them would forget his kindness to Susie when she had lost her job the previous year. Alf took her on as a barmaid and Susie herself would have been the first to admit that she hadn't been the most reliable initially, but he had persevered with her and spoiled her into the bargain.

There wasn't any sign of the landlord, so David leaned on the bar talking to a fellow customer who he had seen in the pub a few times previously. He was a pleasant chap and it wasn't long before David discovered that his name was Richard and that he was the sales manager for a stationery company based in Leeds, who stayed at The Crown whenever business brought him that way. He couldn't praise the place highly enough, saying he found it to be very good value for money and that the food was excellent. David agreed with him and told Richard that he lived next door and how he had bought the cottage from Alf a few years ago.

Finally, Alf appeared. "I see you've been making friends with my paying guest, David," he said. "Richard reckons I run the best pub south of Watford."

All three smiled at that. Modesty was most certainly not one of Alf's qualities. Richard suggested that his expense account should treat them all to a drink. Both Alf and David accepted a large brandy. David then excused himself and headed off to the Gents, where he did a double take, as who should be coming out of the cloakroom and heading for the restaurant, but none other than Jonathan Browne, Susie's ex? What the hell was he doing in The Crown, David wondered. The man hadn't recognised David, but then he had been half-cut the night he had barged his way into Susie's sitting room and it had been a year ago. David knew him all right, though.

After he had used the loo, and when he went back into the bar, David asked Alf what Jonathan Browne was doing in the pub, as he understood that Jonathan didn't live locally. Alf shrugged his shoulders and did his best to change the subject, but David was having none of it.

In the end, Alf said that he'd go through to the restaurant and ask Jonathan why he was in Church Enstone, thinking that at the same time he'd tell Susie to get herself off home smartish as her old man was in the bar asking awkward questions about Jonathan.

David balked at Alf actually approaching Jonathan and told him not to go to that extreme. Maybe he was just being paranoid and it was time that he went home. Telling Richard that he looked forward to seeing him next time he was staying at the pub, when the drinks would be on him, David said goodnight and went home.

***

Susie was enjoying herself with Jonathan. She had had a delicious dinner and rather too much champagne, as Jonathan had bought a second bottle. It was a good job that David was away in London as he'd be bound to notice that she'd had a few, as she felt that she was probably going to be a bit unsteady on her feet when it came time to stand up.

Jonathan topped up her glass again. David was away, so he had no doubt that he would be going home with Susie and getting inside her knickers again. She had always been both silly and amorous after she had too much champagne, and she'd certainly had that now. It would soon be time to make his move. What the hell did that nosey old fool want, he thought to himself as he saw Alf walking towards the table.

"Susie love, could you spare me a moment in private please?" he asked.

"Oh, you can shay whatever you want to in front of Jonathan," she slurred happily.

"I would prefer to speak with you on your own," Alf persisted.

Jonathan was now extremely cross. This stupid old buffoon was getting on his nerves. "For fuck's sake, just spit it out," he said. "You heard the lady. You can speak freely in front of me."

"Speak to me like that again and you're barred, but for now I'll just ask you to leave," said a furious Alf. "Amy, who is the tall, blonde girl behind the bar, will take your money. Goodnight, Jonathan. You can come and apologise to me some other time."

Jonathan couldn't believe what was happening, but as he knew he would need to use the pub in the future, he did as Alf had asked. Fifteen minutes later, he was letting himself into his flat - alone. Not the end to the evening he had planned; particularly with a bill in excess of £150 and no further arrangement to see Susie. Bloody interfering old bastard, that landlord.

***

Susie sat looking at Alf in amazement.

"Whatever's the matter?" she asked. "Sending poor Jonathan away wasn't very ni—"

"Nobody swears at me, Susie love," he replied, "so we'll have less of the poor Jonathan. Now listen to what I've got to say to you. Your David has come home early and has had his supper here in the bar as you were out. He bumped into Jonathan in the hallway, then started to ask me what Jonathan was doing here. I managed to change the subject away from Jonathan, and now David has gone home. You, you silly little girl, have had too much to drink and your David is going to wonder where the hell you've been, so I suggest you try and sober up and come up with a good story to tell him when you get in."

Even though she'd had too much to drink, Susie realised what a mess she'd got herself into. "Could I rent your room tonight, please Alf?" she asked. "I could pretend that I'd gone over to my parents and decided to stay the night."

"That won't work. Your car's outside in its usual place. Anyway, my room is let tonight. You'll have to do better than that. You're going to have to go home, explain where you've been and who you've been with. You're a very silly girl. Take it from me, you don't want to lose a decent chap like David because of that idiot Jonathan Browne."

Susie pouted. How dare Alf tell her how to run her life. Still, she supposed it had been good of him to keep David out of the restaurant.

"I know, I'll tell him I've been out with James. He knows that he's upset about the way Greg's been behaving. I could say that he came over to talk to me and we went out for something to eat, and he's dropped me off and now gone rushing back to Greg, following my advice."

Alf said he would leave her to sort herself out and went back behind the bar, shaking his head sadly.

Airily, Susie waved to Amy and asked for a black coffee. She felt that might help. When she had drunk it, Susie staggered into the Ladies and soaked her elbows in cold water. She was sure that she had read somewhere that helped to sober you up. However, it didn't seem to have any effect on her.

Lipstick - that would make her look better. She didn't want David to know she'd been drinking, if she could help it. Perhaps he'd have gone to bed and be asleep? Susie peered at her watch. It was getting on for 11 pm.

Here's hoping, she thought, as she walked unsteadily down the road. Why did the damn road have to go downhill? That certainly wasn't doing her any favours in her high heels. She wondered if David would think she was a bit dressed-up for a night out with her brother if he was awake. Oh well...

Clumsily, Susie turned her key in the door and stumbled into the cottage.

CHAPTER 44

End of term came and went at The Dragon, with the twins having a wonderful time. They had both excelled at Sports Day and now had the long summer holiday and their mother's wedding to look forward to. They were chattering excitedly as they came down to breakfast.

Angela looked at them lovingly, thinking how fortunate she was to have a new life which was just beginning. It was just over a week until her wedding day, followed by a family holiday at a surprise destination. She loved the fact that Alex was being secretive and had everything under control. She couldn't wait to be Mrs Alexander Drummond.

At that moment, Alex came in, carrying an assortment of croissants, pains au chocolat and other goodies which he placed on the breakfast table. "A special breakfast to start the holiday," he said smiling.

"Where are we going for our real holiday after you and Mummy are married, Uncle Alex?" Emily enquired.

She was told that she would have to wait and see, as he didn't want to spoil Mummy's surprise. Looking disappointed, the twins tucked into their breakfast.

"Have you seen our special dresses, Uncle Alex?" Alice piped up. He assured her that he hadn't and didn't want to be told about them, as he too wanted a surprise on the big day.

"So you see, everyone has their secret," he said. "Nobody knows about everything that's happening, so it's going to be exciting for all of us."

Angela looked at Alex fondly. He was so good with the girls and knew how to get on their wavelength. He was a natural father. Once again, she counted her blessings. How fortunate she was that the coffee shop had been full that day and Alex had sat at her table. That said, she would never have left Jonathan had he not shown her up in front of the whole school by having an affair with Susie Rowlands. Thinking about Susie made Angela wrinkle her brow. She was a little uncomfortable that Alex had invited Susie's parents to their wedding and that they had accepted. There weren't going to be many guests, so she wouldn't really be able to avoid them.

Coming out of her reverie, Angela realised that Alex was speaking to her, reminding her that their wedding was only ten days away. He went on to ask her if there was anything that she needed to do in preparation. She shook her head. Everything was organised, down to the very last detail.

Her dress was hanging in one of the spare rooms, which she had locked and was carrying the key in her purse, so that nosey little girls couldn't have

175

a crafty look. Privately, Angela was very pleased with her wedding outfit. She had chosen a full-length cream lace dress with a matching jacket, topped off by a pretty feathery fascinator.

The twins had matching cream dresses - one with a red sash and the other with a green one, to complement the colours in Alex's kilt. Angela knew that he was wearing dress tartan, and the colours, but she knew nothing else. She would be carrying a bouquet of red roses, with Alice and Emily having small posies of cream and red rosebuds.

The wedding was at midday and would be followed by a splendid lunch - each course being served with a different wine. This would be followed by cake and champagne and then everyone would go their separate ways. The new Mr and Mrs Drummond and the children would go back to the house in Oxford, as they weren't going away on their honeymoon until the following Wednesday. Angela didn't know where they were going - only that they would need their passports and clothing for a hot country. This wasn't entirely surprising, as it would be the middle of July and most places were hot then.

Next, Angela thought of Jonathan. She wondered how he felt about the fact that she was getting married, and pretty quickly after the divorce, at that. She almost felt sorry for him, but gave herself a strict talking to. Jonathan really was the cause of her having gone off with Alex, so she had no need to feel sorry for him. No doubt he was still running a string of women, although she did have to admit to herself that not having a job or a driving licence would not be doing him any favours.

***

The object of Angela's thoughts was in a meeting with Eileen Shaw, discussing staff rotas and how he felt he was settling in. Jonathan had found working in a shop to be a culture shock, but was trying to make the best of it, as being in Enstone kept him close to Susie. He hadn't seen her since the night Alf had unceremoniously demanded that he left the pub and Jonathan knew that he needed to get himself back to The Crown and apologise to the silly old fool.

However, for the moment, he was contemplating Eileen Shaw. She was a woman of mystery, about whom he knew very little. Strikingly elegant, as she had been on the few occasions that they had met, Mrs Shaw was busily pontificating about her various staff members. Jonathan was studying her legs. For a woman of a certain age, they were very good legs; in fact, her whole body, or what he could see of it, looked very good indeed.

Surely she would be grateful for the attention of a younger, attractive man? Eileen Shaw could be a very viable alternative to Susie Rowlands. She obviously had money, but did she have a husband? If he was clever, which of course he was, he might well be able to play one off against the other.

Jonathan leaned forward in his chair to indicate great interest in what was being said to him. Now how could he turn the conversation so that he could ask this woman out to dinner? He wasn't yet on Christian name terms with her, so currently was very much on the back foot. Eventually the meeting drew to a close, with Mrs Shaw suggesting they re-convene in a fortnight's time. Taking the bull by the horns, Jonathan said it might be pleasanter to have the meeting in his flat, rather than in the office. It also took them that bit further away from the shop itself and the possibility of being interrupted. She replied that she would let him know. Definitely, the woman wasn't going to be a pushover.

As he wasn't working in the shop until the following day, Jonathan thought it would be a good opportunity to walk up to The Crown and apologise to Alf for swearing at him the other night. He certainly couldn't afford the risk of being barred.

On arrival, Jonathan was disappointed to learn that Alf had gone out, but that he was expected back. He picked up his pint and carried it out to the garden, where he sat looking at the back of Susie's cottage, wondering where the coming weeks and months would take him. He was aware that Angela would be getting married very soon, as the twins talked of little else when they came to see him.

Alice and Emily thought it was wonderful that Daddy was living over a real shop and that he let them choose their sweets when the shop was closed, which meant they could go behind the counter and pretend that they worked there. They had enjoyed their first visit to Jonathan's new home and were eagerly looking forward to the next one.

Going back in the bar for a second pint, Jonathan was pleased to see that the landlord had returned. He immediately walked up to him, holding out his hand and asking if he could buy him a drink by way of apology for the other evening. Alf gave him an old-fashioned look, shook the proffered hand and accepted a half of Leffe.

"It's nothing to do with me, but I'll still say it, the young lady you were having dinner with the other night is engaged. I suggest you leave her alone, Jonathan." With that, Alf walked away.

Jonathan was seething. How dare the silly old fool warn him off Susie. However, he just had to put up with it if he wanted to use the pub, which he did. Meeting up with Susie in the pub again might be awkward, but he'd cross that bridge when he came to it. He might have missed his opportunity, so maybe would have to spend more time on the internet and also pursue Eileen Shaw.

Joan walked into the bar at that point, and not realising that she didn't particularly like him, Jonathan started questioning her regarding Eileen Shaw.

"I'm sure you know that I'm managing the Village Stores," he ventured. "Do you know the owner, by any chance? She obviously doesn't live above the shop, as I do."

Joan was far too long in the tooth to take Jonathan's bait. She merely smiled and said that yes, she knew Eileen. Jonathan cursed. Clearly the old cow wasn't going to be forthcoming. What was it with these people? He decided to go back out to the garden and enjoy the rest of his drink in the sunshine and ponder his plan of attack.

CHAPTER 45

Stumbling across the sitting room, Susie got the shock of her life when she tripped over David's legs.

"Why the hell are you shitting in the dark?" she slurred. "I thought you'd have gone to bed."

"Oh you would, would you?" asked David, as he got to his feet to turn on the light. "Perhaps I should remind you that I'm supposed to be in London tonight, yet when you came in you were expecting me to be here. Why's that?"

What the hell was she up to, David asked himself. Dressed up to the nines, drunk as a skunk, knowing he was home and expecting him to be in bed. The only people who knew he was at home were those next door in the pub, and Susie couldn't have been there, or could she?

His mind flashed back to seeing Jonathan heading for the restaurant. Surely Susie couldn't have been with him? David's mind was really whirring round now. He was not supposed to be at home tonight, and what had happened? Susie had been somewhere, dressed to kill, which she hadn't told him about during one of their numerous phone calls, and then come home the worse for drink, knowing that he would be there. It didn't make sense, or the sense it did make wasn't worth thinking about.

Shit, shit, shit, she was hardly through the door and she'd already dropped herself in it. She'd forgotten that she wasn't supposed to know that David was at home. How the hell was she going to get out of that one? Trying her best to look sober, Susie sidled up to David and tried to put her arms round him, but he was having none of it.

"I asked you a question, Susie," he said sternly.

"Oh David, dush it matter why I knew you were here? Let'sh go to bed," she replied.

Having had a few drinks himself, and seeing how stunning Susie looked, made the offer very tempting indeed, but David refused to succumb.

"We'll go to bed when you've answered my question, but not before," he replied sternly.

Susie giggled. "What was the question? I sheem to have forgotten. Wash it something important?" Shit, her speech was getting worse. Bloody champagne. It had been lovely though. "All I want to do ish go to bed, David, and I'd like it if you came with me."

Reluctantly, David realised he wasn't going to get any sense out of Susie, no matter how hard he tried. He couldn't bring himself to go next door and ask Alf if he'd seen her or if she'd been in the pub. That wouldn't be fair on the old chap. He might as well admit defeat and go to bed and try again in the morning.

***

Although he had been unable to resist Susie's amorous advances, David spent a disturbed night. His imagination was working over-time, coupled with which he was feeling very hurt. Susie was his world, which appeared to be falling apart. He had a nasty feeling that she had been in The Crown's restaurant with Jonathan Browne. What should, or indeed what could, he do?

He got up early next morning and went for a walk. Susie was still sleeping and probably would be for some time to come. David decided that if she were still asleep when he got back, he would wake her up. There was no reason why she should be late for work, because that affected his father as well.

Walking past The Stores, David decided he would pop in and get a few essentials. Susie was a notoriously bad housekeeper and there was very little milk in the fridge. He did a double take when he saw Jonathan Browne standing behind the counter. So that was why he was in Enstone and no doubt the bloody man would be a frequent visitor to The Crown, giving him lots of opportunity to see Susie. Did she already know that Jonathan was working in The Stores, he wondered. It appeared that the man in question still hadn't a clue who David was. David wasn't sure whether or not to enlighten him, but decided not to, for the moment at any rate, so took his bag of shopping and walked slowly home.

As he had predicted, Susie was still asleep, so he made her a cup of coffee, which he took upstairs. She looked at him blearily, while trying to gather her senses. She suddenly came to them, recalling what had happened the previous night. Shit, she needed a miracle.

David would be bound to start again as to where she had been and how had she had known he was at home. Rubbing her eyes, Susie smiled at him, trying to ignore her thumping head, remarking that he had got up early. She then patted the bed invitingly and suggested he got back in. David shook his head, saying that he would sort breakfast while she got herself ready for work. Once he had gone downstairs, Susie turned over and went back to sleep.

When he realised what she had done, David was angry. He went back upstairs, woke her up again and told her he expected to see her in the office at 9 am. He then stormed out, slamming the door. Susie breathed a sigh of relief. At least he couldn't grill her all the way to Chipping Norton, nor could he be off with her in the office. She had bought herself some time.

Driving to work, Susie rang James and asked him for a favour.

***

Greg and James were driving to Wallingford together when James' phone rang. He was surprised to see it was Susie and even more surprised when she told him what she wanted.

"You really are priceless, Suse," he said. "You always come to me when you're in trouble. Last year it was your debts, and now you want me to ring David and tell him some cock and bull story about you going out with me last night to help me sort out my head? Do me a favour, and go away. When Greg and I had a problem a little while ago you couldn't even be bothered to listen to me, but David did. Why should I crap on him and cover for you? You're a selfish little cow and always have been. Mum and Dad always spoiled you and now the only person you think about is yourself." With that, James put the phone down.

"What was all that about?" Greg enquired. James told him, adding he didn't like the fact that his sister seemed to be playing away the moment David's back was turned.

"He's a really decent chap you know, Greg, and she's supposed to be marrying him in September, for God's sake."

When they got to the Lamb, Annabelle was already there, unwrapping some new stock.

"Hello boys," she called cheerily. "How are you both this morning? You're looking a bit down, James. Is anything the matter?"

James decided to confide in his mother. Without any hesitation, he repeated the conversation he had just had with his sister. Annabelle looked horrified. "That bloody man cost her her job once, surely to God she isn't going to let him cost her her forthcoming marriage," she said. "I think I need to go and see her and talk some sense into her."

"How on earth are you going to do that?" James asked. "You can't let on that I've told you and you can't confront her in front of David."

"Leave it to me, James, and don't worry," replied his mum. "I'm about to take a little buying trip out to Chipping Norton and will call in at the office and take Susie out to lunch. I will explain to the men folk that it's a girly lunch, bat my eyelashes and all will be well." With that, Annabelle picked up her handbag and swept out of her shop.

As it was a lovely day, she put the roof down on her Golf and enjoyed the sunshine. As she approached Church Enstone, Annabelle decided that she would call in at The Crown and see what she could learn from Alf, who, according to James, had told Susie that David was in the pub at the same time she was dining with her ex.

Alf greeted her warmly. "Hello, Annabelle love, how are you, and what brings you here?" he asked jovially.

Annabelle smiled, sighed and said that yet again it was her wayward daughter, asking if he could spare her a few minutes. The two of them went and sat in the garden, with Alf instructing one of his staff to bring them a pot of coffee.

Annabelle got straight to the point, explaining how Susie had phoned James asking for help, going on to say that she had made the elementary mistake of telling David that she had expected him to be in bed.

"She really is as silly as a sheep," went on her mother, "but what I'm more interested in is why the hell she was having dinner with Jonathan Browne. I'm asking you to shed any light on it that you can, please Alf. I don't like to ask you to tell tales, but having a daughter yourself, I'm sure you'll understand where I'm coming from. By the way, I am grateful that you looked out for Susie last night."

Smiling at that, Alf replied that he didn't appear to have achieved anything, despite his best efforts. Susie had definitely had too much to drink, which may or may not have been engineered by Jonathan Browne. He went on to say that he was of the opinion that it was, and if it was, Jonathan no doubt had an ulterior motive, which Susie was perhaps too naïve to see.

"Joan doesn't like him at all, if that's any help," he went on to say, "and she's usually a pretty good judge of character. If you want my opinion, you've summed it up perfectly by saying that Susie's as silly as a sheep. I really do believe that she's only silly and not trying to two-time David. However, that doesn't help her with the mess that she's in now, unfortunately."

Thanking Alf for his time and the coffee, Annabelle got back in her car and resumed her journey to Chipping Norton. Twenty minutes later, she was paying George Timmins and Son a surprise visit.

CHAPTER 46

Working in the Italian restaurant suited Simon rather well. He either had to be there between 10 am and 6.30 pm or 1.30 pm until 10 pm, not too late at all, as the place closed early. Whichever shift he was doing, he was guaranteed a meal, so that saved him a lot of trouble too. Tips were excellent, especially from the old ladies, who fell for his charm and good looks. However, he did need to earn more money, as his stash wouldn't last forever.

He was wondering what else he could do to earn more, when one of the customers said to him, "Hello, are you Simon?"

He replied that he was and wondered why the chap had asked, but as the restaurant was busy, he thought no more about it and got on with his work. He needed the money! Next time he looked in that direction, the chap had gone and the table was ready to be cleared.

That day, his shift finished at 6.30 pm, so Simon decided to have a drink in one of the local pubs before walking home. He was settled comfortably in front of the television, when there was a loud knock at the door.

Feeling annoyed, he went and answered it. To his amazement, the chap who had asked him if he were Simon earlier in the day was standing there with another bloke.

"What on earth do you want and how did you know where I lived?" he asked, somewhat peevishly.

At this point, the chap he had seen earlier flashed a Thames Valley Police warrant card and informed Simon that he was being arrested on suspicion of theft. He was then given his rights and told that his house would be searched. Simon tried to make a run for it, as he didn't fancy going through the courts again, but was no match for the officers, who soon had him in handcuffs.

The search proved very interesting for the police officers. The first thing that they found was Greg's passport. Looking at it, they could quite see how Simon had managed to travel on it successfully as he certainly did look like the man in the photo.

Detective Constable Dickinson then unearthed some bits of silver, which he suggested were stolen goods, as they were hidden in a drawer. Simon shook his head vehemently, but was told not to waste his time as they had a list of property that had been stolen from the Lamb Arcade down at the station, which was where they were heading next. It was also suggested to him that he might like to have a solicitor present.

A very dejected Simon was shoved into the back of the police car and driven away. He could feel the neighbours peeping from behind their lace curtains.

***

No-one was more relieved than Greg when Thames Valley Police phoned him the next day to inform him that they had arrested his brother on suspicion of the theft of Annabelle's earrings. After he had told James the good news, he phoned his dad at the bank. Stephen received the news with mixed feelings.

Disappointed and angry as he was with the way Simon had behaved, the reality hit him that this was his younger son that they were discussing and this was the second crime that he had committed. Of course, he was pleased that Greg, as the innocent party, should now be able to prove that innocence, but he knew how much the news would upset Maria. He also felt that he should tell the Rowlands what had happened, but would leave that until after he had told his wife. After all, Greg and James would be sure to tell them anyway.

James was over the moon and said that they must celebrate. He knew that he could now put all his uncertainties about Greg behind him and concentrate on moving forward. Moving house too, for that matter. He wanted to do two things, neither of which he could do at that precise moment.

He wanted to phone David and make an appointment to talk about house purchase seriously, and he wanted to go and see his parents, taking Greg with him, to explain what had happened. He couldn't ring David in the office because Susie would answer the phone and he didn't want to speak to her and he couldn't sort out going to see his parents because his mum was on her way to see Susie.

That day in the Arcade flew by and it wasn't long before the two boys were cashing up to go home. There was no sign of Annabelle, so James wondered if she had gone straight home from Chipping Norton. Knowing that his mum wouldn't want his dad to know what she was up to, he still didn't call the house, or anyone's mobile, deciding that his and Greg's news would keep until the following day.

***

Susie had the hangover from hell and wasn't sure how she was going to sort out things with David. As usual, James had been no help. She really didn't deserve to be treated like this. James was such a goody two shoes. He had always been bright at school, a model pupil and child and then he had gone on to university, whereas she had scraped through most things in her life.

James was now leading a blissful existence with his lover and to boot was horribly rich, having had a big win on the lottery. She was still paying off her sodding credit card debts which she had run up prior to meeting David. She didn't even have a credit card any more as he had cut it up. Now, to put the icing on the cake, she had just had one dinner with Jonathan because David should have been in London and the shit was about to hit the fan. Life was very unfair to her.

It wasn't as though she had been up to anything other than having a bit of fun. After all, she had been with Jonathan for over a year, and he was a good laugh, whereas David could be a bit serious at times. She really hadn't done anyone any harm, but it looked as though she was going to be the one to suffer. As always.

Feeling very sorry for herself, Susie was trying to concentrate on updating some boring old investment portfolio when she heard the front door open and close. Looking up, she was amazed to see her mother standing there.

"Mummy, whatever are you doing here? Is something the matter?" she asked anxiously.

"Nothing at all, darling," replied Annabelle smiling. "I'm out on a buying spree for the shop and I couldn't think of anything nicer than a girly lunch with my one and only daughter. What time will you be free?"

Hearing Annabelle's voice, George came through into the front office. "This is an unexpected pleasure, Annabelle," he said. "Can we offer you some coffee before you steal our valuable assistant away?"

Annabelle accepted graciously and she and George disappeared into George's office, closing the door behind them. They were chattering away about their children's wedding when Susie brought in the coffee. She put the tray down carefully, then returned to her own office, grateful that David was with clients so couldn't use the time to question her. It was handy that Mummy had come to take her out to lunch, because her lunch break could be another awkward time.

She now had until this evening to get her story straight. Her latest version that she had concocted was that she had bumped into Alf as she was getting out of a taxi and he had told her that David was home. Where had she been to in the taxi and who had she been with? That was the slight problem as James wouldn't be helpful.

She wished her head didn't hurt so much and she didn't feel so queasy. Perhaps a drink and some food would make her feel better. Dear old George wouldn't mind if she was a bit late back as she was going out with Mummy.

Sure enough, as Annabelle and Susie were going out, George told her to take her time and enjoy herself. Susie didn't need telling twice.

"This is a lovely surprise, Mummy," she said, linking her arm through Annabelle's. "Where shall we go?"

Annabelle suggested that her daughter should choose as she had the better knowledge of Chipping Norton. True to form, Susie chose Whistlers. The restaurant was quite busy but she was well known there and they were soon seated.

Susie merrily gabbled away asking her mother about her shopping trip and whether or not she had bought anything. The wine was making her feel better, she decided, as she took a large gulp. Annabelle watched Susie with interest as she sipped her own glass of wine. "You look as though you're enjoying that, darling," she said. "Does George mind you having a drink at lunchtime?"

"For a start, he doesn't know I'm having one, and for seconds it really has nothing to do with him," remarked Susie casually. "I don't ask him what he does when he goes out of the office, or David either, for that matter."

"I didn't see David this morning," Annabelle remarked. "How is he? How did his conference in London go?"

"David's David," Susie said, a touch petulantly, "and I dare say his conference was boring. To be quite honest with you, I haven't had the chance to ask him yet."

"You surprise me," said her mother, "but then I suppose cavorting with Jonathan Browne last night has put lots of things out of your head. I can't wait to hear what the two of you got up to and why you thought it such a good idea to have dinner with him next door to where you live, when you thought your fiancé was away. I'm all ears, so do tell."

Susie's jaw dropped. Her bloody brother must have gone telling tales to her bloody mother. How the hell did she get out of this one – again?

CHAPTER 47

"Annabelle's come in and taken Susie out for lunch," George remarked to David when he came out of his client meeting. "That was a surprise. Come to mention it, you look a bit down in the mouth today, David. Is everything all right?"

David was very tempted to share his misery and concern with his father, but felt he should give Susie the chance to exonerate herself first. Sometimes, he was too fair for his own good.

"I think I'm just tired, Dad," he said. "The conference was quite heavy going and then I hopped on a train and came home last night. Susie wasn't in when I got back, so I went next door to the pub for something to eat and then I had a few drinks. You know what it's like."

George smiled, although he did wonder where Susie had been and whether that had anything to do with his son's long face. It wasn't like David to be down and, putting two and two together, George wondered if Annabelle's surprise appearance had anything to do with his son's domestic situation.

Susie had been a few minutes late into the office, looking worried. Was that because of something that had happened the night before, George wondered? He decided to pop home for lunch so that he could confide his fears in Julia.

Walking into the house, George found Julia in the kitchen preparing salad. She was surprised to see him. "Hello darling, I didn't know you were coming home today," she said. He replied that he felt anxious about David and Susie and needed to talk to her.

"Take us both a glass of wine into the garden. I'll be out in a minute or two with something to eat, then you can tell me everything," she said.

When they were sitting down together, George told Julia of his suspicions. He wondered whether she could ring Annabelle to try and find out what was going on. She said that she couldn't as there probably wasn't anything going on, other than her husband's over-active imagination.

"I could invite Peter and Annabelle over to lunch to have a pre-wedding chat if you like," she said. "That doesn't sound in the least bit sinister and it will also give me an excuse to ring Annabelle. Now, do stop worrying, George. You're probably putting two and two together and making a hundred and seven. No doubt Susie went out because she wasn't expecting David to be at home and he's feeling miffed because he came home and she wasn't there. The two of them probably had too much to drink and are suffering today and feeling sorry for themselves. Annabelle happened to be in Chipping Norton on an antiques hunt and thought she'd have lunch with her daughter. Go back to work, George. Stop worrying. If something is the matter, we'll know soon enough."

George did as he was told. When he got back to the office, Susie still wasn't back. He knew he'd told her not to rush, but she was now taking the biscuit.

***

Susie gaped at her mother.

"Answer me, please, Susannah," said Annabelle sternly. "I know you think you're an adult, but quite frankly you're behaving like a child. You're getting married in two months' time, so what on earth was on your mind last night? Jonathan Browne is trouble with a capital T and you of all people should know that. Fancy having a champagne supper with him at The Crown of all places. What have you got to say for yourself and more importantly, what are you going to say to David?"

Shrugging her shoulders, Susie told her mother it was none of her business, and yes, she was an adult which gave her the right to do what she wanted, when she wanted.

"Yes, you're so grown up that you rang your brother this morning asking him to be your alibi as you knew you were in the wrong. You haven't got a clue what to say to David, which is hardly surprising. You aren't sure whether or not he knows you were with Jonathan, all you know is that you slipped up good and proper when you said you thought he'd be in bed. You really are incredibly stupid, Susie, and what's more, you expect other people to lie to bail you out. You really do need to think about this carefully, you know. Poor David is probably very hurt."

"Poor David," said Susie scornfully. "What about me, Mummy? All I–"

Annabelle cut across her. "What about you, indeed? Sadly, the only person you ever seem to think about is yourself, Susie. I thought you had grown out of all that nonsense when you met David and got engaged, but quite clearly I was wrong. You are selfish and unreasonable and furthermore you're in a right mess. I came here today to try and help you, but it is quite apparent that you don't want my help, or rather, you are beyond it. I just hope that David can both understand and forgive you."

"Forgive me for what? I haven't done anything," wailed her daughter.

"That's good to hear and it means that you'll have no problem in explaining to your husband-to-be why, when you thought he wasn't coming home, you decided to have dinner with your ex, married boyfriend, who dumped you unceremoniously last summer and caused you to lose your job. As you say, Susannah, you haven't done anything at all. May I have the bill, please?" Annabelle added, as she could see a waiter hovering.

***

Driving back to Moulsford Annabelle was too cross to appreciate how beautiful the day was. She had thought that Susie had become a sensible young woman, but realised just how wrong she was. She could see trouble brewing between Susie and David, but felt powerless to stop it. Why had that bloody man Browne raised his ugly head in Enstone? To top it all, she was going to his ex-wife's wedding the following Saturday, which would no doubt be an ordeal.

Still, Peter was keen, as he and Alex Drummond had apparently got on well together all those years ago. The next thing would be that she would be inviting Angela to dinner. She could just see it coming.

Peter was getting out of his car when she pulled into the drive. He was very mellow as he'd had a particularly brilliant round of golf - at least according to him he had. "You're back early from the shop," he said. "Have you had a quiet day?"

"Not the adjective I would have chosen," was the reply. "It's 5 o'clock somewhere. What do you fancy?"

Peter said he'd have a G&T, so Annabelle mixed two large ones and carried them out into the garden. She had decided that she was going to tell Peter Susie's story, but thought a stiff drink might make things more palatable.

As she had expected, her husband was fizzing. "Does she never learn?" he asked in an exasperated manner. "She's going the right way to lose David, if you ask me. What is it with that bloody Jonathan?"

Annabelle said that she didn't know, but that quite clearly there was something. Next thing, her phone was ringing and it was none other than Julia Timmins suggesting they should have Sunday lunch to catch up on the wedding plans. Laughingly, she added that they needed to make sure that their outfits didn't clash. Annabelle struggled to sound up-beat, but they arranged a date for the following weekend, with the Rowlands going over to Great Rollright.

***

George was irritated by Susie's extended lunch break. He had given her the proverbial inch and she had taken the mile. However, he bit his tongue as he was convinced that things were not right between her and David. 5 pm came and the three of them packed up for the evening.

Susie was not looking forward to going home as she didn't know what she was going to say to David. She was a crap liar and he was suspicious.

189

Who could she have been out with? She could say she had bumped into someone from The Crown when the taxi dropped her off, but who the hell could she have been out with?

David's mind was going round in circles too. He needed to find out where Susie had been the previous night and who she had been with. The more he thought about it the more he was convinced that it was Jonathan Browne. But if she'd been up to no good, surely she wouldn't have been in The Crown? She'd know that he'd be bound to find out - one way or another.

The two of them drove home in separate cars with their different thoughts.

CHAPTER 48

After David had left the shop, Jonathan wondered where he had seen him before, as he felt that his face looked familiar. He just couldn't place him, so continued with his daily chores without giving David another thought. It was a fairly quiet morning, so Jonathan started thinking about Eileen Shaw. Dare he phone her and ask her out to dinner, or even cook for her himself? He didn't particularly want to take her to The Crown, and going further afield would incur the cost of a taxi. It didn't occur to Jonathan that Eileen Shaw wouldn't be interested.

Jonathan served customers automatically, making polite small talk as and when necessary. He had to admit to himself that most of them were pleasant enough, with some of them quite clearly interested in his background. Sadly, he didn't feel particularly interested in any of the women who were fishing to find out about him.

Eileen Shaw was classy and without doubt had money. Both of these aspects appealed to Jonathan. Maybe he should ask her for a drink first? He could make some pretext about needing to discuss something with her that he would prefer to do in private. The question was what?

He thought hard about it all afternoon and then had a brainwave. How about a policy regarding pets coming into The Stores? Being in a rural community, people brought their dogs in. Jonathan didn't think that was particularly hygienic, and to push his cause further forward, he thought it would be a good idea to introduce a deli section if they could keep the dogs out. Feeling very pleased with himself, Jonathan picked up the phone.

Eileen answered almost immediately. When she heard Jonathan's voice, her first reaction was that there was some kind of problem that he couldn't deal with himself. Hastily, he reassured her, explaining that he had one or two suggestions for The Stores that he would like to run by her and was wondering if she would be free to discuss them with him that evening.

As she had nothing particular to do, Eileen decided to accept, having to admit to herself that she was just a little intrigued. Jonathan Browne was an enigma. He was educated, but must have fallen upon hard times apart from his divorce, as otherwise he wouldn't be living in her flat and managing her shop. He had struck her as very much in need of money when he had come for the interview. She hadn't missed the fact that Jonathan didn't have a car; what she didn't know was that he didn't have a driving licence.

Shortly after 8 pm, Eileen let herself into The Stores, then knocked on the door at the bottom of the stairs that led up to the flat. Within moments,

Jonathan was opening the door and escorting her upstairs. The sitting room was quite dimly lit by a couple of table lamps. Eileen was surprised by how tasteful everything looked, but Jonathan hadn't been married to Angela for all those years without learning something. Desperate to put his past behind him, Jonathan had soaked up style and knowledge like a sponge, so much so that no-one would have guessed his humble beginnings.

Politely, Eileen remarked how nice the sitting room was looking. Jonathan preened, as he indicated that she sit down.

Not one to beat about the bush, Eileen asked him what it was that he wanted.

"Do let me pour you a drink first," said Jonathan. "Would you care for a glass of wine?"

"Not particularly," was the reply. "Could you just get to the point?"

This wasn't going at all as planned. Jonathan's intention had been to ply Eileen with wine and then attempt to move in on her. Sighing to himself, he outlined his suggestion about a deli counter and the need to keep dogs out of the shop. Rather tartly, he was told that that was something they could have discussed on the phone, rather than waste her time in coming to see him.

After she had gone, a disgruntled Jonathan realised that Eileen hadn't answered his question about either the deli or the dogs; nothing for him there then. He poured himself a large scotch and fired up his laptop. He would have to have another go on the bloody dating site.

***

One of the objects of Jonathan's desire was pushing her food round her plate, wondering what to say to her husband-to-be. He had hardly spoken to her since they had got home and she knew that she needed to clear the air. The question was how did she start?

Looking at David with sad eyes, Susie finally told him that she had seen Alf outside The Crown, who had told her that he was home, but that she really wasn't sure why she had assumed that he would be in bed. "Silly of me, I suppose," said Susie, "but it really gave me a fright when I fell over your legs. Why on earth were you sitting in the dark?"

"I was disappointed that you weren't at home, so I was just sitting there," was the reply. "I didn't think you could have gone far because your car was outside. I was also surprised that you hadn't told me you were going out, as we must have spoken three times during the course of the day. Where had you been, Susie, and who had you been with? You must have had a good time, because you were as drunk as a skunk."

Susie bridled at this. "I really don't like being cross-questioned, David. It sounds as though you don't trust me. That's not fair."

192

"Oh, not the 'that's not fair' card, Susie. You play it too often and I'm bored with it now," replied David. "You're acting as though you've got something to hide, and I don't like it."

"Tell you what," replied Susie, pushing her chair back from the table. "I don't like it either, and I'm not staying here to listen to you. I shall go to Moulsford for a couple of days while you calm down."

With that she swept upstairs, chucked some clothes and toiletries into a bag, and headed out of the door towards her car, leaving an upset and confused David still sitting at the table.

***

Peter and Annabelle were finishing supper when flying gravel heralded Susie's arrival. She let herself in, dumped her bag in the hall, then went to find her parents, who were still in the dining room.

"To what do we owe the honour?" enquired Peter. "Your mother was telling me that you had lunch together today and now you're here. Where's David?"

Susie tossed her head and said she had left David to his own devices as he wasn't being fair to her.

Knowing what he did about the Jonathan saga, Peter was understandably furious. "Life's never fair to you, is it, Susie?" he asked. "You really do enjoy the role of the victim or the martyr. I suppose David was wanting to know what you'd been up to last night, when Jonathan Browne was entertaining you with a champagne supper at The Crown. Or worse still, has David found out and thrown you out of the house? It really would be no more than you deserve. You are so stupid at times, Susie, that I despair."

This was not what Susie had been expecting. She had expected Daddy to throw his arms round her and cuddle her better, then pour her a nice glass of wine. It was unbelievable that James had told Mummy about Jonathan, and that Mummy had now told Daddy, who was very cross indeed. She had been expecting love and sympathy, and look at what she was getting instead. What was more, he was still going on.

"...going to tell David? That's what I'd like to know. It needs to be the truth, but knowing you, you've just come here to see if we can make up some cock and bull story to save your pathetic skin. I really am ashamed of you, Susannah."

Susie began to cry. "You're not being very nice to me, Daddy," she whimpered. "I came here because I need help and all you do is shout at me. You haven't even heard my side of things."

"I don't know what there can be to hear," replied her father. "You have an affair with a married man, which causes you to lose a good job. Married man then dumps you. You get yourself into a lot of debt, then you meet David, who endeavours to put you on the straight and narrow. On top of that, he gets you a job working in his father's business in Chipping Norton, then he asks you to marry him. Your wedding is arranged for September. However, this bloody Jonathan Browne appears out of nowhere, freshly divorced and available. He asks you out to dinner when David is away, so you must have told him that David was going to be away at some previous liaison that the two of you must have had somewhere, and to top it all, the bastard takes you to the pub next door to where you live. Are you out of your mind or what?"

Tears were now coursing down Susie's cheeks as she tried to hiccup a reply. "You just don't understand, Daddy," she wailed. "I really haven't done anything wrong."

Peter glared at his daughter. "At this point in time, I have no more to say to you, Susannah. I'm going to my study for a large brandy and a cigar. Tell your tale of woe to your mother. Maybe she'll be more sympathetic than I am."

CHAPTER 49

Greg was very keen to tell Peter and Annabelle about Simon's arrest and, therefore, his exoneration. After they had supper, he suggested to James that they should pop over to Moulsford and do that very thing. James felt it a bit late to go that evening, so said to his partner that they should invite his parents for dinner the next night.

Greg wasn't too happy with that idea, as he didn't want to have to prepare a decent dinner mid-week for James' parents when he wasn't organised, so in the end they agreed that they would go across to Riverside House after work the following day.

The boys were very surprised to find Susie there, and Greg was even more surprised that David wasn't, although James had a nasty feeling that he knew why.

"Fancy seeing you, Suse," he said when he got her on her own. "Has David thrown you out then?"

Susie's eyes welled up again. Daddy had been horrible the previous night and Mummy hadn't been that much better. She had also been at home all day today, making it more difficult for Susie to mope about. Added to all her problems, she wasn't feeling that well, although had anyone asked her, she wouldn't really have been able to put her finger on what was the matter.

"No, he hasn't," she snapped. "No thanks to you, Mr Unhelpful. You really are the one with the golden balls, aren't you, Jamie? And you just don't give a shit about me. For all you care, David could well have thrown me out. Daddy's ripped me apart and it's all thanks to you running to Mummy, telling her about Jonathan and then, of course, Mummy had to go and tell Daddy. If you can't trust your own brother, I don't know who you can trust."

James sighed. He loved his sister, but at times she really could be totally unreasonable. This was one of those times.

"Did you know I was here? Have you come to gloat?" she went on.

"No, I didn't and no, I haven't," replied the ever-patient James. "The police have notified Greg that they have arrested Simon on suspicion of the theft of Mum's earrings, and for stealing a passport and subsequently travelling on it, and we wanted to come and let them know that Greg was off the hook."

"So everything's lovely in your garden then, is it?" went on his sister nastily. "I'm so happy for you both."

"What's with you, Susie?" James asked in exasperation. "You've suddenly become all nasty again, like you were when you lost your job and were in debt. You're not the same person sometimes."

"Life has been so good to you, Jamie," said Susie with a sneer on her face. "You were always Mummy and Daddy's favourite because you were the youngest and because you were a boy. You were cleverer than me too and went on to uni. You have a great relationship with Greg, and Daddy has even forgiven you for batting for the wrong side. As for me, I'm looked upon as stupid, because apparently I'm always doing silly things. I'm hard up, whereas you've recently had a big win on the lottery."

James stared at her in amazement. She was getting married to David in three months' time, so clearly she had a great relationship too, provided she hadn't been silly enough to spoil it by going out to dinner with Jonathan Browne. OK, he was academically brighter than Susie, but so what? He always had been, so that was nothing new, and yes, he had had a win on the lottery, but he'd given her five thousand out of his winnings, so what the hell was her problem?

He'd gone to court with her when she'd got done for speeding and always listened when the chips were down, but a few weeks ago when he had a fall-out with Greg, Susie had no time at all for him. James felt very sad - for both of them.

"Come on Suse, let's not fall out," he said in desperation.

"It's too late," was the reply. "You wouldn't give me an alibi for David the other night, so you're the one who's fallen out with me. Just go away and go and tell Mummy and Daddy how wonderful everything is in your world now that Simon has been arrested. I think I'll take Allsort for a walk. At least she doesn't spend her life judging me."

***

A sad James went and joined the rest of the family in the sitting room, whilst Susie took herself and Allsort for a walk along the riverbank. When she got as far as the Beetle and Wedge, Susie felt in the pocket of her shorts to see if she had any money, as she thought she would treat herself to a glass of wine, which she could have sitting in the garden and watching the river. She could, of course, have done that at home, but didn't really feel in the mood to be involved with family celebrations. She was also smarting from the fact that David hadn't phoned her. She felt very unloved indeed.

Whilst she was patting her pockets hopefully, but with no success, a chap appeared who also had a basset hound on a lead. "Hi," he said, "fancy you having a basset too. You don't see many of them."

Susie forced a smile and explained that Allsort belonged to her parents and that she was staying with them for a few days. The chap introduced himself, saying that he was called Mark and the dog was called Bertie. Susie reciprocated. They both smiled at the dogs' names. Mark then asked her if she was visiting the Beetle for a drink. At this, Susie shook her head, explaining that she had come out of the house without any money, so she couldn't have one. He replied that it wasn't a problem, asked her what she would like and then handed her Bertie's lead whilst he went to the bar.

When he came back carrying a glass of wine and a pint, Allsort and Bertie were sniffing each other happily. Allsort always was sociable, and Bertie seemed to be equally friendly. Mark and Susie chatted away and she finally began to feel better. Here was someone she could talk to who didn't feel it necessary to judge her.

Accepting her second drink, Susie asked Mark if he lived locally. He replied that he lived quite close by and often walked Bertie down to the Beetle for a drink. He had moved in recently and didn't yet know many people. In return, Susie told him that her parents lived in Riverside House and that she lived in a village on the edge of the Cotswolds called Church Enstone.

Mark found Susie attractive, but couldn't help but notice the ruby and diamond ring on the fourth finger of her left hand. He also felt that there was a sadness about her and wondered why. He decided to take the bull by the horns and asked if her fiancé was also in Moulsford.

At this, the floodgates opened and he got the story of how misunderstood Susie had been, just because she had been out to dinner with an old friend. She decided it was not in her interest to tell Mark that Jonathan had been married and she had had an affair with him. She felt that "old friend" was much more socially acceptable.

Listening to her, Mark decided that Susie could be trouble and that it was probably best not to pursue the friendship. Yes, she was very attractive, but clearly she had loads of baggage and was engaged to another man. That might come to an end, but if it did, it would probably be messy.

Susie, of course, was enjoying herself. She had had two large glasses of wine and was sitting with an attractive man, who was clearly enjoying her company. What's not to like? She had no plans to go home to David the following day, so suggested to Mark that they should meet up at the Beetle again the following evening, when she would make sure that she had money with her, so that she could return the favour of the drinks.

Having decided that he wasn't going to have a relationship with Susie, Mark felt that he could still meet her for a drink the next evening. He replied that that would be lovely, then asked her if she would like one for the road? Of course Susie said that she would, as by now she had lost track of time and the fact that her parents might wonder where she and Allsort had got to.

Finally, a very wobbly Susie bade Mark goodnight and set off to walk back to Riverside House. By now she was feeling very sick. She guessed that would teach her to drink over a bottle of wine when she hadn't really eaten very much during the day.

She staggered back to the house, where much to her horror, she actually threw up in the middle of the lawn, and was observed to do so by the entire family, who were sitting on the patio as it was still warm. Peter turned to Annabelle and wearily asked what the hell they were going to do with Susie. They had had a pleasant evening with James and Greg, being delighted with the news that Greg was now, so to speak, in the clear with the police, and then Susie had to come back, obviously drunk, and show herself and them up.

"I'm so sorry," whispered Susie, "but I'm really not feeling very well." And with that, she was sick again. A very embarrassed Annabelle put her daughter to bed with a bucket beside her and said that she would talk to her in the morning. James very kindly hosed down the mess, before he and Greg drove home to Cholsey.

CHAPTER 50

When he went to the office the following morning, David explained to his father that Susie wasn't well and wouldn't be in for a day or two. Although superficially, George accepted this information at face value, he was quick to ring Julia to tell her that he really did think something was amiss. Patiently, she told him there was nothing that either of them could do and everything would evolve over time.

Privately, she hoped that George was wrong, as she felt that the two young people were very good for each other. David tamed Susie down and she brought David out of his sometimes serious shell. She also had a good family background and the various niceties that came with it. Feeling it might be interesting to observe her son, to see if she could find out what was going on, Julia told George that she wasn't too busy at the moment and could help him in the practice, if he so wished. He thanked her, saying that would be most helpful.

Julia arrived at George Timmins and Son shortly before lunch, to find David on his own in the office, looking rather glum.

"Hello Mum, has Dad decided that we need your help?" he enquired.

"No, no," his mother replied. "When he phoned me to say that Susie wasn't well, I offered my services as my agency is relatively quiet at the moment. What's wrong with her, by the way? Is there anything I can do for either of you?"

David hadn't been expecting either his mother to come to the office or to be asked that question. He couldn't bring himself to lie, so told her the story about coming home early from London and Susie refusing to say where she had been or who she had been with. He then confided his suspicions about Jonathan Browne, going on to say that he was working in Enstone Stores, so looked like being a permanent fixture in their lives. He said he'd told his dad that Susie was sick because it was easier. He didn't want his parents to worry, or be turned against Susie, because of an argument they were having.

Not liking what she heard at all, Julia knew that she had to keep her mouth shut. She assured David that George would learn nothing from her. It would be very interesting to see what Peter and Annabelle's take was on all this, but she'd have to wait another week for that.

As Susie had taken off for Riverside House, she would no doubt be telling her parents her side of events. It did, however, concern Julia that Susie wouldn't tell David where she had been. She hated to admit it, but felt that Susie probably hadn't been up to any good as she had not been expecting David to come home that evening. Surprises weren't always what they were cracked up to be.

Feeling sorry for her son, Julia sat down at Susie's desk and started sorting through some files, thinking as she did so. Was there any pretext that she could use to call Annabelle? Or could she just be blunt and ring her to say that she was worried about things between David and Susie, as she understood that Susie had upped sticks and gone to Moulsford, and ask Annabelle what Susie had to say for herself.

On balance she felt that she couldn't, as she wouldn't appreciate that sort of phone call about either of her children. She'd have to wait until next Sunday when they were having lunch together, but that was a long time away.

After a while, Julia went back into David's office and asked him what he was going to do. He replied that he didn't know. His mother told him that someone had to break the ice and make a phone call. He replied that it wouldn't be him, just yet, as Susie was the one who had walked out, and who he thought had a guilty secret. Julia hoped fervently that her son was wrong.

***

On his way home, David decided to stop at The Stores to get some bits and pieces for supper, although if he were honest with himself, he was really hoping to see Jonathan. He was disappointed to find a young girl behind the counter. When he asked after Jonathan, he was told that he wasn't working that evening and as she was about to close, could David please get on with his shopping as she wanted to lock up and get off home as she had a date. Smiling at her honesty and directness, David did as he was asked.

After he had his supper, David decided to pop next door for a couple of drinks. He felt lonely in the cottage with just George the cat for company. He might also find out something about Susie from Alf, if he were behind the bar. Sure enough, he was and greeted David with the customary, "Evening son. What can I get you? A pint of the usual? Will Susie be joining you?"

David replied that he would like a pint of the usual and that Susie wouldn't be joining him. Alf didn't say anything, but fetched David's drink and put it on the bar in front of him, although he was wondering what had happened when Susie had got home after her dinner with Jonathan. The old boy had noticed that the Mini had been missing since the previous evening, which told him a lot.

He was very fond of Susie, which was why he had tried to save her bacon, but he had a nasty feeling that he hadn't succeeded. All was definitely not right next door. Not wanting an in-depth conversation with David, Alf shuffled off to serve another customer.

This didn't go unnoticed by David, who now felt that Alf was avoiding him, because he knew something about Susie that he didn't want to share. Should he just come out with it and ask him? The very worst that could happen would be that Alf wouldn't reply or tell him something that he didn't want to hear. Could he be bold enough to ask if Susie had been in the pub with Jonathan Browne?

As he was plucking up courage to do that very thing, one of his racing friends came into the bar and they started talking about the Formula 1 carnival. David managed to put Susie to the back of his mind - for a while at least. After a few pints he managed to convince himself that he was being melodramatic and returned home to spend the night with George, deciding to leave things for another night to see if he heard from his wife-to-be.

***

Over supper in Great Rollright, George asked Julia how she thought David was. She replied that she thought that David was busy and a bit worried about Susie not being well. It wasn't too far from the truth as David was worried about Susie, even though that wasn't necessarily regarding the state of her health.

"Kids, eh?" said George. "You never stop worrying about them, do you? The next thing is what sort of a career will Jenny find? She's got a good job working for Marks and Spencer as a management trainee, but I can't help but wonder where that will take her. She doesn't seem to have a serious boyfriend, so we can't marry her off to someone wealthy."

Julia laughed at her husband. "You are feeling serious tonight, aren't you?" she said. "Let's take Honey and Mustard for a nice long walk together to blow the cobwebs away, then we'll come home and finish off the evening with a really good bottle of wine. I'll put something special in the fridge now so that it's lovely and cold when we get home. I shall then get changed and I'll be ready to go."

George smiled after Julia's departing back, reminding himself how fortunate he was in his wife. She was beautiful, sensible and intelligent, and had chosen to marry him, a plain, ordinary sort of chap. All he wanted was for his children to be as fortunate and as happy. Thinking about them prompted him to ring Jenny - just to see how she was. She told him that she was fine, but then she would, wouldn't she? Hearing Julia come back down the stairs, he whistled Honey and Mustard, who came dashing through with their usual exuberance. The four of them set off for a brisk walk.

CHAPTER 51

When Annabelle went to look in on Susie the following morning, she was surprised to see how ill her daughter looked.

"You must have had a skinful last night, Susie. You look absolutely terrible."

"I've been throwing up all night, and have a dreadful headache, Mummy. That can't possibly have been the wine. I think I must have a bug," Susie replied. "I didn't drink any more than usual last night, honestly."

"Stay where you are for the moment and I'll bring you a mug of boiled water and some Paracetamol," said Annabelle. "Perhaps you can then sleep it off, if you've finished being sick."

Susie said that she hoped she had, and that she definitely needed to stay in bed. With that, Annabelle went downstairs and told Peter that they may have misjudged Susie as she didn't seem well at all. Peter merely grunted and poured himself another mug of coffee.

"I'll tell the boys that I won't be going to Wallingford today. I'll stay home and take care of Susie. What are you doing, darling?"

Peter replied that he and a small group of other chaps were going out to lunch with Alex Drummond. Alex felt he was too old to have a Stag Night, but had invited Peter and one or two others out to lunch. He wondered if Annabelle could eventually take him to Cholsey station and then he would get a cab back. He was meeting Alex at Malmaison at 12.30 pm and he didn't want to drive.

"I'll bet you don't," she replied, smiling. "If you like, you can give me a ring to let me know what time you're coming back to Cholsey, and if I'm not doing anything, which I probably won't be, I'll come and pick you up. Anyway, I must take this upstairs to Susie now. She really doesn't look well at all."

Peter wasn't as convinced as Annabelle that there was much wrong with his daughter, apart from a bad hangover. He was very cross that she had shown them up last night, and was relieved that their visitors had only been James and Greg. He was glad that he was going out to lunch. With a bit of luck, things would be back to normal by evening. Annabelle could fuss round Susie if she wished, but personally he would leave her to stew.

***

Susie eventually crawled out of bed at 4 pm, still feeling very much under the weather. She was supposed to be meeting Mark to buy him a drink at 8 pm and wondered how she was going to manage that. Still, she had four hours to pull herself together. Mummy had been very kind and brought her some chicken soup a couple of hours ago. She had managed to keep that down and was no longer feeling sick.

She stood under the shower, letting the water course down her body. After she had lathered herself all over with some Elemis shower gel that her mother must have put in the bathroom as it certainly wasn't hers, Susie felt marginally better. Putting on a pair of navy chinos and a red tee shirt, she went downstairs to find her mother sitting in the garden. It looked as though she were doing a table plan for the wedding.

Susie felt wretched and immediately thought of David. He hadn't rung her either, though. How long were they going to keep this up for? She really felt that she was the innocent party and thought that David should ring her, but then it didn't look as though he were going to!

"Hello Mummy, I'm up," said Susie, stating the obvious.

"Hello darling, how are you feeling now?" enquired her mother.

Susie said that she was feeling better than she did, although still rather wobbly.

"I know that you and Daddy think I was drunk last night, but I wasn't," she said. "I hadn't been feeling that great all day and still don't. Drink wouldn't do that to me. Besides which, I didn't have enough. I only had three glasses of wine."

"Who were you drinking with?" Annabelle asked. "You were gone for rather a long time and I'd be surprised if you drank all that on your own."

"For a start, I took Allsort for a walk," was the reply, "and we landed up at the Beetle. I couldn't buy myself a drink as I hadn't got any money, and there was this nice chap who also had a basset hound with him, called Bertie, who I got into conversation with and he bought me the wine. I'm supposed to be meeting him there again tonight to return the favour. I don't accept drinks without paying my share."

"Let me get this right," said Annabelle. "You had dinner with Jonathan Browne at The Crown on Tuesday when you were expecting David to be in London. You didn't want to tell him who you'd been with, so when he questioned you, you ran here for sanctuary. The next evening, you take Allsort for a walk to the Beetle where a strange man buys you drinks and you arrange to meet him again the next night, despite the fact that you are engaged to David. Have I got that about right?"

"Oh Mummy, you do make it sound sordid, calling Mark a strange man," said Susie wrinkling her nose. "He was perfectly nice."

"You really don't get it, do you, Susie?" said an exasperated Annabelle. "You have been drinking with two different men this week, neither of whom happens to be your fiancé. Does that sound right to you? It doesn't to me, nor will it to David."

"David doesn't need to know, if you think it will cause more trouble," said Susie sulkily. "Personally I can't see what the problem is. You've lived with Daddy for far too long. You're becoming narrow-minded like he is. Of all people, I would expect you to understand. All I've done is have a drink with a guy who has the same sort of dog as Allsort, and if I'm well enough I'll be going back tonight, to have more drinks with him, as I don't want to appear rude and let Mark down."

Annabelle was almost lost for words at this. "Let Mark down," she said. "What about the man who will shortly become your husband? Have you even spoken to him since you got here?"

Susie replied that as David hadn't bothered to phone her, she hadn't rung him either.

Annabelle shook her head in disbelief and said she was going to Cholsey to pick up Peter, which was probably as well, before she said something that she deeply regretted.

***

Peter was pleased with life when Annabelle picked him up. They had had a jolly good lunch and were all looking forward to the wedding the following day. Annabelle did a double-take at this. With all the drama over Susie, she had completely overlooked the fact that it was the Drummond wedding the next day.

Even Peter going out to lunch with Alex hadn't reminded her. She would have to dash into the Arcade in the morning and find a silver photo frame. That always made a very acceptable gift, unless she gave James a call and asked him to choose something for her and drop it round. That would be easier still. His taste was impeccable and it would save her a lot of trouble. She needed to check over her wedding outfit for tomorrow and keep an eye on Susie as well.

Once back home, Annabelle gave James a call, explaining that she needed wrapping paper and a card as well as the photo frame. He told her that was no problem and would come over later after supper with Greg and Zizi. She then went to find Susie, who was still sitting in the garden, looking sorry for herself.

"I'd forgotten it was Jonathan's ex-wife's wedding tomorrow," Annabelle remarked conversationally. "I need to sort out what I'm going to wear. I'd completely forgotten and haven't even got a gift, but James is coming up trumps and bringing me something from the shop after supper."

"He's so wonderful, isn't he?" remarked Susie sarcastically. "It's such a shame that I'm not more like your darling boy, isn't it?"

"I'm really worried about you, Susie," said her mother. "You are fast becoming a nasty, spiteful person, not the beautiful daughter that I know and love. Whatever is the matter, darling? This should be such a happy time leading up to your wedding, and you're just lashing out at everybody and everything. Why are you so unhappy?"

At that, Susie burst into tears. She hadn't realised that she was unhappy and tried to explain that to her mother. She admitted that she wasn't feeling particularly loved, especially by David and her family. All she seemed to come in for was criticism, no matter what she did; the latest being her mother saying that she shouldn't have had a drink with Mark last night.

Annabelle rolled her eyes to heaven. What on earth was she going to do with Susie? The wretched girl couldn't see that her behaviour was atrocious and felt that she was the victim in all this. It was important that she and David should speak soon and Annabelle was wondering whether it was time for her to interfere. She wondered if Julia and George knew about the situation. George must know that Susie wasn't at work, but did he know why? Peter was on a short fuse and it wouldn't be a good idea to tell him about Mark. He really would have a fit.

There was nothing that she could do at this precise moment. She needed to sort out an outfit for the following day, and provide Peter, and possibly Susie, with some supper. She needed to get a move on, as the next thing would be James, Greg and Zizi arriving.

Leaving Susie to her own devices, Annabelle went inside and started beating up eggs to make omelettes. Peter had had a good lunch, so didn't need a lot, Susie might possibly manage to eat an omelette and she was past caring what she had to eat. Mixing up a French dressing for the salad, Annabelle wondered what on earth she was going to do.

***

Susie did manage to eat some omelette, which made her feel slightly better again. She planned to slip out under cover of James and Greg's arrival. She wouldn't take Allsort tonight – that might draw attention to her – but she must go and see Mark. After all, she had promised. She went back upstairs and stuffed a £20 note into her pocket, feeling that a handbag was too obvious.

It wasn't long before excited barking announced the arrival of her brother, his partner, and dog. As they came in through the front door, Susie exited through the back. Waves of nausea were sweeping over her again, but determinedly, she set out in the direction of the hotel.

When she got there, Mark and Bertie were already sitting outside. He was drinking a pint and there was a large glass of wine waiting for Susie. She all but gagged at the sight of it, but what could she do other than try and drink it? Mark commented that she hadn't brought Allsort, to which Susie replied that she hadn't been well and had just popped out to buy him a drink as promised, as she had no way of getting hold of him, and she didn't want him to think she'd taken advantage of his kindness.

Mark was touched by that. Now that she came to mention it, Susie did look a little pale. He told her that he felt it would be best if she just drank the glass of wine he had bought her and then went home. If she really felt the need to buy him a drink, he would give her his phone number and she could ring him when she was feeling better. With that, he passed her a business card, which Susie put in her pocket.

The garden was beginning to go in and out of focus and she was also finding it difficult to concentrate on what Mark was saying to her. Gallantly, Susie picked up her glass to see if some more wine would make her feel better. That was the last thing she remembered.

CHAPTER 52

Why was she lying on the grass with Allsort pushing her nose against her leg? No, it wasn't Allsort, it was Mark's dog, Bertie. Mark was bending over her, asking how she was feeling. Oh God, she'd fainted. How embarrassing was that? Susie tried to sit up, but the garden started to spin again.

"Stay still, Susie. I'm going to fetch you a glass of water," Mark's voice sounded a million miles away. She tried to nod but couldn't, so just did as she was told.

He was soon back with a glass of water, which he held to her lips. He then tried to help her to sit up. This made her feel very nauseous. No, no, no, she couldn't possibly chuck up now. Susie tried taking deep breaths and the nausea eased slightly. She tried to apologise to Mark, but he just held up his hand and told her not to try to talk for a few minutes. By now, he was sitting on the grass beside her. Bertie was still gently nuzzling her leg.

After a few minutes had gone by, Susie's insides began to feel calmer and she managed to sit up with Mark's help.

"The next thing to do is to get you onto a chair," he said, "although that might be easier said than done." Carefully, he tried to help Susie to her feet and at the third attempt got her onto a chair. She was ashen white and complaining that she was feeling sick.

"You shouldn't have come out tonight," he said, smiling at her ruefully. "It was very sweet of you to think about keeping your promise, but you really aren't very well, are you?"

Susie looked at him with tears in her eyes. What a lovely man he was – so kind and understanding. She shook her head and said she wasn't feeling too good at all.

"Not to worry," Mark said. "Once you're feeling a bit better, we'll think about getting you home. You certainly can't walk, that's for sure."

Susie replied that she'd have to, as her parents were entertaining that evening. She didn't say that it was her brother and his partner, or that it would be no problem for someone to come and pick her up, as she couldn't face the scene that that would undoubtedly cause. Her mother had told her in no uncertain terms that she shouldn't be meeting Mark again, and she had slipped out of the house without saying where she was going.

"You're not walking anywhere," was the reply. "Once I think you're OK to be left on your own, I'll go home and fetch my car. I've not even finished my pint, so I'm quite safe to drive."

Susie felt too ill to argue, although she knew that it would cause another scene when she got back to Riverside House if her parents saw Mark, but perhaps with a bit of luck no-one would see him dropping her off and she could pop back into the house unnoticed.

***

At Riverside House, the family was wondering where Susie actually was, although Annabelle had a horrible feeling that she knew. She would have put money on Susie having sneaked off to the Beetle and Wedge to meet this Mark.

Peter raised his eyes to heaven. "One minute she's too ill to get out of bed and the next minute she appears to have disappeared," he said in an exasperated tone.

James had brought a couple of photo frames for his mother to cast her eye over. As she expected, Annabelle was delighted with both of them. "Come on Peter, he's your friend. The final decision is down to you," she said, holding them out towards him. Peter really wasn't in the slightest bit interested in which frame they gave to Alex and Angela, but had more sense than to say so, and did as he was bid.

"Would you like me to wrap it for you, Mum? It would save you a job," asked James.

"Thank you darling, that would be lovely," was the reply. "Maybe when you've done that we'll have managed to find your sister. I'll just go and check upstairs. Maybe she's not feeling well again." Out of sight of the rest of the family, Annabelle quickly rang Susie, but as she expected, there was no reply.

Running down the stairs, she went into the kitchen and grabbed a couple of bottles of wine and some nibbles, which she carried through to the men folk, who were sitting in the garden, making the most of the last bit of sun. Zizi and Allsort were happily chasing each other around.

"Who's driving?" was Greg's immediate question, when he saw the excellent bottle of Merlot.

James said that he would. He then headed for the kitchen himself and returned with a can of lager.

"The present's on the dining room table, Mum. I trust it's wrapped to your satisfaction," he said, grinning. Annabelle replied that she was sure that it would be. "What are you wearing then?" James went on.

Annabelle replied that she wasn't quite sure as she had a choice of one or two different outfits.

"Only one or two?" enquired Peter. "I would have thought that you must have at least seven or eight, plus whatever you've bought for Susie's wedding."

"I shall hardly be wearing my Mother-of-the-Bride outfit to a small wedding in an Oxford College," was the immediate reply. "That was bought for Susie's big day and is extremely special. I shall be much more conservative tomorrow. As I'm only going to get one chance to be Mother of the Bride, I'm really going for it."

"Not long to go until you'll be wearing it, Annabelle," said Greg. "I'm sure you must be looking forward to the day enormously. I know I am. The Rowlands women will be absolutely stunning."

Annabelle smiled faintly at that. If only Greg knew what was troubling her, and the most pressing and immediate thing was where the hell Susie was and whether she was OK. She was desperate to slip away to the Beetle and Wedge herself, but knew that was completely out of the question. Should she suggest that they all walk down there for a drink? Probably not a good idea, as Peter would have a hissy fit if he found Susie drinking with a strange man after the exhibition she had made of herself the previous evening.

***

David was feeling very down without Susie. It was Friday night and he was on his own, apart from pussy cat George. Loving as George was, it wasn't quite the same as having his mistress home. Rubbing the cat's head, David asked him what he thought he should do.

"Should I drive over to Moulsford and surprise her, do you think, George?" he asked. David then remembered what had happened the last time he had tried to surprise Susie. He had had a big shock and that was only three days ago. George merely gazed at him adoringly. He was a very friendly cat, who loved to be fussed.

Biting the bullet, David decided that he would give his wife-to-be a call. They couldn't go on like this forever, and it looked as though he was going to have to be the one to make the first move. Irritatingly, the phone went to answer, so he just left a message saying that he hoped she was OK and that it would be good to talk, so please would she call him back?

"Nothing more we can do at the moment, George," he said, "other than sit and wait. Should I go next door and have a drink, do you think?" George continued to purr. David sat with him for a while, then, when he hadn't heard from Susie within the hour, he decided that he might as well go and see Alf and have a pint.

The bar was busy when he walked in, but then it was Friday night. Who should he see leaning on the counter, but Jonathan Browne. David decided to go and stand next to him. He wished Jonathan a friendly good evening and got a condescending nod in return. That made David's blood boil. Who did the man think he was? From what David could see, he was nothing other than a shopkeeper, and it certainly wasn't his own shop either. How the mighty fell from grace.

When he came into the bar, Alf was surprised to see David standing next to Jonathan. Could that cause trouble, he wondered. Definitely best not to ask after Susie, as God alone knew which of the two men would answer him. Probably as well not to ask David how he was either. There were times when being a publican was a damned sight more complicated than being in the Diplomatic Service. Giving the world at large a smile, Alf retreated to his office. He would venture out again in a while. Things might be better then as either Jonathan or David might have moved on.

David had one drink, which he didn't particularly enjoy as Jonathan's mere presence was an irritant. Should he go to Moulsford after all? He'd only had the one, so could definitely drive. Walking towards his car, David looked at his watch. Thanks to his procrastinating, it was now almost 10 o'clock; far too late to call on the Rowlands. It would be about 11 by the time he got there. He rang Susie again. Still no reply, so he left another message.

Going inside the cottage, David decided that a large scotch and an early night were probably the best course of action. He could then go to Moulsford in the morning and see if Susie was ready to come home.

CHAPTER 53

Susie sat there shivering after Mark had gone for the car. This evening certainly hadn't gone according to plan. She felt as sick as a parrot and had made a fool of herself by passing out. There was now little chance of her getting back into Riverside House without someone seeing her and there would be more arguments.

She wondered if she could walk home and then no-one would be any the wiser. Cautiously, Susie got to her feet, but sat down again immediately because she felt so wobbly. She took another sip of water. What on earth had she caught? Whatever it was, it was a vicious little beast.

After what seemed like an eternity, Mark was back. "You're going to have to walk to the car, I'm afraid," he said. "I've brought it up as close as I can." With that, he started to help Susie to her feet. She looked extremely unsteady, so he put one arm round her for support and held onto her hand. Very slowly, and carefully, they walked to the car and he helped her in.

Susie opened the window as she felt that she needed air, then fastened her seatbelt. Mark looked at her out of the corner of his eye. She still looked ashen. Gently, and slowly, he drove off. Within five minutes, he was turning into Riverside House's drive. He picked the same moment to arrive as the one when James and Greg were leaving, being waved off by Annabelle and Peter.

They all looked surprised to see his red Vauxhall pulling into the drive and more surprised still to see Susie in the passenger seat. Peter turned to Annabelle and asked her what the hell was going on. Although she had a good idea, his wife just shrugged her shoulders.

Parking the car, Mark walked up to the assembled group and introduced himself. He went on to say that he had been having a drink with Susie at the Beetle and Wedge when she had fainted, so he had gone home to fetch his car so that he could drive her home, as she quite clearly wasn't capable of walking.

Peter started to thank Mark, who quickly assured him with a smile that no thanks were necessary and said he would help Susie out of the car. It would be difficult to say who was the most horrified of the group, when, as he pulled her to her feet, she vomited all over him. Annabelle dashed forward and removed the sobbing Susie from Mark's grasp, whilst he stood there looking somewhat shocked.

"James, do you having anything that you could lend Mark to wear?" asked a very embarrassed Peter. Then, turning to Mark, he went on to say,

"I can only apologise for my daughter. She started being ill last night, so what on earth she thought she was doing by going out for a drink, I can't imagine. However, do please come in and at least let us offer you something to drink and a change of clothes."

James had gone scooting off upstairs and came back with some tracksuit bottoms and a sweatshirt. "I know they aren't very glamorous," he said, "but at least the bottoms will be flexible because of the elastic waist, as we probably aren't the same size. The downstairs loo is just through here." With that, James led the way through the hall.

Mark and Annabelle reappeared at the same time. "Please give me your clothes so that I can wash them for you," she said. Mark thanked her and asked after Susie. Annabelle replied that she had put her to bed, as she had done the previous night.

"Come through into the sitting room and let me get you a drink," she said. Mark replied that he would like a cup of coffee as he had had the best part of a pint already and had to drive home. Annabelle showed him into the sitting room, leaving him with Peter, praying that the latter wouldn't bite off the former's head, before going to the kitchen to make a pot of coffee.

Peter and Mark appeared to be chatting amicably enough when Annabelle walked in with the coffee. After she had passed around the cups, Peter waved the brandy decanter. Mark declined, whilst Annabelle accepted a small one.

"So, how do you come to know my daughter?" Peter asked in a conversational tone. Inwardly he was seething, but accepted that this man deserved some courtesy. He had been kind enough to bring Susie home after she had passed out, and then the wretched girl had thrown up over him.

Mark told the story of how he and Susie had met at the Beetle the previous evening, the connection being Allsort and Bertie. He went on to say that Susie hadn't had any money with her, so he had bought her a couple of drinks. Not wanting to be in his debt, she had said that she would return the favour the following evening, and that Peter and Annabelle knew the rest. Mark finished off by saying that he was new to Moulsford, having only moved in a few weeks ago.

Peter nodded at this and thanked him again for bringing Susie home. Mark took the hint and bade them goodnight.

When he had gone, Peter looked at Annabelle and asked her if she knew any of this. She told him that she had dragged the information about Mark from Susie, then given her a lecture on the fact that she was engaged to David, yet drinking with someone else only a couple of days after she had had dinner with Jonathan Browne. What was more, she had told Susie unequivocally that she wasn't to go back to the Beetle and meet Mark again.

Drily, Peter told her that her lecture hadn't worked. Once again, he asked his wife what the hell were they going to do.

***

Meanwhile Susie was in bed, feeling absolutely wretched. She had been sick again another couple of times and was unbelievably sorry for herself. She couldn't believe that she had thrown up all over Mark, but at least she now had his phone number so could ring up and apologise. After all, he had been so kind when she had fainted.

He seemed to be the only person who didn't want to judge her. Mummy and Daddy weren't being particularly nice, James was horrid, and David didn't really understand her. She ought to speak to him, but didn't feel well enough at the moment. Susie turned over and tried to go to sleep.

The next thing she knew, there was a tap on her door and Daddy was asking if he could come in. As she wasn't going anywhere anytime soon, she didn't really have a choice, so in he came. As she expected, Susie got a lecture on her behaviour. She really couldn't remember when she'd seen her father so exasperated and angry. Immediately, she started to cry, but was told in no uncertain terms that she could dry her eyes, as tears wouldn't wash with him. She tried to tell him how poorly she felt, but it was quite obvious that he wasn't listening. Eventually, he went back downstairs.

After he had gone, Susie reached for her phone and dialled David after all. She didn't get a reply, which struck her as very odd, so left a message explaining that she wasn't well, and would really like to talk to him. As an afterthought, she added that she missed him. Hopefully that would do the trick, and David would forget that he was cross with her and everything would blow over. Feeling that she had done the best she could, Susie once again tried to go to sleep.

CHAPTER 54

When she woke up on Saturday morning, Angela was pleased to see that the sun was shining. After all, this was her wedding day! She was alone in the house with the twins, as Alex had spent the night at The Randolph. She wanted the day to be traditional, which meant that Alex should not see her in her dress until the ceremony. She had a long soak in the bath, before going downstairs to get breakfast. Understandably, the twins were very excited and couldn't wait to get dressed in their wedding outfits.

Once the breakfast dishes had been stowed in the dishwasher, Angela sent the girls upstairs and told them both to wash their hair, as the hairdresser would soon be there. Sure enough, it wasn't long before Claire, the hairdresser, arrived.

Explaining that she would like the twins' hair to be French plaited, Angela then went and washed her own hair. She was not doing anything elaborate with it. As it was shoulder-length, she was just going to have it turned under, and Claire would put her fascinator in the right place, making sure it was very secure so that it couldn't slide out.

Whilst she was waiting her turn with Claire, Angela very carefully applied her make-up. She was wearing a little more than usual, but still wished to look natural. It wasn't long before Claire appeared to blow dry her hair and put in her fascinator. Angela was beginning to feel excited now, and was delighted with the appearance of the person looking back at her from the dressing table mirror.

Next thing she knew, the florist was ringing the bell. Angela smiled when she saw her bouquet. It was quite perfect. The roses were beautiful and the girls' posies were also lovely. Going back upstairs, she decided to see how the twins were getting on. They were nearly ready and were looking so pretty. Angela told them this and asked them to go and wait for her in the sitting room, saying that she wouldn't be long.

She carefully stepped into her dress and pulled up the zip. She then slipped on the lace jacket, pushed her feet into her shoes and picked up her small bag. Surveying herself in the mirror, Angela had to admit that she was pleased with the result. She went downstairs to find her daughters, who oohed and aahed when they saw her.

Hugging them close, Angela fought back the tears. Fortunately, the car soon arrived to collect them, so she had to pull herself together. The three of them picked up their bouquets and walked out to the vintage Rolls Royce where Angela's father was waiting for them. He told his daughter that he was a very proud man and that she and the twins looked absolutely beautiful.

***

As soon as she got up on Saturday morning, Annabelle donned her Nike running gear, collected Allsort and went out. When Peter woke and found her missing, he knew that his wife was uptight. She always felt the need to run problems out of her system. He guessed that was what she was trying to do now with Susie.

He went downstairs and started to make coffee, knowing that Annabelle would be glad of it when she came home. Sure enough, she was soon running up the lawn with a tired Allsort doing her best to keep up. Smiling at him, Annabelle accepted the steaming mug of coffee, which she carried upstairs. She had a quick shower and blasted her long, dark hair dry, before going to look in on Susie.

As she was still asleep, Annabelle decided to leave her and go and have some breakfast, before deciding what she was going to wear and what she was going to do with her hair. She found Peter on the phone to James, arranging for him to pick them up after the wedding. He was instructing him to catch a train to Oxford, so that he could drive them home in the BMW, as he didn't want Annabelle having to squash herself into James' Mini when she was wearing a posh frock. She smiled to herself, then started preparing breakfast.

Breakfast over, Annabelle made a mug of boiled water, popped in a slice of lemon and put it, together with a slice of toast and a dish of butter onto a tray, which she carried up to Susie. Her daughter was now awake and looking slightly better than she had the previous evening.

"I don't have time to talk to you now, Susie," said Annabelle. "I've got a wedding to go to and I need to sort out what I'm going to wear. Suffice it to say that you made a complete exhibition of yourself and us last night. I'm not the only one who is cross. Your father is absolutely furious and will have something to say to you. I can't believe you went and met Mark after all I said to you.

"Anyway, enough of that for now. As I said, your father and I are going to your ex-lover's ex-wife's wedding, so I shall see you early evening, I would imagine." With that Annabelle swept out of the bedroom, leaving a very stunned Susie behind her.

Rummaging through her wardrobe, Annabelle settled on a fuchsia pink silk shift dress, which had a patterned sheer silk jacket to go over it. The jacket had several colours in it, one being apple green. She topped the outfit with a huge pink hat and accessorised with apple green sandals and clutch bag.

218

Quickly, she put heated rollers in her hair to give it some body and bounce, as she decided to wear it down. From her jewellery box, Annabelle chose a long string of pearls and a pair of pearl earrings. Her engagement ring, Omega watch, and a gold bangle completed her outfit. Whilst her hair was curling, Annabelle applied her make-up, sprayed herself generously with Coco Mademoiselle, and chose her underwear.

Twenty minutes later, she was ready and went to look for Peter. As expected, she found him in his study, smoking a cigar and reading *The Telegraph*. He wolf whistled when he saw her. "You looking stunning, Belle," he said. "But then, when don't you? Have you seen our daughter this morning?"

Annabelle replied that she had and that she had told Susie that they would be speaking to her later. Peter merely nodded his head. Collecting James' beautifully wrapped package and their card, the couple headed for the car, remarking that it was a beautiful day for it.

***

Once she had heard the car leave the drive, Susie decided that she would get up. She certainly wasn't hanging around for a bollocking from her parents, so she would go home. David would be bound to be pleased to see her. She wouldn't ring him. This would be her surprise this time. If he returned her call from last night, all well and good, she would tell him that she was coming home, if not, she would just go home. Still feeling very nauseous, Susie tottered to the bathroom and was promptly sick. This really had been going on long enough, she thought to herself. If she wasn't better on Monday, she would have to see the doctor.

She ran a warm bath, frightened that a hot one would make her dizzy again, and climbed in and out of it with great care. Slowly, she towelled herself down and even more slowly got herself dressed. So far, so good. Next, she shoved her clothes into her overnight bag, which she carried downstairs. Sod the fact that she hadn't made the bed or carried down her tray, but Mummy could damn well see to that.

She was so self-righteous and it would give her something to complain about. She was getting out of Moulsford while the going was good. She didn't need to leave a note. It would be obvious that she had gone home - that's if anyone cared that she was missing.

Carefully, Susie got into the Mini Cooper, then put the hood down. She would definitely need fresh air in order to drive all the way to Church Enstone. Cautiously, she turned the car round, then edged out of the drive.

The journey home wasn't as straightforward as Susie had hoped. She felt very sick and had to stop the car a couple of times. Eventually though, she made it and was pleased to see David's Alfa Spider was at home. Parking behind it, Susie got her bag out of the car and opened the cottage door.

David was hoovering the sitting room, but stopped when he saw Susie. She looked dreadful - very, very pale. "Are you all right, Susie?" he asked anxiously, momentarily forgetting how cross he was with her.

She dropped her bag on the floor, shook her head and started to cry.

***

Alex and Angela's wedding was both beautiful and simple. She looked radiant and he looked very proud. The twins were having the time of their lives. They recognised the Rowlands from Buckingham Palace and made a point of asking how Miss Rowlands was. "We've never been bridesmaids before," Alice told Annabelle. "Have you ever been one, Mrs Rowlands?" Annabelle confessed that she hadn't and went on to tell Alice that Susie was getting married in three months' time. The child nodded her head and said she was sure that Miss Rowlands would look very pretty, just like Mummy.

A marquee had been set up on the South Lawn, where the wedding breakfast was served. Everything was just so, from the canapés at the beginning, to the wedding cake at the end. The wines and champagne were perfect too.

Annabelle had to admit that Alex and Angela looked right together. He was wearing a dress kilt and Angela a demure cream lace dress. With the twins, they made a lovely little family. Annabelle wondered if perhaps Susie had done Angela a favour, but kept the thought to herself. Peter was in his element with the gourmet food and fine wines. He and Alex seemed to be enjoying their flying reminiscences too.

All in all, it hadn't been such a bad day. Angela's friends and family were very correct, but it was good to see people with standards. Everything had been arranged to perfection, which Annabelle approved of heartily. She felt that Angela looked so happy, and after all, that was what weddings were about and how the bride should look. Annabelle prayed that Susie's big day would be as successful and that Susie would be as happy as Angela looked.

Peter came and took her by the arm, whispering that James was waiting outside. Arm in arm they strolled up to the happy couple, wished them much happiness and thanked them for inviting them to be part of their special day. They then went to find their son.

Driving home to Moulsford, Peter said how much he had enjoyed himself and that maybe they should invite Alex and Angela to supper. Annabelle smiled to herself. The smile soon disappeared when she discovered that Susie and her car had gone.

CHAPTER 55

David was concerned to see how white Susie looked and didn't much like the fact that she was crying. Gently, he folded her in his arms, led her to the sofa and tried to soothe her, rocking her like a child.

"You didn't even phone me back," she gulped. "Not even after I left you a message last night that I wasn't well." David replied that he'd also left her a message and she hadn't called back either. He knew that now was not the time to question her about Tuesday evening.

"What's wrong, anyway, poppet?" he asked.

Susie explained that she hadn't been well for two days and kept throwing up. She told David that on one occasion she had also passed out. "Whatever I've caught, it's a vicious little bugger," she said ruefully.

Looking at her, David felt she would be better off in bed and said so. Susie didn't argue and let him help her upstairs. It wasn't long before George joined her. Returning with a glass of water, David suggested that she try to sleep and said he would be back up to check on her later.

Curled up with George, Susie started to feel safe. David had obviously forgotten about the other night. All was rosy in her garden again. Smiling to herself, Susie drifted off to sleep, accompanied by George purring softly. He had missed her and intended to make his feelings known.

David checked on her throughout the afternoon. He was pleased to see that she was sleeping and hoped that when she woke up, Susie would have recovered. She came downstairs shortly before 6.30 pm, and told David that she felt a little better. He told her to go and put her feet up, saying that he would bring her something to eat and wondering if there was anything in particular that she fancied? Susie said that there wasn't and she would leave it up to him.

It wasn't long before he appeared with a tray of scrambled eggs on toast, which he placed on her lap. Suddenly hungry, Susie ate with enthusiasm. However, she regretted it, as soon she was feeling sick again. Struggling to her feet, Susie went outside to the garden, hoping that fresh air might make her feel better.

This really was no fun at all. It looked as though she would have to go to the doctor on Monday. Just to put the icing on the cake, she was starting to feel dizzy. When David came out to join her, Susie told him how bad she felt and asked him to help her back to bed.

Meanwhile, her phone was ringing, which she didn't feel well enough to answer. It was her mother, ringing to make sure that she was all right.

Annabelle was sure that Susie had gone home in order to avoid her and Peter, but for peace of mind had to make absolutely sure. When Susie didn't answer, Annabelle tried David. He wasn't in a position to answer at that very moment, but once he had got Susie settled, he called her back.

David was surprised how angry Annabelle sounded, but put it down to the fact that she was probably worried about Susie. He hastily reassured her that her daughter was safe, although clearly Susie wasn't at all well. Promising that he would ring Annabelle the following day with a Susie update, David rang off.

***

Kicking off her shoes, Annabelle told Peter that Susie had gone home to David. He felt that that was one problem solved, as at least the two of them were back together, and would hopefully overcome their differences. They were sitting together in the Snug, when the doorbell rang. Looking surprised, Peter went to answer the door.

He was even more surprised to see Mark standing there with James' clothes folded up in his arms. He held them out to Peter, asking how Susie was. Peter invited him in, explaining as they walked through the hall that Susie had gone home to her fiancé. There, he thought to himself, that makes things perfectly clear with that young chap. Annabelle looked surprised to see Mark. She thanked him for returning James' clothes, apologising for the fact that she had not yet had the opportunity to launder his, explaining that she and Peter had spent the day at a wedding.

"Will you join us in a drink this evening?" Peter asked. "We really are grateful that you went to the trouble of bringing Susie home last night." He was keen to find out something about Mark and how he came to know Susie. Mark accepted the offer. Being new to the village, he felt it would be good to get to know a few people, and the Rowlands were as good a place to start as any. They would be sure to have a large social circle.

"What will you have?" Peter continued. "I think we have most things, so name your poison." Mark asked if it would be possible to have a beer. Peter replied that it most certainly would and went off to fetch one.

"You said that you had only moved here recently," Annabelle said. "How are you settling in?"

Mark replied it was a slow process as he was out at work all day, and his days were long. This prompted Annabelle to ask what he did. He told her that he was Sales Manager for a computer company, which meant he did a lot of travelling which limited his ability to get to know people.

He had been living in Reading, he went on, but wanted to get away from town life, so had bought a property in Moulsford. He enjoyed being close to water and he hadn't moved too far away from his Head Office in

Bracknell, so all in all it was a win/win situation. She had to admit that the more Mark talked, the more she liked him. He struck her as very genuine and she felt slightly guilty that she had thought ill of him.

Peter returned with a beer, a glass of Chablis for Annabelle and a gin and tonic for himself. He was quite surprised to find his wife deep in conversation with Mark, and seeming to be very relaxed. Perhaps this chap was all right after all. He had brought home Susie, who had thanked him by throwing up all over him, and it hadn't seemed to faze him.

Annabelle brought Peter into the conversation by telling him what Mark had just told her. Peter then asked Mark if his property had river frontage, if he liked being close to water. Mark replied that sadly it hadn't, saying how beautiful Riverside House was with its extensive river frontage, adding that it would also be well outside his price range. Peter had to admit to himself that Mark seemed straightforward and unpretentious, which he liked. Perhaps the chap wasn't after Susie at all, but had genuinely done her a good turn.

They spent a pleasant half hour chatting generally, then Mark said that he must be getting back home to Bertie, explaining that he, too, had a Basset hound. Allsort, who was a total trollop, remembered Mark from the Beetle and Wedge and had spent a large part of the evening sitting on his foot, whilst he scratched her ears.

After Mark had gone, Peter asked Annabelle what she thought of him. She replied that she thought he was a genuinely nice man, who was new to the area and looking to make friends, which was quite difficult due to all the travelling he did with his job. She didn't think he necessarily had any designs on Susie at all.

Peter nodded his head, saying perhaps they should invite Mark around for a drink and introduce him to James and Greg. Annabelle looked most surprised by this, saying that Mark might not be interested in the gay scene. There were still times when Peter had the ability to astonish her.

CHAPTER 56

Greg had been fascinated by Susie being driven home by a "strange man" and kept onto James saying that he must ring home to see if there were any new developments. James asked him whatever he meant, saying that there couldn't possibly be any "developments" as Greg called them, when his dad was around.

To appease him, he said that Greg could grill his parents himself when he came to collect him from Riverside House after he had done his taxi service. Needless to say Greg didn't, although he did comment to James that Susie must be feeling much better as she had gone home. It didn't go unnoticed that Peter and Annabelle were surprised that their daughter was no longer at Riverside House.

When they got back to Cholsey, Greg could contain himself no longer. "You'll have to ring Susie and find out what's going on," he said. "She obviously thinks that David is the lesser of the two evils, your parents being the more evil! I wonder if she's confessed yet?"

"Stop it, you old Queen," said James. "I'll ring Susie tomorrow to see how she is, but not before. Let's concentrate on our own business. We keep talking about looking for another house, but do nothing about it. We should be studying the property pages in the paper rather than worrying about my sister. What's for supper, anyway? I'm starving."

Greg smiled. James was always starving and ate like a horse without putting on weight. Come to mention it, all the Rowlands had good figures, but he knew that Annabelle ran and worked out with a personal trainer in order to keep in shape.

"Sausages and mash," he replied eventually. "I've had a busy day and didn't know what time you'd be through with picking up your parents, so it had to be something simple."

"Fine by me," James replied. "I'll sort out the table while you crack on with the cooking."

***

Susie had a wretched night. When she wasn't throwing up she felt that she was going to and spent most of the time in the bathroom. David was concerned. Surely a bug should be a lot better by now. Maybe it was gastro-enteritis, in which case she ought to see a doctor.

As she didn't seem to be much better on Sunday morning, David decided to call a doctor, saying that this had been going on long enough. Feeling dreadful, Susie didn't argue with him. It was a terrible palaver getting through to a duty doctor on a Sunday, but David finally managed it, and eventually a doctor appeared, although by then it was mid-afternoon.

Dr Barrett seemed kind and professional. She offered Susie an injection to combat the nausea, which she accepted gratefully. Perching on the end of the bed, having taken Susie's pulse, temperature and blood pressure, the doctor asked all sorts of questions and said she would take a blood test and a urine sample to ensure that nothing untoward was going on. Susie asked the woman what she thought was wrong with her.

At this, Dr Barrett smiled, saying she had no reason to believe it was anything sinister, but her tests would rule out any possibility. She wondered if Susie had eaten any suspicious shellfish or been to a dodgy restaurant. Susie laughed at this, replying that the last meal she had out had been at The Crown next door, where Alf was renowned for his food. The doctor replied that she knew that, as in fact she had just joined a doctors' practice in Chipping Norton. The Crown had been highly recommended by one of the partners. When asked which practice she had joined, Dr Barrett confirmed that it was the one that Susie used.

Smiling at the patient and telling her not to worry, Dr Barrett got off the bed and went downstairs to see David. She reassured him, saying she was sure it was nothing nasty and that she had given Susie an injection to quell the nausea. She went on to say that she had got samples of both blood and urine and would be in touch with Susie about them in a couple of days' time. David thanked the doctor and showed her to the door.

He then went upstairs to see how Susie was feeling. She replied that she was very tired, so David suggested she stay where she was for the rest of the afternoon and that he would bring her something light to eat later on. He was relieved that the doctor had been, and pleased that she didn't seem concerned. He started ringing round the family to tell them the good news, whilst pointing out to his dad that Susie wouldn't be back at work the following day.

***

"That's a relief," George said to Julia when he put the phone down. "David's had a doctor out to see Susie. She won't be back at work tomorrow, but it doesn't sound as though it's anything serious."

"And to think you thought something peculiar was going on," replied his wife. "I told you, you were imagining things that weren't there. No doubt you'd be glad of my assistance a little while longer then?"

George agreed that he would, then stuck his head back in *The Financial Times*, muttering to himself as he read. Julia smiled, doing her best to ignore the mutterings. However, for whatever reason, she couldn't, so decided to take the dogs for a walk.

Whilst she was strolling through the pretty village, Julia decided to phone her son to see what more she could find out about Susie. She drew a blank, as David wasn't very forthcoming. She finished her call by asking him to tell Susie not to rush back to work, as she had everything under control. David thanked his mother before ringing off.

Julia walked on, deep in thought. Not about Susie and David, but about a holiday. She and George hadn't been away for a while and it would be good to fit something in before David went away on honeymoon. She knew that her help would be needed in the practice again then. It seemed ages since they had been to La Petite Maison and the house was definitely beckoning. She would talk to George about it as soon as she got home.

When she did get back, George was sitting just where she had left him, still reading. Julia asked him if he had nearly finished, to which he merely grunted. Taking that as an affirmative, she went into the kitchen and made a pot of tea, which she put on a tray along with her delicious lemon drizzle cake, and carried it through to George.

Putting down his paper, George accepted a cup of tea and a large slice of the cake. Once he was munching happily, Julia told him that she thought they should have a holiday before the wedding, otherwise she couldn't see them getting away until late October. Much to her surprise, her husband actually agreed with her. He said he would look at his diary first thing the following morning and give her some dates.

***

Annabelle was also pleased to hear from David. She wasted no time in telling Peter that David had called out a doctor to see Susie, even though it was Sunday, and that hopefully their daughter would be feeling better soon. She went on to say that they really must have misjudged her as regards to the drink.

"Tell that to the chap who she vomited all over," suggested Peter.

"That was the following night," Annabelle replied crossly. "Can't you just cut her some slack for once, Peter?"

"Susie's behaviour doesn't always make me feel tolerant," he said. "Don't forget that Susie came here in the first place because of a potential row with David over Jonathan Browne. I wonder if that little incident has now resolved itself, or whether she's been able to avoid mentioning it due to being poorly? David's far too kind to badger her when she's not well."

Annabelle knew that what Peter was saying was true, but neither did she know the answer to the question. She'd ring Susie in the morning when David had gone to the office. She ought to be able to find out something then. She must also get Mark's clothes back to him. They had been washed that morning and were ready to go. Perhaps she and Allsort should go for a walk? Mark had given them his address the previous evening.

"Do you fancy a walk, Peter?" she asked.

"Why?" he enquired. "It isn't Allsort's usual time." Annabelle explained that she was thinking of taking Mark's clothes back to him and the walk would do Allsort good anyway. He replied that he wouldn't bother as he hadn't finished reading *The Sunday Telegraph* and that he would see her later.

Annabelle went through to the utility, collected Mark's clothes, which she placed in a bag, and called to Allsort. Shouting "bye" to Peter she set off down the road, with a very happy dog beside her.

CHAPTER 57

Monday came and went with Susie feeling only marginally better, with waves of nausea still sweeping over her, and she was actually sick a couple of times. She also continued having the dizzy feelings. All in all, she was extremely sorry for herself and felt that nobody understood how ill she felt. David was concerned and was quite pleased when Susie told him that Dr Barrett had telephone and asked to see her the following day.

"I just hope I can get to Chipping Norton and back without throwing up," said a very weary Susie. "I hope nothing nasty's come out of those tests, which is why the doctor wants me to go and see her."

David did his best to reassure her, although he was also wondering why the doctor had sent for Susie. Surely they could have discussed whatever was wrong with her over the phone? This had been going on for the best part of a week now and surely it was time it cleared up? He was also quite surprised that he hadn't caught whatever was wrong with Susie and could only conclude that she must have extremely severe food poisoning.

As her appointment with Dr Barrett wasn't until Tuesday evening, Susie spent the day quietly. She had secretly hoped that David would offer to go with her, but he had an early evening client meeting so wasn't able to. She had told Annabelle that she had to go back to see the doctor, and her mother had been quite comforting, telling Susie that she was sure it was nothing to worry about, as Susie was never ill. She went on to say that maybe it was a virus and the doctor wanted to do some more tests to see if it was on its way out. Susie replied that the amount of times she was throwing up, that didn't seem terribly likely.

George was her biggest comfort. He could sense that something was wrong and spent most of his time curled up beside her, occasionally patting her with his paw. When the afternoon came, Susie took herself out for a little stroll – up past the church and back round. She found that was quite far enough, feeling weak and exhausted by the time she got back home. What the hell was the matter with her? She really wasn't used to being ill.

Eventually, the time came for her to go to see the doctor and, very carefully, Susie drove herself to Chipping Norton. She was feeling rather resentful that David hadn't offered to change his client appointment so that he could go with her, but she was forgetting how much her fiancé was hurting following their argument the previous week.

Dr Barrett kept her waiting for what seemed like an eternity, but eventually Susie went through into her consulting room. Smiling at her, the doctor invited Susie to sit down. She then proceeded to ask her how she was feeling. Susie replied that she didn't feel an awful lot better, as she was still being sick and feeling dizzy. She said she had to stand up quite slowly. Dr Barrett took her blood pressure again, and said that it was very low indeed and that Susie must be careful when going from sitting to standing, as she could feel very dizzy indeed and even faint.

Susie replied that that had already happened to her and she'd prefer for it not to happen again. She went on to ask the doctor what was wrong with her and when she might expect to feel better. The doctor's reply stunned Susie, as her condition was life-changing. The poor girl burst into tears and said that she didn't know what she was going to do. Dr Barrett passed her a box of tissues and suggested she make another appointment the following week, when they could go through the available options. Muttering her thanks, a stunned Susie stumbled from the surgery.

She couldn't actually remember driving home, but obviously she did. When she got there, David's Alfa was parked outside, but there was no sign of him. Starting to cry again, Susie curled up on the sofa with George and a mug of tea. It wasn't long before she had to rush to the bathroom.

***

David's client meeting had been a tough one. Mr had wanted to proceed with the suggested investments, but Mrs hadn't. He hated it when couples started wrangling in front of him. After about an hour, they had compromised and agreed to invest half the sum that they had originally discussed. So, it hadn't been a waste of time, although not exactly the result he had been hoping for.

He wasn't entirely surprised to find that Susie wasn't yet back. Evening appointments with doctors could be lengthy and they usually kept you waiting at the end of the day anyway. Feeling that a drink was in order, David popped into the cottage to dump his briefcase and feed the ever hopeful George.

That done, he walked next door to The Crown. He was surprised that there was no sign of Alf, but then he supposed it was relatively early, and the old boy liked to be around when the pub was busy. He noticed that Jonathan Browne was at the far side of the bar, seemingly engrossed in trying to chat up the barmaid. Did that man never give up?

David asked for a pint of Abbot which he carried to a small table. He held the glass up to the light. Alf certainly knew how to keep his beer. He drank appreciatively. The first pint went down well, so David decided to have a second. Susie probably wouldn't be up for much to eat, so he didn't need to hurry.

As he enjoyed his beer, David's thoughts turned to the previous week and the fact that he and Susie hadn't sorted out their differences as she hadn't been well since she had come home after her sudden departure to Moulsford.

The next thing David knew, Jonathan was standing by his table, leering at him in an unpleasant manner.

"I knew I knew you," he drawled, "and I've finally managed to place you. You're the loser who's engaged to Susie Rowlands. When you came in the shop the other morning I felt that I recognised you. I bet you didn't know that the little tart spent the night with me when you were up in London on that course last week, did you? She was really pleased to see me, let me tell you. Lost none of her magic, as far as I'm concerned. Has to beg the question why she wanted to see me, don't you think? Clearly you don't come up to scratch.

"I'm guessing it's in the bedroom department. Susie always was keen on lots of sex. Have you found that? Perhaps you have and she's discovered that you aren't man enough for her. Probably that's why she was so pleased to see me. I'm a real man, you see, and don't have any problems at all in that department. I find it interesting that she can't be bothered to come to the pub with you either. She always came with me, but then of course, we had a very passionate and physical relationship. Probably didn't want to let me out of her sight. Quite clearly she doesn't have that problem with you, you pathetic little wimp."

David was horrified. He longed to punch Jonathan, but that would only bring him down to the level of his tormentor and he wasn't going to reply as that would only start a slanging match. With as much dignity as he could muster, David got to his feet and walked out of the pub.

He could see that Susie was back as the Mini was parked behind the Alfa. However, he just didn't know what to do. Jonathan had certainly solved the mystery of what had happened last week, but what he had just said was too awful to believe.

As David was thinking about what he should do, his phone rang. It was one of his mates, going on and on about a proposed trip to the Nurburgring. David answered mechanically and suggested that Paul mailed him the dates and he would get back to him.

Knowing that he couldn't put it off any longer, David let himself into the cottage, where he found Susie in the foetal position on the sofa with George curled up next to her. It was very apparent that she had been crying – again.

They both spoke at once.

"I've had amazing news from the doctor. I don't know how you're going to feel about this David, but I'm expecting a baby."

"I'm sorry Susie, but in view of what happened last week I don't think I can marry you."

Now read what happens next to the Rowlands family in this sample chapter from the final volume in Antonia Abbott's *Emotions trilogy*:

ENDURING EMOTIONS

CHAPTER 1

The family certainly hadn't planned on spending the evening of Christmas Day in Coronary Care at the JR, anxiously watching the flashing lights and beeping machines. They'd all been enjoying the delicious Christmas pudding when the old man had started to rub his chest. At first, they thought it was indigestion, but then they very quickly realised it was something much more serious. An ambulance had been called and now they were in the Coronary Care Unit of the John Radcliffe Hospital in Oxford.

Nurses in scrubs came and went quietly, checking drips and machines. They were very calm and seemed satisfied with what they were seeing. But then he wasn't their husband, their father, their grandfather. Each person was lost in their own thoughts; some were remembering happy times, others were worrying about the future. The old man's wife was very upset and frightened. Their daughter was doing her best to comfort her and to generally hold things together. That's what she usually did.

It wasn't as though this was the first time. The old chap had had a scare a few years ago, but it had been nothing like as serious as this appeared to be. Still, he was a tough old boy, so hopefully all would be well. It was far too early to know anything conclusive.

Only two were allowed at the bedside at any one time. As there was four of them, they were taking it in turns to either sit with him or to pace up and down in the waiting area. Every so often one of them would ring home to update the rest of the family, who were holding the fort at home. Not that there was much to say, but contact with the outside world seemed very necessary.

They realised that they would have to sort out what was going to happen next. Were any of them going to stay all night? Were they going to do half the night each in pairs or what? The old chap's daughter asked a member of the nursing team what she thought they ought to do. The staff nurse replied that the patient was stable at the moment, and that she didn't think much could be achieved by them all staying there. Of course, they would be called immediately should there be any change in the patient's condition.

The family went to the Waiting Room and talked quietly together. There was a part of each of them that felt they were letting the old chap down if they went home, but equally they all realised that they couldn't really achieve anything if they stayed. This could be a long job, so it was best if they conserved as much energy as possible. Decision made, they went to find the nurse to explain what they planned to do.

The next nightmare was getting a taxi back home. Two of them had travelled in the ambulance and the other two had followed a bit later in a cab. Christmas Day was not a good time to be looking for one, and now that it was late evening rather than late afternoon, it was that much harder still. Eventually, they managed to get hold of one who was willing to go out to the village and they all piled in.

Those who had stayed at home were pleased to see them back, but obviously concerned about the old man. Almost every member of the family had a large glass of brandy and then went up to bed, each with their own thoughts.

***

It was shortly after 2 am when the house was roused by the urgent shrilling of the telephone. The old boy had had another heart attack and they were advised to go into the hospital. Quickly, they dressed, and this time five of them drove off to Oxford. One of them stayed behind, feeling it inappropriate that he should be there, and anyway only five would fit in the one car. He also had a deep dislike for hospitals and said that he would be better occupied looking after the house.

Even at that time in the morning, parking was horribly difficult and it seemed as though hours had elapsed before they finally made it to Coronary Care and rang the bell to be admitted.

The old man looked like a wax model, he was so pale. The machines were still beeping away and nothing much looked as though it had changed. Immediately, a nurse, this time the ward sister, came and took them to one side. She explained that her patient had had another attack, and at this point it was not possible to ascertain what damage the attack had caused. However, the immediate danger had passed and he was now stable. Everyone looked very relieved. Sister suggested that they stay for a little while and then go home to catch up on some sleep.

***

The next few days were spent to-ing and fro-ing. The whole family was, by now, heartily sick of the John Radcliffe Hospital. However, progress had been made. The old man was well enough to be transferred to a ward. He was coherent and his prognosis was good. They now had to plan for his coming home in about a week's time.

As his wife was in her late seventies, it was agreed that she could not possibly be expected to cope alone, particularly as she lived a good two hours away from her only daughter. It seemed as though the pair of them would have to move in with their daughter and son-in-law, at least in the short term. Fortunately, they had a large house, although whether they welcomed the arrival of permanent house guests would remain to be seen.

However, the son-in-law put his foot down, saying it would put an unreasonable burden on his wife, who wasn't a nurse. Father-in-law should have a month in some sort of care home before they could contemplate looking after him. He wanted to be sure that the man could go up and down stairs, for example, as he had no desire to install a stair lift. It would look hideous parked at the bottom of their beautiful staircase.

This did cause some controversy, but he was adamant, and he was also used to getting his own way. Fortunately, there was a suitable care home in the village, which also offered nursing care for convalescence. That meant that his father-in-law could be admitted there, whilst mother-in-law stayed with them. Visiting would be easy, as it was so local. They were in the fortunate position where money wasn't an issue, so subject to getting the old fellow booked in, everything was hunky dory.

The old man's wife and daughter went to sort out the formalities, having ascertained that they were very fortunate in that a room had just become available. The woman who had been staying there had been recovering from a stroke and was now well enough to go home.

It was the beginning of the second week in January when the move took place. To his credit, the old man settled in very quickly. One or more members of his family visited him every day. He was also surrounded by women, as there were only two other male guests. Being a bit of a flirt, he enjoyed the attention, although was always on his best behaviour when his wife was due to visit.

He stayed there for a month, and at the beginning of February went to stay with his daughter and her husband. By now he was much stronger and really feeling quite well. What could go wrong?

Enduring Emotions: will be published in late 2015.

ALSO BY ANTONIA ABBOTT

The Emotions Trilogy

Book one: Mixed Emotions: An Oxfordshire Affair

Get the book at: **http://getBook.at/mixed_emotions**

Or if you have a smartphone, scan the barcode below:

Book three: *Enduring Emotions* coming end 2015

CONTACT DETAILS

Visit the author's website:
www.antoniaabbottauthor.co.uk

Follow on Twitter:
twitter.com/Antonia_Author

Like on Facebook:
facebook.com/AntoniaAbbottAuthor

Cover Design by: www.StunningBookCovers.com
Cover photography © Arenaphotouk | Dreamstime.com

Published by: Raven Crest Books
ravencrestbooks.com

Contact us on Facebook:
facebook.com/RavenCrestBooksClub

Printed in Great Britain
by Amazon